"FOR WE KNOW IN PART...

Scientists today can answer thousands of questions quickly and completely. However, we are still faced with many questions about basic matters which only appear to be simple. . . . It is time that we realize how many gaps there are in our knowledge and how insignificant we are.

"We have the desire and perhaps the right as well to learn why our world exists and what it is like. We want to learn the answer to the question: Where am I? And when we learn this answer, we can face the ancient philosophical question: What am I, what is man?"

—F.L. Boschke

PUBLISHED BY POCKET BOOKS NEW YORK

F. L. BOSCHKE

THE UNEXPLAINED

THE UNKNOWN WORLD IN WHICH WE LIVE

Translated
from the German by
JAN VAN HEURCK

PUBLISHED BY POCKET BOOKS NEW YORK

POCKET BOOKS, a Simon & Schuster division of
GULF & WESTERN CORPORATION
1230 Avenue of the Americas, New York, N.Y. 10020

ISBN: 0-671-80983-0

First Pocket Books printing October, 1978

1 2 9 8

Trademarks registered in the United States and other countries.

Printed in the U.S.A.

Translated from the German DAS UNERFORSCHTE:
DIE UNBEKANNTE WELT IN DER WIR LEBEN

1. Auflage 1975

"What we see is beautiful,
what we know is more beautiful,
but most beautiful of all is what we do
not yet understand."

Niels Stensen (1638-1686), Danish scientist,
anatomist, geologist, priest, and founder of
paleontology

CONTENTS

FOREWORD

The Unexplained

SCIENCE DETERMINES the way we live and now it even determines whether or not we are born. It is no wonder then that we are interested in the progress of scientific research. In countless textbooks, writers attempt to explain the latest medical and scientific data. This book also discusses the new frontiers of science; but at the same time it asks whether in our zeal to forge ahead we haven't sidestepped important problems. It may surprise us to learn that we still have a great deal to learn! We still lack the answers to many urgent questions. There are many natural phenomena about which we know a great deal, but which we do not completely understand and cannot totally explain. For example:

- Do we know so little about our universe because we think that the earth is the best place that exists?
- Do we feel that we are helpless to defend against earthquakes and volcanic eruptions, and does this explain why we do not know more about them?
- Are we content with our ability to forecast tomorrow's weather more or less accurately, and has this ability prevented us from intensively investigating tornadoes, thunderstorms, and torrential rainstorms?
- Have we relied on the Bible to tell us how life on earth was created?

- Have we neglected certain phenomena because we simply lacked the necessary instruments of measurement?

- Have we thought that the answers to many questions would be too expensive?

This book urges scientists to reconsider these "forgotten" questions.

There is one other thing which I would like this book to do. I would like to awaken interest in, even love for, everyday natural events. We live in the largest laboratory in existence. Nature is continually performing new experiments here, experiments to which we are witnesses. Often all we need to do in order to understand some event and to enrich and renovate our image of the world is to observe and then think about what we have seen. We can all share the joy of discovery, as well as the joy of research.

We are only beginning to find out about our world, and thus the history of science abounds in curious stories. Eccentric people and astonishing events are part of the tale this book tells. Dreamers arise and make incredible claims, and credulous people believe them. No less "amusing" to the true scientist are the powerful men of the earth who make impossible demands and proclaim laws which run counter to natural law.

This book is the story of a beginning. If it causes the reader to reflect as much as it did the writer, it will have fulfilled its purpose.

F. L. Boschke
January, 1975

THE UNEXPLAINED

Chapter One

OUTER SPACE

Inflexibility and error

THE SCIENCE we learn in school is simple and orderly and contains no contradictions. We learn a system of rules and laws we believe are accurate and basic. Later we realize that the laws we spent so much trouble learning are dubious simplifications or even worthless generalizations, and we must revise our knowledge from the ground up, beginning all over again. Also, the rate at which we hear about great scientific discoveries—discoveries we marvel at rather than understand—and the rate at which our knowledge seems to become obsolete leave us with the impression that we live in an age unique for its scientific progress.

But it is impossible for us to test this impression or to know whether the sum of knowledge is really growing as fast as we would like to believe. The sheer abundance of new facts makes it impossible for us to understand them. So we join in the general enthusiasm and stop trying to understand. Fragments of information and comforting remnants of knowledge we learned at school stick in our memories and cover up our doubts and skepticism. It would be hard to say just when the stifling mass production of "science" really began. The only thing we know for certain is the name of the man who coined the rousing slogan, "We must measure what can be measured and find a way to measure what cannot be measured." This

Galileo Galilei (1564-1642), a clever advocate of our modern world view. Without intending to, he instituted the modern method of research, which is based primarily on measurement.

man was the Italian Galileo Galilei, and he turned science in a new direction.

Galileo's time, like our own, was filled with great events. Exciting news traveled swiftly from place to place. Spitsbergen and Bear Island were discovered in the North Sea; Spain took possession of California; men began to explore the vast reaches of Canada. The isle of Manhattan had already been settled. The decimal system was adopted for money, measurement, and weights. The microscope opened up the world of tiny organisms, and Harvey discovered the circulation of the blood. Kepler calculated the laws governing planetary orbits. St. Peter's Cathedral was completed in Rome. Frans Hals, Rembrandt, Rubens, and other painters created a golden age of art. Russia, France, Austria, and China were torn by peasant revolts, and Gustavus Adolphus, Wallenstein, Richelieu, and Cromwell were helping to wage the Thirty Years' War.

The mathematician Galileo Galilei, a native of Pisa, lived in this tumultuous age. He was a talented young man who, without much attention at first, occupied himself with various exercises in physics: the law of falling bodies, astronomy, and the science of fortification. But the young man was not very modest, and he knew how to put on a performance. His great hour came when he heard of a new invention, the telescope. Soon he was holding a simple two-lens telescope which he demonstrated with full dramatic effect while standing high on the belfry of St. Mark's Cathedral. The amazed council of Venice watched from below. The long telescope, draped in red and white cloth, looked very impressive, and Galileo did not neglect to show the representatives of Venice, a major sea power, the nautical and military significance of the invention. His presentation made him a famous man. He became a professor for life and his salary was doubled. He also received various honorariums.

Did Galileo perform a show-business stunt and nothing more? He did not invent the telescope himself, but what does that matter? He was informed and up to date, recognized new possibilities, and made sure that people took advantage of them. Today we know how rare these talents are.

Until that day—August 21, 1609—no astronomer had ever observed the heavens with a telescope! Neither Tycho Brahe nor Kepler nor Copernicus could use a telescope. This is precisely what Galileo did, and six months later his dumbfounded contemporaries could read what he had seen:

- There are mountains and valleys on the moon.
- Four moons orbit Jupiter.
- There are many more stars than we knew of until now.
- The theory of Copernicus is correct: the earth moves around the sun.

Galileo could still look forward to years of significant discoveries. However, it remained his principal goal to prove the accuracy of the Copernican world view. We might regard him as a zealous propagandist of modern astronomy.

Then in 1633, the reaction set in: the Inquisition. Four hearings were held, and Galileo was imprisoned and threatened with torture. He knew what this treatment betokened, for thirty-three years before, Giordano Bruno had been sentenced to death in the same church where Galileo was imprisoned and had then been burned at the stake. To be sure, Galileo was a famous scholar, but he was sixty-nine years old. What could he do? To save his life, he read aloud and solemnly swore to a theory which everyone present knew was false—the theory that the earth was the fixed center of our planetary system.

Two more dates are important in relation to Galileo. Two hundred two years later, in the year 1835, his major work was removed from the Index of forbidden books. Then, three hundred thirty-five years after his forced perjury, in the year 1968, at a colloquium of Nobel Prize-winning physicists in Lindau on Lake Constance, Cardinal F. König stated that the Church was considering the possibility of "rehabilitating" Galileo. However, any "rehabilitation" of Galileo has long been unnecessary. The theories of Copernicus were accepted without it.

Galileo's demand that everything in nature be measured has proven much more important than his defense of Copernicus. Since his time we have been flooded with new and increasingly refined measurements, a vast quantity of unrelated facts. Unfortunately, it is easier and more comfortable to take measurements than to understand them. Whereas in the past people believed that they could understand things by means of a few experiments and much careful reflection, now people think that if they just take enough measurements, someone else will be able to make sense out of them. But gradually we are realizing that most of the measurements we gather remain meaningless and have no scientific value. *The following chapters will show how little, despite all our efforts, we know about commonplace natural events.*

What is the origin of the universe?

Let us begin with what we know or do not know about the cosmos, the world around us.

The Danish astronomer Tyge Brahe, usually known by the Latinized form of his name, Tycho Brahe, built an observatory in 1576. His "celestial fortress" on the island of Hven contained only large "quadrants" or clinometers to determine the path of the stars. It is remarkable that, despite the fact that he observed the stars with the naked eye, he was able to gather material which correlated to a high degree with the Copernican view of our solar system. Later, after Brahe's death, Kepler was able to derive his laws of planetary motion from Brahe's data! But what had Brahe and Kepler really achieved? Mere knowledge of the solar system did not advance us much beyond the level of the ancients, who expressed their thoughts about the origin of our world in sagas and myths. To understand a thing we must know how it came to be, and neither Kepler's laws nor the observations of Brahe and Galileo tell us anything about the origin of the universe.

There are three scientific ways to answer questions about the origin of the world.

The first way is to investigate *one* object from as many angles as possible. If its present form and composition are the result of past events (*i.e.*, if the law of cause and effect is valid), then by studying it we must be able to penetrate the past. For example, we may pick up a stone from a muddy field. The stone did not come from the place where we found it. It is flat and rounded and worn. Since it is flat, the wind did not beat the sand against it; instead, it must have been water that made it smooth. Water also carried it to the place where we found it. It contains the remains of small animal shells. Thus, it was formed at a time when such creatures were alive. The stone is made of limestone and thus derives from the shell limestone period of our earth's history. It must be around 185,000,000 years old. Finally, we can precisely determine what caused the stone to be formed. The events which formed it must in turn have had a cause, and by exploring these events we can learn about events which occurred long before our stone came into being. Recently we successfully tested this technique—the attempt to read the story of creation from

God created the sun, moon, and stars. (Painting from Codex 1179 of the Österreichische Nationalbibliothek, Vienna)

a few fragments of stone—in our investigation of the moon.

If we do not succeed by measuring as many details as possible about an object and deriving important conclusions from these measurements, then we must take the second approach. Instead of examining one object, we measure as many objects as possible, always gathering those facts which can be measured with maximum precision. The sum of the measurements enables us to draw conclusions, and these conclusions permit us to understand the origin, development, and history of the object under investigation. One example of this research technique is astronomers' continual search for new stars.

Both methods of research are ideal rather than real. Unfortunately, in practice neither suffices. Again and again researchers confront the uncomfortable fact that they do not possess the methods or the necessary precision of measurement to use the first technique, and that not enough appropriate objects are available for them to use the second. Thus, many scientists must strike a compromise between a high degree of precision on the one hand and universal statements on the other. The compromise remains uneasy, and at times precision and universality are incompatible.

When we ask what was the origin of the world, we see that the third approach to the problem is also inapplicable. This third approach is the favorite of chemists, who try to artificially create the object they wish to investigate and thus to test their theories concerning its origin and properties. Unfortunately—or fortunately?—we cannot yet create a new universe.

So three hundred fifty years after Galileo, we still confront the question: What is the origin of our universe? What we know about this subject is scarcely worth mentioning. As evidence of how little we do know, scientists are still debating the merits of two completely opposite theories. Which is correct?

At the beginning of our world all the matter in the cosmos was united in a gigantic lump, which exploded and formed the stars.

Or:

The universe was always the way we see it now, and the stars, their density, and their motions in space have remained, on an average, the same.

The big bang

Devotees of the first theory speak of an explosion and of a ball of fire which contained particles of our world and an antiworld. In this ball, matter was converted into radiation, and finally the cosmos we know developed from the ball. According to this theory, some two seconds after the big bang, protons and neutrons were formed at temperatures of around 10,000,000,000 degrees. In the following eleven minutes (the time it takes free neutrons to decay), atomic nuclei of the heavy elements formed by capturing neutrons and protons. After approximately 10,-000 years, hydrogen and helium atoms developed. After the universe had been expanding for about 10,000,000 years, portions of the gaseous matter which had uniformly filled the universe until that time began to converge. Then star systems or galaxies formed out of the gaseous clouds.

As our galaxy evolved, a large portion of the original cloud of gas was transformed into stars. However, at a certain point in the development of massive stars, part of the mass they contained rejoined the interstellar matter.

Scientists believe that at some point the entire process reverses itself. Thus, the universe must experience recurrent cycles of growth and destruction, and we live in a state of perpetual oscillation.

This theory does not paint a pleasant picture! The notion that our world began with a primal explosion and will one day perish by its opposite, an implosion, is disturbing enough. But the thought that afterward all these events will be repeated again and again resembles a bad dream. The process would, of course, involve the recurrent birth and destruction of an earth and an epoch of human existence. Perhaps each time the universe was reborn, each of us would have to exist all over again.

The steady state

The second theory, that of an eternally constant universe, or the "steady state" theory, seems more appealing. For many years, one of its most engaging champions has been the English astronomer Fred Hoyle (born 1915). Until the beginning of 1972, Hoyle was director of the Institute for Theoretical Astronomy in Cambridge, England. He was among the leading scientists at the Mount Wilson and Mount Palomar observatories in the United States. Moreover, he was a well-known British "television professor," and he also won worldwide fame as an author of textbooks and outstanding science-fiction stories.

Like many of his colleagues, Hoyle has repeatedly attempted to classify, order, and systematize the abundance of cosmic phenomena: stars, asteroids, meteorites, cosmic dust, nebulae, radio sources, pulsars, quasars, interstellar gas. The steady-state hypothesis suggests that all these phenomena exist in a constant balance of forces and masses. Thus, though a few stars might be destroyed, something new would form in another place, so that the picture as a whole remains the same. This hypothesis was bound to fascinate a man like Hoyle and he continually invented new arguments in defense of the theory. In his role as astronomer, physicist, and mathematician, he created a picture of the steady-state universe which many of his colleagues found convincing. Even non-scientists were entranced by this theory. The image of a gigantic universe which grows out of itself and yet always remains in good order is really very appealing. However, despite the most elegant formulations and impressive mathematical proofs, in the end the theory convinces only a few specialists. The real problem with both the big-bang and steady-state theories is that they show us a world which is neither "complete" nor in a state of rest. Moreover, both theories must explain a fleeing motion on the part of all heavenly bodies, a motion which clearly exists.

All non-scientists expect some sort of "solid" theory, as simple, clear, and comprehensible as the world our physics instructors seduce us into believing exists. Unfortunately, scientists cannot offer us such a "seamless" theory of the creation of the universe.

We should also keep in mind that any truly workable theory of the creation of the universe must fulfill two conditions. First it must describe the origin of our world. Second, we must be able, without encountering contradictions, to derive from it the entire history of the cosmos. Every new discovery, every cosmic event, must be consistent with this theory, and it should also enable us to predict phenomena accurately.

Our galaxy

Granted that we know nothing conclusive about the origin of the universe, the next question is: How much or how little do we understand about the origin of our own galaxy? Our galaxy is a smaller universe which surrounds us and serves as our immediate "neighborhood."

First we should realize that we have not yet even established the approximate number of galaxies in the vast reaches of the universe. This is understandable, for we have only known for about half a century that other galaxies exist. Only one thing seems certain: we are surrounded by millions of galaxies, and many of them may be substantially larger than our own. But if we modestly restrict our questions to our own galaxy, are there some things we can know about it for certain? The answer is disappointing. Although we are relatively certain of many facts concerning our cosmic "neighborhood," there is a great deal more that we do not know.

To begin with, we do not even know how large our galaxy is. Authors of popular science books usually take the easy way out and speak of a "discus shape," 1,000 light-years thick and 100,000 light-years in diameter. They do not forget to mention that one light-year is the distance which light, traveling at about 186,000 miles per second, travels in one year, or 5,878,900,000,000 miles. It may be helpful if we add that a light-year is more than 60,000 times the distance from the earth to the sun. However, the term is still incomprehensible unless we have a number to compare it with. The following comparison may be helpful: it takes light around eight minutes to travel from the sun to the earth. In other words, when we see the edge of the sun disappear beneath the horizon, the sun has really "set" eight minutes ago. And when we see the first sunbeam in the morning, the sun has already been in the sky for eight minutes, for the light takes that long to reach us.

It takes 4.3 years for light to reach us from Proxima Centauri, the star nearest our sun, and the radiant Sirius is around nine light-years away. Some forty stars are located sixteen light-years away, and the famous star Vega twenty-seven. Light requires three hundred years to reach us from the Pleiades. However, astronomically speaking, the Pleiades are still among our closest neighbors. Rigel, the splendid bluish star in the constellation Orion, is five hundred forty light-years away. If an astronomer lived on this star and could record the weak gleam of the earth and change it into pictures, then right now he might see the burning of the Maid of Orléans or the fire which destroyed the Mayan capital in Mexico; the light that would be reaching him had shone on the earth around 1430 A.D.

But what do these five hundred forty light-years matter compared with the 100,000 light-years which comprise the diameter of our galaxy? We cannot grasp such distances, and if we note that it is 2,200,000 light-years to our nearest galactic neighbor, the so-called Andromeda nebula, we still have no conception of the distances involved or of the emptiness of the world around us. One is almost tempted to say that we are fortunate in this, for anyone who tried to measure these numbers with absolute precision would be terribly frustrated. Most estimates of cosmic distances are quite inaccurate. In fact, we can only come within twenty percent of measuring the size of our own galaxy!

The shape

Granting that we do not know how many stars surround us and our sun, do we not at least know the *shape* of our galaxy? A great abundance of similar galaxies exists in our universe. We see them from the side, from above, or from below—assuming that we can speak of an "above" or a "below." Some galaxies have no clearly defined structure but look like bright, nebulous, round expanses or long, drawn-out shapes. The aptly named "spiral nebulae" look very different. They resemble the spring of a clock and are relatively flat. Their round, flat shape makes them resemble a discus, but their "arms" make them look like a spring. These arms comprise two, three, or more long, curved accumulations of stars. Sometimes the arms are short and not clearly distinct from each other. The whole formation rotates like a lawn sprinkler, the inner regions very fast, the outer regions slowly. For example, our solar system rotates around the center of our own galaxy at a speed of around one-hundred-fifty-five miles a second. No one knows why this is so.

If an inhabitant of such a star family, or galaxy, looks along the plane of the discus, he sees many stars, a brilliant "Milky Way"; but if he looks above or below, he sees a dark night sky with far fewer stars.

How does our galaxy, our spiral nebula, our Milky Way look from a long distance away? Probably we will never have the chance to take a picture of it. To do so we would have to be able to leave our galaxy in a spaceship, and it is unlikely that we can ever fly as far as that. We have no choice but to laboriously construct a picture of it from inside by means of countless measurements with optical and radio telescopes. And we have done this with modestly successful results. We have learned that our solar system lies in one spiral arm of the galaxy and that two other arms surround us, one in the middle of the galaxy and another along its outer perimeter. But despite

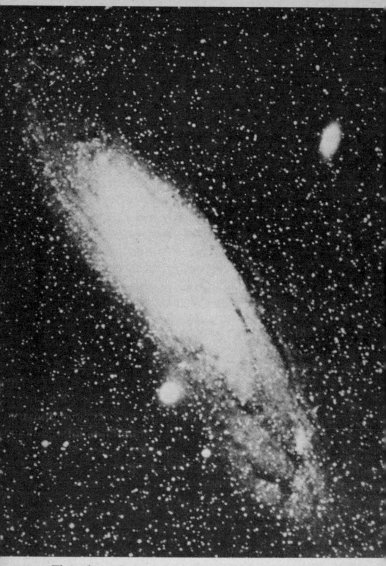

The galaxy closest to ours is the Andromeda nebula. It is around 2,200,000 light-years away. (MPG newspaper photo)

the fact that spiral arms do exist in this galaxy, we cannot go so far as to assume that it is as beautifully shaped as other galaxies are.

Speeding through the universe

We may make one additional, somewhat unsatisfactory statement about our galaxy: as it whirls around, it may be hurling its outward borders into the depths of space, and at the same time it is also flying through the cosmos. Where are we, the earth, the sun, and some 30,000,000,-000 stars all flying to?

A few years ago astronomers believed that they could answer this question fairly precisely: the galaxy is traveling in the direction of the star Sirius at a rate of ninety three miles per second. Now scientists are no longer certain that this theory is correct. They changed their minds because of the shifting toward red of the spectral lines of starlight—the phenomenon that the faster a star is moving away from us, the more the color of its light shifts toward the red part of the spectrum. The only credible explanation for this phenomenon is that the universe is flying apart faster and faster the farther away it is. If this is true, it seems a matter of indifference where our galaxy is going.

Recently the situation has become even more difficult. Not only do we not know the answer to the already more or less classical question of where our universe is headed, but also recent observations have unexpectedly complicated matters. We must now try to answer the following questions: What are radio galaxies and quasars? What role do Seyfert galaxies play in our image of the universe? Are the Seyfert galaxies stars surrounded by vast, glowing masses of gas? What is the nature of the "compact galaxies" which were discovered by the Swiss scientist F. Zwicky in 1961? And what about the other galaxies described in astronomical literature?

The more questions there are, the fewer clear-cut answers we can find.

Compared with the universe as a whole, our galaxy is nothing. If there are astronauts living elsewhere in the vast reaches of space (and there is no reason why there should not be), they would not even notice it if our galaxy were to disappear; or if they did, they would notice it only a long time afterward. The same holds true of us: if one of the millions and millions of galaxies in the universe were to disappear, we would hardly notice.

If we compare the size of our galaxy with that of our solar system, the result is the same: the inhabitants of other solar systems would hardly notice if our solar system suddenly vanished from the galaxy. No one would miss us if we were gone. However, if we wanted to attract the attention of the rest of the cosmos, our best course might be to arrange for a supernova to appear somewhere nearby. A supernova is such a striking event that one attracted the attention of Chinese astronomers in the year 1054, when science was still young. In that year a new "star" appeared in the sky. It was so radiant and bright that for twenty-three days it was visible even in bright daylight. European scientists did not record the presence of the "guest star," as the Chinese called it, but apparently the North American Indians were better observers. A cave in northern California depicts something like a configuration of stars, along with the moon in a specific position. One of the stars in the formation appears to be the cloud of glowing gases that we now call the Crab nebula, a brilliant supernova.

Neighbors in space

Our solar system is important to us for two reasons: first, because it is our home, and second, because we know some important things about this region of the cosmos. Of course, our knowledge of the solar system primarily results from the fact that it is a clearly defined region consisting of a central sun around which a number of planets rotate in (relatively) fixed orbits. No expansion takes place here, no creation of new matter, and no noticeable loss of substance. Above all, the solar system is of such a size that we can easily observe it. Whereas a ray of light takes 4.3 *years* to travel to the nearest star, it takes only 6.5 *hours* to reach the outermost planet of our solar system. Astronomers know so much about our solar system that they have filled whole libraries with books on the subject. All this is very satisfying and strengthens our tenderly nurtured faith in scientific progress.

However, we are not standing on as solid ground as we

may think. After all, Kepler, Copernicus, and Galileo knew of the existence of only six planets. How many theories and speculations were based on the assumption that there were only six! Is our own time any different?

The seventh planet, Uranus, was the first planet to be discovered with the aid of a telescope. It was found—quite accidentally!—by the astronomer Wilhelm Herschel in 1781. Herschel was actually a musician whose father played the oboe in the Hanover regimental band. Before war broke out in Europe he fled to England, where he became the most famous astronomer of his time. He had not been educated as an astronomer but was a self-educated man who built his optical instruments himself: a musical stargazer. Later he advanced to the post of "Royal Astronomer" and was dubbed "Sir William." In addition to his other achievements, he now showed a flair for business. He became so successful at the manufacture of telescopes that he could have lived well on the income from this sideline alone. No new planets had been discovered since the time of the Babylonian astronomers. Thus, when Herschel discovered Uranus on March 13, 1781, he at first believed that he had seen a comet. His discovery breathed new life into the science of astronomy.

Astronomers had difficulty in computing the planetary orbit of Uranus. The planet did not move in accordance with astronomical theory, and soon astronomers decided that another planet must be affecting its orbit. Then in 1846 they actually succeeded in finding this new planet, which they called Neptune. But still the orbit of Uranus was not what it should have been. Then finally in 1930 a third new planet was discovered, the planet Pluto. We now know of the existence of nine planets, but this by no means implies that we have found all the planets in our solar system. We do not even know the mass of Pluto, unless we are satisfied with the vague assertion that it is somewhere between .11 and one times the mass of the earth.

Thus, we are far from having completed our investigation of the immediate neighborhood of our earth. Another example: between the years 1895 and 1961, astronomers tried fifteen times to determine the mean distance between the earth and the sun. None of the fifteen measurements agree, even allowing for the margin of error involved in each technique of measurement! Not until the invention of radar did astronomers make some progress in measuring the distance from the earth to the sun. Then they corrected the closest estimates by a span of about 31,000 miles. Moreover, they corrected former estimates of the distance to our close neighbor Venus by some 186 miles. Let us now try to orient ourselves a little. So that the numbers do not become so vast that we cannot comprehend them, we can use the earth as a unit of measure.

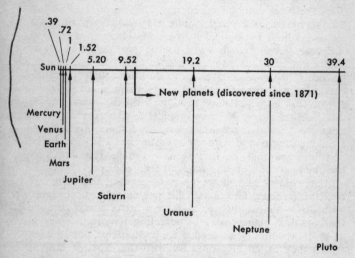

Diagram of the distances in our solar system. The distance from the sun to the earth is the unit of distance and is equal to 1.

The diagram makes it clear that before the discovery of Uranus, we had discovered only one-quarter of our solar system, for Saturn is 9.52 units away and Pluto is 39.4 times the distance between the earth and the sun.

The following table shows us the mass of the various planets, all evaluated in terms of the mass of the earth:

Mercury: .06

Venus: .81

Earth: 1

Mars: .11

> Thus, Venus and the earth are approximately equal in mass, whereas Mercury and Mars are tiny in comparison. In fact, Mercury has only some five times the mass of our moon. But now come two giant planets:

Jupiter: 318

Saturn: 95

> Jupiter is uncanny. Not only does it possess three hundred eighteen times the mass of our earth, but it also has a diameter eleven times as great. Surrounded as it is by twelve moons, two of which are larger than our giant moon, Jupiter resembles an entire solar system in itself; for the planet resembles a sun in that it probably radiates more heat into outer space than it absorbs. We know that Saturn gives off heat; but its rings present us with some uncomfortable riddles, for we know very little about their origin, their substance, their density, and their function with regard to the planet.

Uranus: 14.5

Neptune: 17.5

> These planets are gigantic compared with the earth. It seems amazing that we noticed them so late.

Pluto: .2

> We are so uncertain of our facts about this planet that many astronomers believe it is possible that Pluto is not a

"genuine" planet, but rather one of Neptune's moons which has become separated from its parent planet.

No one knows for certain whether there are other planets in our solar system. Repeated attempts have been made to find a tenth planet, but until now they have met with no success. However, a tenth planet may exist, and astronomers would not be surprised if one were discovered.

On the other side of Mars a ring of rock chunks circles the sun. These are asteroids. Their mass must be substantially smaller than that of our moon. However, some of the rock chunks orbiting the sun are many miles across. They are angular objects which have been baptized with their own names:

- Ceres, around four hundred miles in diameter
- Pallas, three hundred miles in diameter
- Vesta, two hundred fifty miles in diameter
- Juno, one hundred miles in diameter.

These asteroids are almost small planets. However, most of the matter composing asteroids consists of rock fragments, some of which are the size of dust particles. Some of the larger asteroids have strange orbits which bring them close to the earth.

Do the meteorites which strike our earth and moon represent rock and metal fragments from this asteroid belt? There is some evidence that most meteorites do originate from there. However, we know so little about these wanderers in space that it is equally possible that they constitute remains from the early history of creation, or that they are the remnants of one or several planets which exploded long ago. On the other hand, it is possible that asteroid material will give rise to a new planet which will have the mass of the planet Mercury! No one knows for sure. Perhaps we can understand the origin of asteroids if we know more about the formation of our solar system, its size, age, and motion through space.

Rumors and hopes

There are many other great mysteries in our solar system besides the quest for remote outer planets and speculations about the origin of asteroids and meteorites. From time to time we hear reports that scientists have observed and photographed planet-like material near the sun. Do planets really exist in that area? Is it true that the space between Mercury and the sun is not empty? Almost one hundred years ago the Parisian astronomer Urbain J. J. Leverrier, famed for discovering the planet Neptune, believed that another planet must be located in this area. He even gave the planet a name, Vulcan. Meanwhile, during solar eclipses we have observed various "objects" near the sun. Apparently these objects are not comets, as was first suspected, but may move along orbits resembling planetary orbits and thus may actually be something resembling planets. Astronomers disagree about the meaning of their observations.

How much more must we investigate, measure, observe, and compute in order to draw a picture of our tiny solar system? Such a picture would serve as the basis for our image of the universe. Unfortunately, it seems that we are further from our goal than ever before.

The moon

Some scientific questions are so old and venerable that we almost succeed in forgetting them—that is, we forget that they have not yet been answered. For example, there is our moon. It is of such a size and such a distance from the earth that during a solar eclipse it conceals the sun itself but not the gas which surrounds the sun. Is this an "accident"? Hardly. And if it is no accident, why is it so?

As we know, the same side of the moon always faces toward the earth—that is, the rotation of the moon on its own axis and its orbit around the earth coincide. Is this an accident? And if it is no accident, we must ask whether the size and motion of the moon were created when it was formed. In other words, where does the moon come from? Was it born long ago at the same time as the earth? Did it travel through space until it was captured by the earth? Or was it hurled away from the earth at a time when our planet was rotating very fast?

The spectacular American moon flights give us no answers to these old questions. We must now append a new question which sounds strange only because it was first voiced as recently as 1973: Why does the moon have no moons? Computations of the masses of the earth and the moon and of their rotation and flight paths are too complex to present in detail here. However, these computations appear to indicate that once upon a time the moon was orbited by "little moons" which gradually slowed down until they finally crashed into the moon. When this happened, pieces of the smaller moons one hundred sixty miles across may have struck the moon's surface. In fact, the giant craters called Mare Serenitatis and Mare Crisium may have been formed by these falling chunks of little moons! Perhaps small quantities of debris, remains of the tiny moons, are still orbiting the moon.

These speculations lead us to wonder if one day our moon will fall onto the earth, and how long it will be before the first planet falls into the sun.

Many scientists hoped that our direct investigation of the moon would at least solve a few riddles or give us a couple of clear-cut answers. But apart from a few details about surface structures, we already knew about or at least had predicted everything we found on the moon: dead stone, meteorite remains, craters, waterless plains, no atmosphere, dust, desert. Naturally, these somewhat unsatisfactory results do not change the fact that the flight to the moon was a great adventure involving what for our time were fantastic technical achievements. But we were deeply disappointed in our hopes that, as an American physicist expressed it, we might be able to read the history of our solar system in a little piece of moon rock. Today we know no more about the origin of our moon than we did twenty or thirty years ago.

Our modern "space flights" resemble the first awkward movements of a child. If we reduce the distances within the solar system to human scale, the flight to the moon corresponds to a movement of just one and one half inches, i.e., less than we move our fingertip when we bend a finger. If we compare this with the distance from the earth to Pluto, at present the outermost edge of our solar system (this is still a tiny distance on the cosmic scale), we would have to travel over six hundred yards. If we wanted to journey to Pluto in one of today's conventional space-ships, it would take us almost eight and a half years to complete the trip. The space probe Pioneer 10, which radioed some interesting data from Jupiter, took six hundred forty-one days, or around one and three-quarter years, to travel this short distance. On the other hand, the message it sent, which traveled at the speed of light, reached us in only forty-three minutes, less than three-quarters of an hour.

Is astronomy just beginning?

One of the exciting developments of recent years has been the story of Cygnus X-3, or, as the astronomers call it, Cyg X-3. Perhaps never before in the history of astronomy have so many unexpected and incomprehensible phenomena been discovered in such a short space of time. Cygnus means swan, and the object in question is a heavenly body in the constellation of the Swan, which is located at the edge of our galaxy.

In 1967 the "object" Cyg X-3 was discovered as a point which emitted X rays. Nothing, not even the tiniest shimmer, could be discerned there. The only thing which astronomers knew about the source of the X rays was that it must be many kiloparsecs away. One kiloparsec is around 3,000 light-years.

On September 2, 1972, the subject of Cyg X-3 suddenly became quite exciting. A Canadian radioastronomer, P. C. Gregory, was waiting for a star to rise, and to avoid boredom he pointed his instrument toward Cyg X-3. During the last days of August astronomers had barely been able to measure the X rays it was emitting. Now suddenly Gregory's instrument recorded such intense X rays that the astronomer had to reduce its sensitivity! Was his equipment broken? Quickly he called up another team of researchers: "Would you believe that the intensity of Cyg X-3 has increased twenty times?"

A few moments later it became clear that whereas a few days before the X rays had reached an intensity of .01, their intensity was now around twenty. All the observatories around the world were alerted. A Dutch astronomer assumed the responsibility of telephoning his colleagues in Europe, and soon hundreds of astronomers at dozens of institutions, along with several satellites, were busy investigating the strange phenomenon of Cyg X-3.

It soon became clear that the intensity of the radiation emitted by Cyg X-3 fluctuates markedly and that the longer waves of radio emissions also fluctuate in intensity. Something we do not understand takes place in Cyg X-3. What appear to be hot gases and magnetic fields spread out from this source at one-tenth the speed of light, and in a few days they develop into "bubbles" which are perhaps 12,400,000,000 miles across. (The radius of the earth's orbit, or the distance from the sun to the earth, is only 92,500,000 miles.) Thus, these bubbles are truly beyond comprehension. After they form, they disappear again.

But the surprises were not at an end. Occasionally a radioastronomer hit on the notion of leaving his heated and well-lighted observatory and going outside to look through a normal telescope and see whether he could not discover a tiny point of light in the area of Cyg X-3. However, even with the aid of the finest telescopes, no one saw anything for a long time. Then on October 3, 1972, an astronomer found a source of light. It was not in the visible spectrum but was infrared! However, the most exciting event occurred in July, 1973, when astronomers discovered that the infrared radiation fluctuated markedly. This was the first time that astronomers had seen something like this take place in the universe.

To summarize everything we now know about Cyg X-3, it appears to be an incredibly large object which contains a highly compact nucleus, which is surrounded by masses of hot gas, which emits X rays, radio waves, and infrared waves, which may be a double star system, and which may have something to do with a "black hole." Cyg X-3 is so different from everything previously known that in the end it may not only compel us to ask countless new questions but may also force us to reexamine many theories which we had previously assumed to be true.

Compared with the mysteries of Cyg X-3, the discussion of the moon's peculiarities and the debate as to how fluctuations in the sun's behavior (the solar wind, the interplanetary magnetic field, geomagnetic storms, and sunspots) may affect the weather and, in particular, the development of storms seem relatively insignificant.

Demonstration of ignorance

At the end of 1973 and at the beginning of 1974, the comet Kohoutek demonstrated how little we really know about the world. On June 20, 1973, the headlines of one German newspaper read: GIANT COMET RACES TOWARD THE EARTH. A German astronomer was said to have discovered an "Envoy from the Beginning of the Solar System." It was predicted that in September people would be able to see the comet through a telescope and then with the naked eye, and that finally the comet's tail would be visible across one-sixth of the sky. During Christmas of 1973, a gigantic "star of Bethlehem" would be shining in the sky. And soon the usual prophets of doom, as bleak as seers of the Dark Ages, predicted that the comet would bring war, pestilence, and famine to the earth, and rumors began to spread of what might happen if the comet actually struck the earth or if the earth were to fly through the glowing comet's tail.

All these headlines and predictions were false. It was not a German but a Czech astronomer, L. Kohoutek, attached to the Hamburg Observatory, who discovered the comet as he was looking through photographs of the sky that were already ten days old. Moreover, the comet was not racing toward the earth, but was destined to fly past it.

When it was all over, the comet had not been an "impressive cosmic phenomenon" at all. In fact, astronomers had barely been able to see it. The disappointment was so great that astronomers would gladly have forgotten all about the comet. However, it is important that we not forget, but keep several things in mind:

Despite the fact that the comet might have represented the ultimate disaster to the earth, it was discovered only by accident.

Astronomers miscalculated its flight path.

Astronomers overestimated the degree to which the comet would be visible.

For the most part expensive research programs set up to investigate the comet represented money spent in vain.

Even more painful is the fact that we know very little about comets in general. In fact, we are forced to guess the following facts about them:

- Probably comets are composed of dust, metallic particles, ice, and frozen gases.
- Probably approximately several billion comets exist in our solar system.
- Probably the comets move like a cloud around the border of our solar system.
- Probably the majority of these comets possess a diameter of only a few miles. (Kohoutek was estimated to have a diameter of twelve miles.)
- Probably all the comets together do not possess the mass of our earth.
- Probably comets represent the remains of the creation of our solar system.
- Probably from time to time some of them are diverted from their course by planets which sail by them, and their change in course takes them into the interior of the solar system.
- Probably the gigantic, glowing tail of the comet poses no danger at all. (As recently as 1974, a mineralogist estimated that a comet's tail would shatter hundreds of miles of the earth's surface.)
- Probably a relationship exists between comets and meteorites ("falling stars" and micrometeorites).

The comet Kohoutek demonstrated the fact that we are just beginning to find out about the universe.

If we make relatively little progress, it is perhaps because although we can describe many phenomena, we still do not know enough about them to convert them into exact figures. To compute the relationships between things, we must have information in exact figures. When scientific controversies arose, the great Anglo-Indian all-around scientist J. B. S. Haldane (born 1892 in Oxford, died 1964 in Bhubaneswar) used to say that an ounce of algebra was more convincing than a ton of impassioned arguments. It is this ounce of algebra which we too often lack.

Science fiction?

What appeals to the imagination of scientists is the saga of the growth and aging of stars. Stars are born from "hot" gaseous clouds which slowly cool and contract.

When very large masses of gas are present and begin to contract, the force of gravity exerts a powerful effect on the gas particles. Moreover, when the mass is sufficiently dense, changes occur in the atomic nuclei. These changes create heat and lead to high temperatures. The increasing heat and motion of the particles resists the further contraction of the gas, and as long as the nuclear reactions continue, a balance is established between the forces of contraction and the nuclear explosions which cause the gas to expand. The balance between expansion and contraction depends on the mass of the system, just as activities within a nuclear reactor depend on the "critical mass." In any case, when the nuclear energy is exhausted, the balance becomes unstable and the star must collapse as the mass falls inward. This collapse can be slowed down by the mutual repulsion of electrons, which have the same charge, and finally a new equilibrium is achieved. Astronomers call the end product a "white dwarf," which is a small star that is slowly cooling.

On the other hand, if the original star possesses substantially more mass than our sun did at its birth, the force of gravity can prove stronger than the power of the electrons to repel each other. When the star's mass "falls" through the cloud of electrons, the nuclear forces interact, and energy is hurled into space, creating a dazzling flash of light. What remains may be a neutron star, a little dot ten kilometers across. Perhaps the pulsars discovered in 1968 are really such neutron stars.

We enter a true fantasy world when we try to imagine what happens when a star's original mass is so great that neither a cloud of electrons nor nuclear reactions are capable of halting gravitational collapse. What happens when a gigantic mass relentlessly collapses into a point? At this point scientific theories begin to surpass the fables of science-fiction writers.

A fantastic idea

Among the scientific works which have postulated these new dimensions and new worlds are those of the brilliant German astrophysicist Karl Schwarzschild. There have been many spectacular scientific careers, but in our century it is truly remarkable that a schoolboy should publish scientific articles in well-known technical journals, enter the university at sixteen, become a university lecturer at twenty-six, and a professor and director of a world-famous observatory at twenty-eight.

In 1916, the year of his death, Schwarzschild produced a formula according to which the acceleration of gravity could become *infinitely* great in relation to a motionless observer. One of the strange inferences drawn from this formula was that the light of a star which suffers total gravitational collapse eventually *fails to reach the observer*. The observer no longer sees what is taking place! The only thing he is aware of is the gravitational field, the effect of gravity. Astrophysicists have a name for such collapsed bodies, which are invisible and therefore would appear black in the sky. They call them "black holes."

The distant observer of such a gravitational collapse would not be harmed. But what would happen to someone on the surface of a star that underwent collapse? Assuming that he could consciously experience what took place, he would find himself hurled into the midpoint of a star, a region in which spatial coordinates (length, breadth, and height) would have the nature of *time*. He would be in "another world" from which he could never return! He would have to remain in another universe, a universe which mathematicians believe can never communicate with ours.

If we expand on this theory and assume the existence of symmetry in our universe, we can derive another phenomenon, the opposite of gravitational collapse: a ceaseless expansion. We should note that astrophysicists believe that antigravitational expansion must be a phenomenon observable in our world. In case it does occur, they have prepared a name for it: a " white hole."

What will be the world-view of the future? Surely the modern relativistic image of the world is not the final one. Once the world was just the earth and some lights in "Heaven." Then it became the solar system, then the galaxy, then the limited but infinite space containing many galaxies. Now we are thinking in terms of "gravitational worlds."

Are we only just beginning to find out about our world?

Chapter Two

THE EARTH IS STILL INCOMPLETE

"And darkness was upon the face of the deep. . . ."

OUR EARTH is a relatively young planet. Astrophysicists estimate the age of the universe as anything up to 20,000,000,000 years, but they estimate the age of the earth as 5,000,000,000 years at most. (The exact estimate is around 4,700,000,000 years, but scientists cannot be certain. The oldest known earth rock is around 3,750,000,000 years old.) The solar system as a whole cannot be much older.

Why and how did our solar system and our earth come into being 5,000,000,000 years ago? Scientists have repeatedly come up with new theories which enabled them to interpret findings they considered significant. However, they frequently disagreed about what "significant" findings were.

For example, here are just six of the many attempts scientists have made to explain the origin of our solar system:

Comets: A comet crashed into the sun and caused the planets of our solar system to split off from it [1749].

Meteorites: Assemblages of meteorites formed the sun and the planets [1755].

Nebulae: "Nebulae" [dust] came together to form the sun; gases were hurled outward and formed the planets [1796].

Collisions of stars: Various theories have been suggested.

Double stars: The sun had a twin from which the planets developed.

Planetary planes: Since all the planets move around the sun in a plane, the entire solar system developed from a flat "nebular disk."

Once again, these theories show us that although we know a great deal, we lack much basic information. The world appears simple and clear only in our schoolbooks, which simplify the true state of affairs.

Schoolbooks never admit doubt

Can we at least expect an answer to the question of how our old familiar earth came to exist? Once again, our schoolbooks seem to know all about it; but scientists do not. In schoolbooks we usually read that, like all planets, the earth was born from a cloud of glowing gases. A white-hot molten mass separated out from this cloud and began to rotate (why, we are not told). Then the earth's crust formed and cooled, while the interior of the earth remained hot.

Meanwhile scientists are discussing a number of possibilities, of which I will mention only a few:

- The earth formed from cold meteoritic material that was heated by the energy freed when it crashed together.
- The earth formed through the agglomeration of cold chunks of cosmic matter. It was heated by atomic nuclear decay when the radioactive substance on the earth reached "critical mass."
- Large masses of meteoritic iron massed together to form the earth's core. Masses of stone were attracted to the iron by the force of gravity and gathered around it.
- Iron and nickel condensed from a cosmic "nebula" and formed the earth's core. Then sulfides

and silicates condensed to form the outer layers of the earth.

None of these possibilities can be absolutely discounted, but at the same time none of them is much more convincing than the others. All the theories have one thing in common: they agree that the earth was formed by a catastrophic event.

Two questions confront us. First: Was the birth of our earth a meaningless event, an "accident," or was the earth created according to a plan we can understand? Second: Is the earth's creation at an end, or are we living on a planet which is still being transformed by brutal acts from outer space?

Was the earth created "accidentally"? If we equate an "accidental event" with an "incomprehensible event," we must answer yes, for we do not know what events led to the formation of the earth. However, if we mean more by the word "accident" than the admission that we do not know enough to understand a certain event, we must answer no. Doubtless the earth was formed in accordance with immutable laws of nature, and one day when its time runs out, it will be destroyed by laws just as immutable.

It is more difficult to answer the second question—whether the earth's creation is complete. Is the time when the earth was subjected to brutal attacks from space really past?

Naturally we are inclined to believe that we humans represent the ultimate goal of the creation, so that now that man has appeared, the earth—*our* earth—must be "complete."

Why do we believe this? Why do we assume that everything was made for us and that it was made as well as it could be?

There is no reason for this assumption. Our belief that we can live in peace, without fear that our planet is about to go into labor once more, is based on the fact that our lives are so short that many generations of men can live and die without experiencing any major catastrophes. If some cosmic power had worked its wrath on our planet within recorded history, we would take a more modest view of things.

No planet to live on

A moment's reflection will tell us how insecure our planet really is. Let us pretend that we are inhabitants of another planet sent here on a mission: to determine whether it is worthwhile to found a civilization on earth. Slowly we would approach the large bluish planet Earth, and at once we would notice its uncommonly large moon. The moon seems the ideal place to stay while observing the earth. Once we landed on the moon, we would see what a barbaric region it is: deep layers of dust, absolutely dry, no animals, no plants, no water, dead rocks, and everywhere craters which show how dangerous it would be to stay there very long. Moreover, there is an unhealthy amount of radiation. On the horizon, shrouded in mist, is the cold, blue earth, rotating much faster than seems desirable. We see that the climate on this planet will not be moderate. Then we glimpse a nearby meteorite. It is

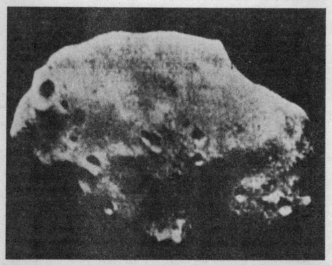

Like all known planets, Phobos, the little moon belonging to Mars, is covered with meteorite craters. Phobos is approximately twenty-two kilometers long and eighteen kilometers wide and is about the size of an asteroid.

Eskimos named this iron meteorite, which was discovered in western Greenland in 1818, Agnighito, or "the tent." The piece of meteorite weighs fifty-nine metric tons and is now in a New York museum. Presumably it was part of a meteorite shower consisting of three or four similar large iron meteorites and hundreds of smaller chunks of iron. (Photograph taken from F. Boschke's *Erde von anderen Sternen/Der Flug der Meteorite*, Econ Verlag, 1965)

only two or three yards in diameter and thus is no giant; nevertheless, it shatters a patch the size of a football field on the moon's surface, creating a new shallow crater. For almost an hour a cloud of dust hangs over the area where the meteorite struck. Clearly, great quantities of meteorites, chunks of stone and iron, and clouds of cosmic dust move about near the earth.

Soon we see comets and asteroids, the remains of stars, coming dangerously close to the earth! Then there is an earthquake on the moon, and we perceive that the moon is not a very stable body. Every thirty-six hours or so, we experience another quake. Making a few measurements, we learn that a danger zone is located between the old observation stations of Apollo 12 and Apollo 13. Quakes are especially frequent in this zone, and apparently they are triggered by gravitational attraction between the earth and the moon. Gas and dust eruptions make us wonder whether there is any point in continuing our investigation of the earth's suitability for colonization. Our stay on the moon has demonstrated that this is an unstable region of the cosmos, a place for adventurers, not for establishing a planned society.

What would alien visitors really think of our planet? Of course, we can only guess. However, we are all too convinced that the earth would be a paradise if only we humans could behave more rationally. Probably aliens judging whether the earth was suitable for habitation would regard it much less favorably than we imagine.

One reason for their unfavorable judgment would be that, no less than the moon, the earth is subject to the constant bombardment of meteorities. Every day some five to six tons of good-sized meteorites fall to the earth. Each weighs as much as several pounds. Moreover, every day over 10,000 tons of cosmic sand and fine dust land on the earth. Over the course of millions of years, such huge quantities of this material have traveled to the earth that doubtless all the humans, animals, and plants that live here contain extraterrestrial matter. If you look you can find tiny new-fallen meteorites in snow and rainwater, and perhaps you will find even more in your swimming pool. Unfortunately, so far no one has done a statistical analysis of how many roof tiles have been shattered by falling meteorites.

We tend to assume that meteorites have created relatively few craters on the earth. This assumption is partially correct, for although even small meteorites create craters on the moon, most of them burn up in the outer layers of the earth's atmosphere, so that all we see of them are "shooting stars." Are the earth's craters at all similar to craters on the moon?

The mysterious crater

In Germany alone there are two craters larger than many craters on the moon. Between the Swabian and Frankish mountains lies a round plain, the Nördlinger Ries. Its diameter is twelve to fifteen miles. For decades scientists agreed about one thing: the plain did not belong there. What really belonged there were mountains two to three thousand feet tall. So scientists debated about what had created the plain. They suspected that the Nördlinger Ries might be the floor of a huge ancient volcano. There were various reasons for believing this. The Ries contains lava-like stone, vitreous rivers of molten material. It appeared that a mighty volcano must have been active here. Thirty or forty miles away, south of the Danube River near Augsburg, people found stony debris from the crater.

For a hundred years geology students were taught that the Nördlinger Ries had been formed by a volcanic eruption. But was this true?

Then a group of scientists formulated a second, quite different theory: the Nördlinger Ries was not formed by a volcano, but was the crater left by a falling meteorite.

Other scientists protested, asking where anyone had found the iron and stone remains of a meteorite. Moreover, they said, such large meteorite craters cannot exist on earth, for everyone knows that meteorites of a size to make such a crater would explode in the atmosphere.

Finally, in April, 1966, scientists from all over the world met to debate on the subject. They met in the medieval town of Nördlingen, in the middle of the mysterious crater. They sat on long benches in the dancehall of a modest inn and discussed the Ries, and then they went out into the crater to test their conclusions. Here they picked up their geologists' hammers and pounded at the stones. After a while someone picked up a multicolored rock, a breccia. Then everyone knelt down in the soft blue-gray sediment and eagerly searched for small black bits of glass. Professors, their assistants, and their students were all trying to answer the same question: What is the mysterious Nördlinger Ries? The younger generation believed there was only one answer: a meteorite crater. The older men were more cautious. But all of them were guided by the facts, and finally they gained a clear picture of what must have happened.

A meteorite over a half-mile in diameter and traveling at the fantastic speed of nine miles a second crashed into the mountains at a thirty-degree angle. It is not clear whether it touched the earth, was vaporized before it struck, or simply compressed the air in its path so violently that the air acted like a solid body, separating the meteorite and the stone below. Some three cubic miles of rock were catapulted from a crater more than a half-mile in depth. Fissures one to three miles deep were dug in the mountain. Enormously high temperatures melted the rock so that it resembled lava, and large, dark, viscous drops of molten glass were hurled two hundred fifty miles away. They fell as far away as Brünn, in Czechoslovakia. The collision created a central cone in the middle of the crater similar to those we find in craters on the moon. We know this cone as the Steinberg, and it is one thousand six hundred feet high. Compared with such a meteorite crash, the explosion of a hydrogen bomb is relatively insignificant; for the energy released in creating the Nördlinger Ries corresponds to the explosion of 100,-000 megatons of TNT. (One megaton = 1,000,000 tons.)

The inhabitants of the ancient imperial city of Nördlingen, the site of fierce combat during the Thirty Years' War, are not much interested in an event which took place 15,000,000 years ago. However, in reality they owe the existence of their town to this cosmic catastrophe. When the mountains were leveled, the way became clear for traffic between the north and the south. The area around present-day Nördlingen was settled even in Roman times. The existence of the crater made farming possible. The masses of molten rock proved ideal for use in building and were easy to work with. For example, a church in Nördlingen was built of this stone. Moreover, when the rock was ground to a fine powder, it proved an excellent raw material for the manufacture of fireproof dishware. Around the edges of the crater lay crushed stone which could easily be carted away and used to build roads. In places where fissures had been cut into the limestone cliffs, the rock lent itself to use as raw material in the making of cement. The crater has proved disadvantageous to the city in only one respect: because so many fissures were dug into the crater floor and have only partially healed, rainwater does not remain on the surface, where the plants are growing. Thus, the Ries sometimes suffers from a water shortage.

The Ries crater is an unusual, but not a unique, phenomenon. Just thirty kilometers west of the border of the

Nördlinger Ries lies the Steinheimer Basin. This is a shallow limestone basin three kilometers in diameter. In its center is a knoll like those we see in craters on the moon. Here, too, scientists at first assumed that the basin represented the remains of a volcano. However, drill samples revealed no trace of volcanic rocks, but only split rocks which had later been cemented together—*i.e.*, breccia. Then rock debris formed by violent impact, along with other evidence, made it clear that the basin had been formed by another meteorite crashing into our earth!

Our present information suggests that the Nördlinger Ries meteorite and the meteorite which formed the Steinheimer Basin must have flown through space together and landed on earth at almost the same time. We know that the earth has sometimes been bombarded by meteor showers containing thousands or hundreds of thousands of rocks. Millions of years ago they no doubt moved through our solar system in "closed formation." Huge masses of meteorites still fly through space today. Thus, any minute one of them may create another large crater somewhere on earth. The inhabitants of this planet are not safe from catastrophe.

The forgotten risk

When a small meteorite one or two inches in diameter strikes the moon, the fine, loose dust rises in a cloud, and even years later we can still see a small crater. Since gravity is much weaker on the moon than on earth, even a slight impact leaves clearly visible traces. Moreover, the moon has no atmosphere to slow down the meteorite. Thus, even tiny meteorites smaller than a pinhead beat holes in the rocks on the moon. These holes can be seen only under a microscope. In the tiny craters we can detect the wall where the rock melted, a discoloration of the stone, rock chips, cracks, and fissures. When a large object strikes the moon's surface, a cloud of gray dust hangs over the point of impact for hours.

On earth, on the other hand, small meteorites and micrometeorites disappear almost completely as soon as they reach the earth's surface. Even meteorites weighing twenty or thirty pounds leave holes no deeper than one or two feet. People often do not even notice that they are there. Sometimes meteorites have been filmed at night by several cameras so that it was possible to calculate their point of impact to within a few hundred feet. Nevertheless, the meteorites were never found, despite the fact that students, schoolchildren, and other volunteers spent days looking for them.

If we do not find the point of impact within a few days after a meteorite falls, we will search in vain, for rain, snow, leaves, and wind quickly obliterate all traces. On earth the only craters which remain visible for longer periods, *i.e.*, for periods meaningful in geological terms, are those created by the removal of large portions of earth. The diagram shows what we now know about meteorites on earth. The number of craters proven and suspected to have been created by meteorites amounts to more than one hundred.

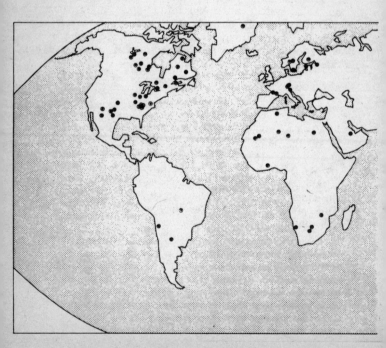

There is some debate about a giant crater in South Africa known as the Vredefort Ring. The inner zone of shattered earth has a diameter of twenty five miles and thus is uncommonly large. Further effects can be observed within a radius of seventy-five miles. This area corresponds to that of the largest moon craters. (The famous crater Copernicus has a diameter of only fifty-six miles.) Naturally, we hesitate to admit that such large tracts of land can be destroyed, today as in the past, by the collision with a meteorite.

The threatening universe

An even more uncanny phenomenon is Hudson Bay, in northeastern Canada. This is a gigantic round basin, located south of a group of islands, which looks as if it

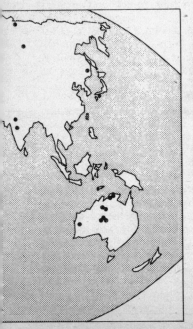

Meteorite craters on earth. The earth would be covered with meteorite craters like the moon if rain and wind did not swiftly efface them. Thus, the black circles in the diagram designate only those craters which we can still detect in our time. If they appear to be less abundant in certain regions, it is due to the fact that no one has searched for craters in those regions.

had been the site of an explosion. Was Hudson Bay created by a gigantic meteorite? We live in a region of the cosmos in which such surprising events are possible. Moreover, much though we might like to do so, we cannot deny the possibility that an asteroid might one day collide with the earth. Here are the relative diameters of meteorites, comets, and asteroids:

Meteorites	Comets	Asteroids
dust and fragments up to a half-mile	from a half-mile to six miles	from a few miles to four hundred miles

If we admit that things similar to what happens on the moon can happen on earth, then in 1971 we discovered something new to fear. In that year we learned of an event which took place on the moon. This event overwhelms our imagination; we can record it but not understand it. Here we are confronting forces and powers which transcend everyday points of reference. Samples brought back by the moonship Apollo 12 reveal that an asteroid around one hundred twenty miles in diameter struck the moon, creating a giant crater. Large expanses of the side of the moon turned toward us were covered with debris exploded from the crater. Lava, molten rock buried more than sixty miles beneath the surface, flowed upward, filled the crater, flowed over the crater walls, and flooded wide areas which had already been covered with rock debris. This is the story of the birth of what we now know as Mare Imbrium!

Later, when another collision formed the crater Copernicus, the new onslaught pierced the old layer of cooled lava and shattered the rock debris which had piled up around Mare Imbrium. A heavenly body one hundred twenty miles across can no longer be designated a meteorite. It is an asteroid. The creation of Mare Imbrium took place some 3,800,000,000 years ago, but this does not mean that a similar event could not occur now. Much larger asteroids are still moving through our solar system today.

Unfortunately, we cannot calculate the orbits of asteroids and thereby cannot reassure ourselves that no collision with the earth will occur. For example, in 1971 astronomers were amazed to discover that the asteroid Torro, three miles in diameter, was describing great *loops* around the sun as it was diverted from its orbit first by the earth, then by Mars, and finally by Jupiter. Torro was attracted by various planets when they approached the asteroid along their own orbits. Quickly astronomers calculated Torro's movements until the year 2020, and at present it appears that the asteroid will not collide with the earth. But what new surprises lie in store for us? We have only known of the existence of Torro since 1964!

As yet no one can predict where Torro will end up. Perhaps one day it will be captured by Venus. If this

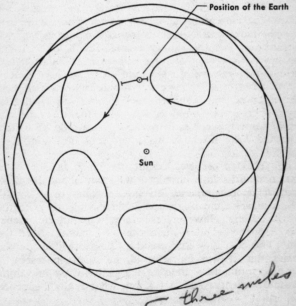

— Position of the Earth

Sun

three miles

The asteroid Torro, which was discovered in 1964, has a diameter of five kilometers. In the time that it takes the earth to orbit the sun eight times, Torro orbits the sun five times. During these orbits Torro is diverted from its course by the earth and other planets, which explains the dizzying loops of its flight path. Eventually the asteroid may be "captured" by a large planet like Venus. We now know of five asteroids whose orbits trace such curves.

happens, Venus may suffer the same effects as the moon during the creation of Mare Imbrium. And what if Torro is "captured" by the earth? Or what if one of the other four wayward asteroids discovered in 1973 collides with the earth? We would like to believe that such a catastrophe could not occur. However, asteroids and meteorites travel in the same region of our solar system, the so-called asteroid belt between Mars and Jupiter, and meteorites from this region collide with the earth every day. Why should asteroids not do so, too?

No one knows why meteorites leave the asteroid belt and strike out on new orbits, and sometimes on a collision course with the earth. The completely unexpected appearance of the comet Kohoutek demonstrates what surprises the universe has in store for us. On March 7, 1973, no one knew that this comet existed, much less that the giant heap of cosmic matter, mixed with ice and wreathed in a cloud of gas and dust, would cross the earth's orbit on November 26 of that year. No one knows whether an asteroid could have shifted the comet's orbit so that sooner or later it would collide with the earth. If the asteroid were as large as Torro, our fate would be sealed. We would have no hope of discovering the asteroid in time.

The repeated debates about the Siberian, or Tunguska, meteorite show how little we know about this field. One fact is indisputable: on the morning of June 30, 1908, a gigantic glowing mass collided violently with the earth in Siberia. However, even now it is not clear what really happened. Did a meteorite or a comet strike the earth? This theory seems credible. Less credible are the theories that it was an asteroid, an alien spaceship, a piece of "antimatter," or a "black hole." Only one thing is certain: scientists do not know what really happened in Siberia.

If we humans live contentedly on our earth, it is because we know mercifully little and because our lifespan is so brief that each of us can hope to live out the few years allotted him in a time when the earth is secure from cosmic threat.

But let us forget the danger in which we live and investigate the question of whether our earth is a solid, well-constructed planet.

The diary of the corals

Every year a tree grows a new ring under its bark. The width of the ring depends on the amount of sun and rain and on the temperature and humidity for that year. Decades after the tree is cut down, the rings tell us whether the climate in each year was good or bad. In the cross-sections of their trunks, trees preserve many facts which we short-lived humans quickly forget. To learn about the past, all we have to do is to learn to read tree rings. For example, the rings of trees whose bark was roasted by the bright flash of the great "Siberian meteor" show what trees can tell us. When we cut down one of these trees, we see that no rings were formed in one area of the trunks. (See illustration.)

When the Tunguska meteorite struck the earth, the bark of a nearby larch tree was damaged by the heat or the dazzling light or the blast. (No one knows the exact cause.) The damage disrupted the normal growth of the tree, as is evident from this cross-section of the trunk.

But trees are not the only living things on which visible marks of each year's growth are traced. Such marks are visible on corals, too. And, in one respect, corals are superior to trees as indicators of past events: they survive not for centuries, but for *millions of years,* and thus they can tell us about the ancient history of our earth.

On March 25, 1966, astronomers, geologists, and zoologists met at a conference in London. It was unusual for scientists of such divergent disciplines to meet together, and their discussion was equally unusual. They talked about only one thing: petrified, fossilized corals.

Scientists had discovered something very exciting. The rings in the limestone skeletons of corals told them more than the simple succession of the years! To be sure, the dark and light stripes represented annual rings, and scientists could clearly read their sequence, but there were also many more, much finer rings within the zones that marked the years. What did they mean? Soon scientists realized that the bands within the annual rings must constitute monthly rings which reflected the phases of the moon. However, between these monthly rings were even finer rings. Could these rings signify *daily* growth? Could the bands in the corals represent something like a calendar in which scientists could read every single day? Did the fine discolorations constitute a life history of every single day of the corals' growth? Or were the rings made by high and low tides?

When scientists counted the rings they discovered that each year contained between three hundred eighty and four hundred five "diurnal rings." In any case, a year contained more than the three hundred sixty-five days that make up our calendar year. Moreover, the evidence suggested that when the corals lived, the year must have contained 13.04 months instead of 12.4 months, as it does now. (We arrive at this figure by calculating the periods it takes the new moon to become a full moon and then a new moon again.) Thus, at that time the moon must have orbited the earth faster than it does today!

The petrified corals confirmed the fact that in the geological epoch known as the Cambrian Age (around 570,000,000 years ago), the year may have consisted of four hundred twenty-eight days instead of three hundred sixty-five. Thus, while completing one orbit around the

Stromatolites. These layers were formed by algae growing 2,000,000,000 years ago. The sequence of layers enabled scientists to decipher the effects of the moon on the earth. (Photograph from the National Science Foundation)

sun, the earth turned on its axis four hundred twenty-eight times instead of three hundred sixty-five.

But was this evidence conclusive?

As soon as a scientist makes a discovery, his colleagues try to test his theory so that they can confirm it or disprove it. Thus, the scientific world soon responded to the new theories about corals. In 1972, G. Pannella, a scientist at the University of Puerto Rico, made a study of stromatolites, strange, finely layered limestone deposits which appear to be around 600,000,000 years old. For a long time scientists had puzzled over the meaning of the stromatolites. Had algae made the fine bands on the limestone? Had the stromatolites been created by mats of algae growing on reefs along the shore? Then a scientific miracle occurred. Suddenly everything became clear: the mysterious stromatolites were layers of limestone which marked the course of a year four hundred twenty-five days long.

The earth is getting tired

Before these discoveries were made, astronomers had already realized that days on earth were getting longer, that the earth was rotating more and more slowly. They had learned this by computing and comparing the dates of lunar eclipses. The eclipses appeared to be occurring earlier than computations suggested they should be. Was this disparity caused by the moon? Was it turning faster now than before? Or was the disparity caused by the earth? Was the earth rotating more slowly? No one likes to think that our earth is "wearing out," that its rotation is slowing down, that in the distant future there will be no more intervals of day and night and that the earth will have a dark side and a sunny side. When this happens there will be long days of burning heat and equally long nights of deadly cold! Now we know for certain that the length of our days is increasing. To be sure, after one hundred years their length has increased only .00164 seconds, and this seems an insignificant amount, but the fact remains that the earth is slowing down.

We now know the reason for this. The earth does not rotate in empty space, but in a gravitational field strongly influenced by the moon. The moon attracts the ocean waters and its gravity creates the tides. The earth must, so to speak, move under a mountain of water. To do so the earth must possess rotational energy, and as this energy is used up, the earth turns more and more slowly on its axis and our days grow longer.

The situation is much more complex than I have outlined. In 1970 scientists saw just how complex it is. They had already suspected, and measurements had to some degree proven, that the land participates in the tides as well as the oceans. But they did not know the whole story until geologists from Columbia University systematically measured the effects of gravity along the fortieth parallel. They followed a course across the North American continent. The results were clear: like the oceans, the continents rise and fall in a twelve-hour rhythm!

Every twelve hours, the attraction of the moon raises North America an average of thirty centimeters. A "tidal wave" made of stone rises and sinks just like the water in the sea. Along the coastline the situation is confusing, for at high tide masses of water are deposited along the edges of the continents, and the tide in the water and the tide on land overlap.

What happens when the rocky structures on the land and in the mountains are subjected to the stress of the tides? Scientists believe that the movements of rock may help to trigger earthquakes, but as yet they cannot prove it. In any case, enormous quantities of energy are expended in moving the continents, and it is important that we study the forces involved. One question which has not yet been answered is this: What happens to the deeper waters of the oceans when the water on the surface is moving around the earth?

Due to the fact that the earth's rotation is affected by the tides, and due to a number of other factors, as well, the rotation of the earth does not serve as a reliable measure of time. (At least it is not a reliable measure of cosmic time spans.) The other factors include seasonal influences like the relative distribution of air masses and snow on the earth's surface. In spring the days are somewhat longer, in the middle of the year they are shorter, in autumn they are longer again, and at the beginning of the new year they are somewhat shorter than normal. Naturally, we are not aware of these fluctuations, but

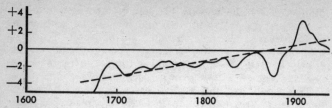

Fluctuations in the length of the day since around 1670. The scale is in 1/1000 second.

scientists using refined techniques of measurement have proved that they occurred over a period of fourteen years.

All in all, the earth now rotates more slowly by about sixty rotations a year than it did in the Cambrian Age. However, some changes in the earth's rotation, in the length of our days, obey no distinguishable pattern. We can do no more than guess at the causes of these changes. Perhaps they result from the irregular disposition of air masses on the earth's surface.

Is the sun slowing us down?

An even more mysterious relationship may exist between the rotation of our earth and the sun. Because scientists have not yet hit upon a better explanation, they are trying to link the phenomenon with changes that sunspots cause in the sun's radiation. However, as yet they can only guess, for they do not know enough about sunspots or about what occurs in the upper layers of the earth's atmosphere.

The best way to describe sunspots is to say that they are uncanny. They represent the most violent explosions of energy which take place in our vicinity, and they may have more influence on our lives than we believe.

One of these mysterious eruptions of solar energy began on August 4, 1972. Physicists in the observation station of Kiruna, in northern Sweden, were warned by a change in the level of short-wave activity. Finally, the chronically bad weather permitted them to send a balloon probe into the air, and they were amazed at the measurements it brought back. At a height of twenty miles, the intensity of the radiation had increased about a thousandfold. The instruments of measurement had broken down because they were not built to record such high readings.

At 6:41 A.M. on the same day, radio astronomers at the Max Planck Society in the Eifel region of West Germany suffered a shock. They were making routine observations of the radio waves which reach us from the sun. Then the intensity of the waves became double what it had been! Precise measurements and a fix on the locus of the disturbance revealed that the intensity of radio waves on the sun had increased ten thousand times in a certain area of the sun.

For days the cause of these phenomena was clearly visible to everyone, a large, dark "sunspot." It could be photographed with simple cameras and recorded on scientific instruments until it disappeared at the upper right corner of the rotating sun.

Sunspots are not dangerous to us on earth because we are shielded by our atmosphere. However, the gases expelled by the sun and the magnetic storms which they cause to rage around the earth represent vast quantities of energy which make themselves felt in various ways.

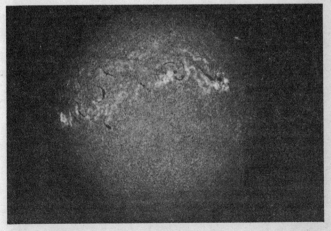

If we photograph the sun through an appropriate light filter, in addition to sunspots we can detect a rough kind of structure. This photograph was taken September 22, 1966. (Photograph from Zeiss-Informationen 65, 1967)

For one thing, they disrupt short-wave and ultra-short-wave radios. The earth is not just a ball of stone. It is also a magnet rotating in space. A change in the strength of the magnetic field must influence the rotation of the earth, and thus the length of our days.

Probably the first scientist to postulate a relationship between eruptions on the sun and the length of our days was the French astronomer A. Danjon. He had observed that in 1959 an unexpected change in the length of the day occurred just after an eruption on the sun. Some of his colleagues accepted his hypothesis; others rejected it. No one knew that soon another powerful eruption would give them the opportunity to test Danjon's theory. The eruption which occurred in August, 1972, was even more powerful than that which had taken place in 1959. Moreover, contrary to general expectation, the eruption clearly affected the rotation of the earth and thus the length of our days! The day of August 8, 1972, was ten milliseconds longer than August 7. This deviation was greater than any which had yet been measured for the length of a single day. In the weeks which followed, the earth, so to speak, "ran slow." Then slowly it regained its old tempo and turned as fast as before.

Now scientists are confronted by a number of questions, the most important of which are these: How did sunspots slow the rotation of the earth? How do sunspots affect the oceanic, continental, and atmospheric tides? Do giant sunspots also affect the weather?

The Chandler wobble

Scientists will spend many years, perhaps decades, puzzling over a phenomenon which in schoolbooks appears to be already settled. As early as 1844, scientists suspected the existence of some irregularity having to do with the earth's axis. A mathematician is responsible for discovering the nature of this irregularity, although he did not discover its cause. Seth Carlo Chandler, who was born in Boston in 1846 and died in 1913, studied at Harvard. He completed his studies there at the age of fifteen and was fortunate enough to be chosen to help run the Harvard observatory. For some time Chandler worked at various jobs and among other things served as an actuary for an insurance firm. In 1891 he published the work for which he is famous, the work in which he described the "Chandler wobble."

The term "Chandler wobble" describes what our earth does: it wobbles. The position of the poles fluctuates to a distance of up to fifty feet. One might think that such slight fluctuations are a matter of little interest. However, the phenomenon presents us with two disturbing questions: What causes the fluctuations? Why do they occur in fourteen-month cycles? Once again, we do not know the answers. Perhaps—but only *perhaps*—large earthquakes cause around ten percent of the fluctuations; and some scientists believe that earthquakes are responsible for as much as thirty percent of the "wobbling." However, we still do not know why the wobbling occurs or what its consequences may be. Perhaps the earthquake theory has reversed cause and effect. Are the earthquakes actually the result, rather than the cause, of the wandering of the poles?

We still confront the question of how the length of an earth day changed over the course of history and how the moon, the planets, and the sun influenced the change. Did the planets play a role, too? Scientists have long doubted this, but it would be foolish to accept the fact that the sun, the earth, and the other planets form a "system" and then to deny that they influence each other. In fact, in 1967 scientists succeeded in proving that the revolution of the planet Mercury influences sunspot activity. Moreover, attraction between the sun and Mercury, Venus, the earth, and Jupiter causes tidal effects. Thus, it is only logical to assume that the planets influence each other, too.

Hope in al-Biruni

On the basis of his investigation of stromatolites, G. Pannella has suggested that once, when the moon may have been only 18,600 miles from the earth (it is now around 230,000 miles away), the days on earth may have been only five hours long. The American scientist R. Newton, of Johns Hopkins University, hopes to clarify the problem with the aid of notes made in the year 1017. At that time Mahmud of Ghazni, Sultan of Afghanistan, gave a certain sum of money to the great scholar al-Biruni. Today we would call this money a research grant. It was al-Biruni's task to precisely determine the direction leading from Ghazni to Mecca so that faithful Moslems would not pray in the wrong direction. Among other things, al-Biruni recorded data concerning the motion of the sun. If, with the aid of old and revised Persian and Christian calendars, Newton succeeds in determining the relationship between this nine-hundred-fifty-year-old data and our own times, his findings may prove more interesting than our scientific data would be to an astronomer living in the year 2920.

It would be wrong to suppose that all the effort and speculation relative to the earth's rotation express nothing more than academic curiosity. When we still used the sun to measure the time of day, or when a burning glass was used to trigger the firing of small cannon at noon in nobles' pleasure gardens, people had no difficulty in telling the correct time. But now that we possess precise clocks, every couple of years we have to correct the time. To make up for irregularities in the earth's rotation, we make the first minute of a new year a little longer or a little shorter. If we did not do this, our descendants would one day have their "noon" at midnight. For example, to keep it from being too short, we had to lengthen the year 1973 by one second, so that its last minute contained sixty-one seconds. In 1974 it was again necessary to compensate for the earth's irregular rotation by lengthening the year by one second.

In the foreseeable future, will we succeed in establishing the basic facts about the history of our earth viewed as a planet in our solar system? As long as we continue to know so little about the solar system, this is not likely.

And how will our solar system look a billion years from now? Will the earth have ceased to rotate on its axis? Will our moon travel through space far away from the earth? Whatever we say in reply, some scientists will agree with us and others will not. We know almost as little about the history of our planet as we do about the universe in which we live.

Chapter Three

THE EARTH HEAVES

A fragile spaceship

WE ARE part of an unknown, incomprehensible creation over which we have no power. Our home is a tiny, reeling, unstable ball, and we are traveling from chaos into an unknown future. From time to time we try to imagine what our world is like and what, if any, meaning lies within it; but we can glimpse only a tiny piece of our world for only an instant. We should realize that our little Spaceship Earth can easily be shipwrecked. We continually see amazing transformations taking place in the cosmos, and so we have to wonder how much time we have left. How stable is our earth?

We know so little about the interior of the earth that we must wonder why scientists have devoted so little attention to the problem. Apparently the earth is not only a small and "wobbly" planet, but also fragile and unstable.

We can sum up the situation in one sentence—*No one knows what makes up the core, the interior, of the earth.* If a student taking his college entrance examinations were to be asked what was inside the earth, he would be quite justified in answering "iron." If he said "an iron-nickel alloy," the answer would be no better and no worse. If he answered "solar matter," this answer, too, would be acceptable. Since 1970 he would get an "A" for answering "a sulfur-iron compound."

53

If a teacher were to ask the student whether the earth's core is solid, soft, or liquid, any answer he gave would deserve an "A," for any of the three is possible.

We do not even know how thick the relatively solid outer crust of the earth is. All we can say is that it appears thin in relation to the core. If I wanted to draw a circle on one page of this book to represent a cross-section of the earth, I would cause the printer severe problems; for no printer could print a line thin enough to accurately represent the earth's crust. Even if he could, the reader could only see the line under a magnifying glass. Thus, it is small wonder that this absurdly thin crust is covered with cracks, tears, and breaks, and is shaken by earthquakes. In short, the earth's crust is very unstable, and it is amazing that it can support life.

Science-fiction writers delight in describing how the earth could break up if we do not treat its crust with sufficient care. For example, H. Dominik wrote a splendid, technical science-fiction novel depicting the building of a super-canal across Central America. In this novel the danger exists that tensions released by the building of the canal may cause North and South America to break apart. (In the end the catastrophe does not occur.) Other stories touch on a similar theme: the possibility that the earth's supposedly liquid interior might erupt into a large mine shaft or excavation. All these stories suggest that man may destroy the earth by carelessly breaking through its thin crust.

Will Helgoland explode?

In 1947, after the end of World War II, plans were made to blow up great quantities of ammunition and explosives on the island of Helgoland. Scientists were very excited. Would the explosion of over 4,000 tons of ammunition create a gigantic hole in the sea floor? Geologists recorded the waves from the detonation, but Helgoland remained intact.

Waves which develop from the impact of large explosions spread through the earth's crust like waves on the surface of a pond. These waves became famous and were even the cause of a military and political tug of war. The whole thing began very simply.

On July 16, 1945, near Alamogordo, New Mexico, the first "small" atomic bomb was exploded on a metal scaffold one hundred feet high. Its effects were twenty times as extensive as the observing physicists had anticipated. An unexpectedly powerful shock wave struck the observers. It was 5:30 A.M., and suddenly a bright light spread across the sky. The light was visible one hundred twenty miles away. However, the shock waves in the earth's crust traveled farther. Seismographs recorded the shock throughout the southwestern United States!

In 1957 scientists exploded the first underground atomic bomb. It had the force of some 1,700 tons of TNT. (One thousand tons is defined as one kiloton $= 10^{12}$ cal. or 4.18×10^{19} erg.) It shook the entire western United States, and the detonation was even felt in faraway Alaska.

In 1961 a bomb almost twice as powerful was set off in a New Mexican salt mine. It shook the entire United States, Canada, and Sweden, and its effects were felt as far away as Finland.

A big heap of pudding?

In 1965 an atomic bomb with the force of 80,000 tons of TNT was exploded underground in the Aleutians. More than two hundred eighty seismic stations on all continents recorded the event.

We can make the earth tremble like a dish of pudding! Actually, only five to ten percent of the energy released by these "medium-sized" bombs create seismic waves. The remaining energy is converted into heat, and its effects are felt only in the immediate neighborhood of the detonation. It splits the rock, raises it, and spreads it out to form a circular hole, and the molten walls of this hole form a subterranean sea of liquid rock.

The similarity between earthquakes and shocks caused by atomic explosions impeded negotiations to halt atomic testing. It was difficult for scientists to tell the difference between the two kinds of shocks. However, few governments would permit a special commission to enter their countries to investigate the causes of shocks, for such a commission would have to know more secrets than a major atomic power would like to reveal. Eventually, scientists learned to detect slight differences between seismic shocks and those caused by atomic explosions.

The final trick

Then scientists learned new, surprising, and disturbing facts about the earth's fragile crust. On July 20, 1971, seismographs all over the earth recorded a shock. Was it an earthquake? Instruments in Alaska, Brazil, Australia, and Europe showed that the earth had been shaken by a quake that measured 4 to 4.5 on the international scale. (This scale extends from 0 to 10.) What had occurred?

Without announcing it beforehand, a small group of scientists from the University of Edinburgh had set off a comparatively tiny quantity of explosives. They used only ten metric tons of explosives, but the earth quaked! The detonation occurred in the North Sea at a depth of six hundred feet. This event proved two things. First, much less energy was required to cause shock waves than had formerly been supposed. Second, it was very important just *where* an explosion took place.

Now scientists learned what soldiers had always known: the "where" makes the difference! For example, an explosion in soft volcanic limestone produces very different effects from an explosion in hard primitive rock. An explosion in alluvial soil has only one-tenth the effect that the same bomb would produce if it were exploded in granite or in a bed of salt.

Moreover, the explosion in the North Sea confirmed something scientists already knew: shock waves travel differently on the surface of the earth than they do in the interior. This fact indicates that the interior of the earth is composed of a different substance from the crust. However, scientists can only speculate about what this substance is. We know nothing about the innermost core of the earth. We cannot even say whether it is composed of different chemical compounds from the outer portions of the core or whether it is different merely with respect to pressure and temperature.

A couple of guesses

Scientists are somewhat more in agreement about the structure of the upper part of the earth's crust. However, they do not know how thick the layer really is and they disagree about its structure. Textbooks list various zones in this region which are named after people who believe that they exist. But do these zones really exist? Again and again we read that this or that zone logically "ought" to exist. In other words, scientists have no proof and are obliged to guess.

The hope of using deep-drill samples to investigate the upper zones of our earth proved vain. The cost of drilling increases with depth. Scientists also had to discard the idea of drilling in the ocean to save the expense of drilling the first two or three miles. Technical difficulties made it impossible for drilling ships to drill much deeper than a half-mile into the bottom of the sea. Millions of dollars were spent without contributing relevant information. Naturally, scientists did discover a number of surprising facts, but it is doubtful that this data justified the expense of drilling.

A more hopeful prospect is the possibility that one day we may find material from the interior of the earth which geological conditions have forced to the surface. But the material normally expelled by volcanoes comes from a depth of twenty-five or thirty miles at most, whereas the radius of the earth is 3,963 miles!

Thus, we know very little about the structure and composition of our planet. All we can say is that scientists have developed certain theories about what may exist in the uppermost twelve miles of the earth. For several centuries miners have testified that the temperature gets warmer as one descends deeper, but no one can tell us whether the interior of the earth is in a molten, liquid state.

San Francisco will perish

The land masses on the earth's surface have been moving around for at least 200,000,000 years. Hot gases, cinders, and molten rock rise from the depths; the earth's axis vibrates; cold and heat cause gigantic masses of ice to form and fruitful fields to become lifeless deserts. Man has had to learn how to survive on earth. He has paid dearly for his knowledge, but today he could, if he chose to, avoid many dangers. Instead, he chooses to ignore them.

If there is any place where it is absurd to build a house, begin a family, and run a business, it is San Francisco. Nevertheless, the city grows and thrives. A person who builds his house at the edge of a crater can at least reassure himself that the volcano may not erupt for another one hundred or five hundred years. However, both scientists and everyday experience tell people who live in San Francisco that they are playing with their lives.

Every week in San Francisco the earth trembles, and it will keep on trembling until another earthquake destroys the city like those which destroyed it in 1857 and 1906. We know what this quake will cost: all of southern California, including San Francisco, Los Angeles, and their environs, will be destroyed, and the damage will cost some $20,000,000,000! How many people die will depend on whether they decide to stay in their homes or leave the area. And science and common sense agree that those who wish to survive should not hesitate to leave southern California, for the deadly earthquake will probably take place before the end of this century.

Why is this so?

The stone is making a crackling sound

Let us go back 30,000,000 years in the earth's history, or thirty minutes in our scale model. The continent of North America is slowly drifting south. Before it lies the eastern part of the Pacific sea floor. However, the sea floor is moving north. (See illustration.) The two blocks of land rub against each other, are pressed together, and push and shove. Finally, the anterior corner of North America breaks free. A crack opens up, the waters of the Pacific enter the crack, and a peninsula develops. Its name is "Baja California." Thus, the Gulf of California formed just 4,000,000 years ago, or four minutes ago in our scale model.

However, the friction between the two land masses continues, threatening to tear loose a strip of the North American continent where Los Angeles and San Fran-

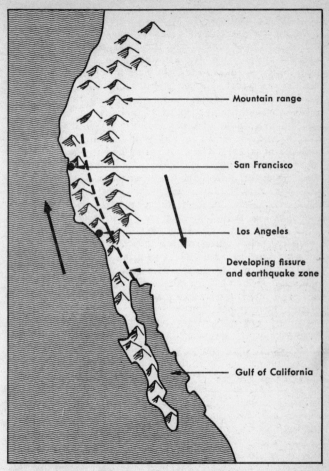

Mountain range

San Francisco

Los Angeles

Developing fissure
and earthquake zone

Gulf of California

The Gulf of California will grow along the lines of the
growing fissure. If the cities of Los Angeles and San Francisco survive, they will be located on a peninsula.

cisco are located. We can already see the location of the
future fissure: a deep ravine already exists at the north of
the Gulf of California.

Surely the geological forces acting in this area would
long since have lengthened the Gulf of California and
turned the peninsula of Baja California into a mountainous island 600 miles in length, were it not for two mountain chains which anchor the tearing land masses like
two giant nails. These mountain chains are the San
Bernadino Mountains (up to 11,000 feet in height) and
the Sierra Nevadas (14,000 feet high). We do not know
what is happening in the depths of the mountains, in the
continental layer of North America and in the Pacific sea
floor. However, we may safely assume that the forces at
work here are quite capable of grinding down immense
blocks of stone, pulverizing rock debris, rubbing land
masses together, heating them to the melting point,
and pressing mountain-sized rocks so that they burst,
split, are broken in pieces, carried away, pressed from
above and below and never left in peace.

To be sure, as a rule all these processes take place very
slowly. Land masses do not move more than two inches a
year. But here and there blocks of stone "get their hooks"
into each other and stay that way until one of them gives
in. Finally, one block yields with a sudden jerk, and the
masses of rock move many feet up, down, or to the side.
Whenever this happens, the earth above the rock
"quakes." If the subterranean movement is slight, the
earthquake is hardly noticeable. However, if two rock
masses have been struggling for a long time without giving in, their eventual shift in position can leave its marks
on the surface. Often the ground above the fault plane
moves many feet up, down, or to the side. Faults can be
hundreds of miles long. In 1857 there was a fault in California which was thirty feet wide and two hundred fifty
miles long! In 1906 rock moved only twenty feet along a
fault plane, and San Francisco was demolished by this
comparatively minor earthquake.

The Baldwin Hills, in the northwestern part of the Los
Angeles basin, show that earth masses do not move only
along horizontal planes. Thirty-six thousand years ago
the site they now occupy was still ocean. Calculations indicate that the land rose an average of less than one
inch a year.

Nowadays people are trying to protect themselves against earthquakes. However, even with the aid of computers we cannot predict exactly how earthquake-proof a building will be. In the course of their earthquake-ridden history, the Japanese have devised a few rules of thumb about the building of "earthquake-proof" houses. Until 1962 the Japanese were not permitted to build houses taller than one hundred feet. The first Japanese skyscraper was built in Tokyo in 1967. It was an office building with thirty-six stories.

Los Angeles architects try to make use of the knowledge of Japanese engineers. In 1971 a minor earthquake destroyed a clinic which had just been built in Los Angeles, but a sixteen-story office building designed by the Japanese remained standing. The seismographs on the ground floor and the eighth floor of the Japanese building recorded the quake and themselves remained undamaged. Apparently the Japanese approach is to make the inner and outer portions of the building as uniform as possible so that the stress placed on them by the quake is equally distributed. This theory is no more than a rule of thumb, for who knows what might happen during the next earthquake?

For example, in April, 1973, a group of Los Angeles underwater divers went to the center of the earthquake which was then taking place a little northwest of the coast. The divers looked for fresh cracks or fissures in the sea floor. Instead, they found countless small craters around three feet wide and twenty inches deep. "None of us had ever seen anything like this underwater before," they reported. So far no scientist has been able to explain how the earthquake could have created these mysterious craters in the sea floor.

Fear and hope

But let us return to the fact which really disturbs geophysicists: approximately once every fifty years, San Francisco is plagued by a "major" earthquake, an immense discharge of tension in the depths of the earth. Statistics indicated that a major earthquake should have occurred in the area by 1970 at the latest. Why did it not happen?

The hope that the geological processes, the motions of

the continental masses which produced the earthquakes, might have come to an end is no more than a dream. Optimists hope for something else. They hope that so many minor discharges of tension have taken place that there has been no serious build-up of tension in the subterranean rock. Their hope resembles that of people who live at the foot of an active volcano and watch calmly as little curls of smoke rise from the crater. The people who live near the volcano believe that the smoke testifies to the continual release of internal pressure, but they are deluded. Pessimists—and many scientific experts fall into this group —fear that just the opposite is true. They fear that greater pressures and tensions are now building up and that this time the resultant earthquake will be even more devastating than in earlier periods. They predict that the Golden Gate and Oakland bridges will collapse and that the streets of San Francisco will become one mass of ruins. They have described how the earth will rise and fall in waves several yards high, how the waves will travel as fast as a man can walk, and how people will find it difficult to stand up. They have also told how the air will ring like a bell and how cracks will appear in the pavement. But no one will leave the danger zone and the authorities will issue no warning.

Who will answer for the dead and the damage?

A precarious existence

The earthquake of 1906 cost San Francisco almost a thousand lives. It does not take much imagination to picture how the next earthquake would affect a city which since that time has grown much larger. Earthquake statistics resemble the lists of death tolls in battles:

1755	Lisbon	32,000 dead.
1783	Calabria	30,000 dead
1896	Sanriku [Japan]	27,000 dead
1908	Messina	83,000 dead
1920	Ping-liang [China]	200,000 dead
1923	Sagami Bay [Japan]	157,000 dead
1932	Kansu [China]	70,000 dead
1935	Baluchistan	60,000 dead
1939	Anatolia	32,000 dead
1939	Southern Chile	30,000 dead

In case this list leaves you with the impression that earthquakes are fairly rare, here is a list of more-recent quakes:

September, 1962	Western and Central Iran	12,000 dead
July, 1963	Skopje [Yugoslavia]	more than 1,000 dead
August, 1966	Eastern Turkey	2,500 dead
August, 1968	Northern and Eastern Iran	around 7,000 dead
September, 1968	Khurasan [Iran]	around 10,000 dead
July, 1969	Swatow [China]	3,000 dead
January, 1970	Yünnan [China]	several thousand dead
March, 1970	Gediz [Turkey]	2,000 dead
May, 1970	Northern Peru	around 70,000 dead
May, 1971	Eastern Turkey	over 1,000 dead
April, 1972	Southern Iran	around 4,000 dead
December, 1972	Nicaragua	around 10,000 to 20,000 dead

Anyone who wishes may continue this list of horror and sudden death, because in reality the list is far from complete! More than one hundred major earthquakes occur each year. Moreover, often an earthquake does not last for just a few hours or a day, but new tremors occur for days on end. Fortunately, the quakes often occur in areas where there are few people, or the damage is not great.

China's buffer

We have seen that the earth is as soft as butter, and thus it would be easy to mention many places where the "solid" earth is in motion and where its pushes and jerks manifest themselves as earthquakes. However, it would be very tedious to enumerate all these places. Nevertheless, geologists and geophysicists would never forgive me if I did not write briefly about Japan, the land of earthquakes *par excellence*.

Like California, Japan lies on the border between two slabs of the earth's crust. In the west it is attached to Asia. In the east the Pacific sea floor presses against the continent of Asia. The pressure is so great that the upper corner of the Pacific has been wrenched upward. What we

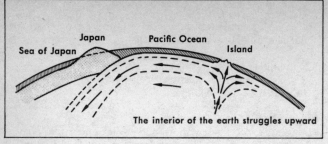

Sea of Japan   Japan   Pacific Ocean   Island

The interior of the earth struggles upward

Japan acts as a buffer for China. (Not drawn to scale.)

see riding above the waves are the islands of Japan. But unlike California, Japan strongly resists the pressure of the Pacific floor, and the ocean floor is forced to yield! It can bend in only one direction: downward. It shoves itself into the depths *beneath* Japan, into regions so hot that the land melts and mingles with the earth's core. The pressure cracks the stony mass of Japan, permitting lava to well up from volcanoes and causing constant earthquakes.

The pressure the Pacific exerts on Japan passes through the islands to China. Thus, it is no wonder that China has always been racked by great earthquakes, or that Chinese scientists long ago invented one of the finest and most precise seismometers, or instruments used to measure earthquakes.

The dragon urn

Supposedly this earthquake detector was invented by the mathematician, astronomer, and geographer Chang Heng, who lived from 87 to 139 A.D. The principle is simple. The lid of an urn-shaped bronze vessel is made into a pendulum with eight arms. If the earth quakes, the vessel tips, but the pendulum remains in the same position. The pendulum arms trigger a ball to fall in the direction in which the vessel tips. (See illustration.) The ball falls out of the head of a dragon and into the mouth of a toad. However, the dragons and the toads are merely artistic embellishments. The important thing is that this instrument records an earthquake and the direction in which the earth moves.

European scientific know-how was inferior to that of the Chinese. When the first German earthquake observatory was established in Hohenheim in 1893, the seismograph was a jar containing a thin stick. During an

The dragon urn, a Chinese seismograph.

earthquake the stick was supposed to fall down, and the direction in which it fell indicated the direction of the quake. This was an extremely primitive apparatus. However, since that time we have devised excellent instruments for measuring earthquakes. All seismographic stations now possess seismometers which enable us to precisely determine the strength, direction, and location of earthquakes.

When the hour strikes

Scientists are still not able to predict earthquakes. One would think that since the forces leading up to an earthquake build up for a long time, it should be possible to predict them ahead of time and warn people to leave the threatened area; but it is not. Even in San Francisco and Los Angeles, scientists can do no more than predict that the next quake will be a big one.

The Japanese hold a folk belief, bordering on superstition, that an earthquake will occur when there is lightning in a clear sky. In other words, if there is no storm but sheet lightning or even ball lightning appears in the sky, the earth will quake soon after. Disturbing as the fact may be to scientists, this rule of thumb apparently holds true. Unfortunately, scientists cannot understand the reason. To be sure, one might imagine that damned-up forces in the rock beneath the earth's surface trigger a piezoelectric effect, but how does this lead to the development of the vast electrical field which is discharged in the flashes of lightning? Everyone who owns a cigarette lighter is familiar with piezoelectric effects. In a lighter a tiny quartz crystal or a tourmaline is briefly compressed, creating an electrical charge, and the resultant spark lights the gas in the lighter. However, how could even extreme geological pressures create a comparable reaction inside the earth? The more scientists thought about this matter, the more certain they became that the lightning preceding an earthquake was not caused by a piezoelectric effect. It is a pity that this is so, for the explanation was one which everyone who owns a lighter could readily understand.

Reading coffee grounds would tell us almost as much

Scientists have tried many approaches to the prediction of earthquakes: using compasses, observing the movements of trigonometric reference points, recording the speed at which small earthquake waves spread across the ground, keeping statistics, and investigating rock formations. Time, effort, and money have not been spared, but to little result. Even when various signs indicate that an earthquake is going to occur, scientists cannot predict the time or force of the quake.

Earthquakes influence many aspects of nature. This influence begins before the actual quake occurs. For example, the secretion from the earth of gases like radon and methane increases, the electrical conductivity of the ground alters, and even the curvature of the earth changes to a measurable degree. Geophysicists are always searching for signs which would enable them to warn people of major impending earthquakes, but so far they have had little success.

As mentioned, the Japanese regard lightning in a clear sky as the signal of an impending quake, and people elsewhere believe that the restlessness of house pets means the same thing. Such beliefs are not much different from reading coffee grounds to prophesy the future; but scientists cannot offer us anything more solid. Perhaps the most promising approach to the problem so far is to regard the increased secretion of gases as the signal of an earthquake. Measurements made in southern Germany indicate that this approach may prove useful. In Bebenhausen (the first part of the name means "quake") the increase in the secretion of gas from the earth coincides with the appearance of small earthquakes, which occur regularly there.

Perhaps a connection may exist on the moon between quakes and the discharge of gas. On February 28, 1971, a lunar quake occurred following a secretion of gas.

An earthquake experiment

Since we are unable to accurately predict the location and force of an earthquake and to warn people of its coming, many scientists are searching for ways to prevent earthquakes. In some cases it may actually be possible to do this. For example, whole series of small earthquakes have followed the explosion of underground atomic bombs. Between December, 1968, and March, 1970, five bombs were exploded underground in Nevada. After each explosion, seismometers located around ten kilometers away recorded small tremors for weeks on end. We may take the pessimistic view and assume that the explosions created pressures beneath the earth which were discharged in the tremors; or we may take the more optimistic view that these pressures had existed all along and that the explosion caused them to harmlessly discharge themselves, preventing a major earthquake later on. In short, scientists have theorized that every couple of years we might set off an atomic bomb underground in areas such as Los Angeles and San Francisco, where earthquakes are prevalent, in order to discharge stored-up tensions and pressures before they build up and create a devastating quake.

But only a genius or a fool would dare to use the earth as a guinea pig. After all, we have only one earth, and we cannot afford to lose it.

Since 1973 we have known what powerful quakes we might create with atomic explosions. In that year we learned that even during normal earthquakes, our earth's axis of rotation rocks back and forth. If we created a super-earthquake by suddenly discharging the tensions in a large earthquake region, the earth's axis of rotation could become permanently "askew." We do not know for certain what would happen.

Questions, nothing but questions. Perhaps just the opposite is true. Perhaps earthquakes do not cause the

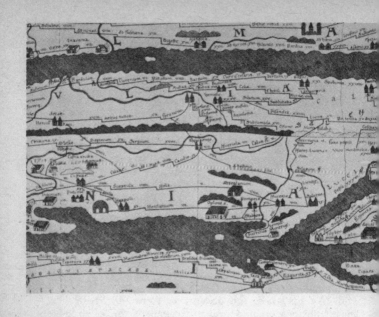

earth's axis of rotation to vibrate, but instead slight changes in the earth's rotation trigger earthquakes. Or are the two phenomena inextricable parts of a whole? If this is true, what happens to our notions about continental drift and the change in the position of the earth's magnetic poles? Guesses, possibilities, and uncertainties: Is this all that our image of the earth comes down to? We still have much to learn about the planet we live on.

For Babylon's revenue office

We have seen that many gaps exist in our knowledge of the universe, our galaxy, our solar system, and even of the tiny ball, the earth. Let us go one step further and consider what we know about the *surface* of our earth, which seems so familiar.

The first people known to have recorded data about at least a small portion of our earth were the Babylonians. Around 2,300 B.C., some Babylonians engraved the borders of certain low-lying regions on clay tablets. The tablets were used in tax assessment. Thus, the first map

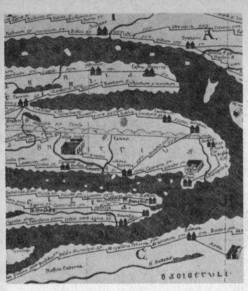

This map represents a segment of the famous Peutinger Tablet, named after Konrad Peutinger, a man who owned it around 1500. It may have been drawn before the year 670. It is a map of streets and places which was used for military purposes. This segment (north is to the left) shows the coast of Africa at the bottom, above it Italy, and at the top the Adriatic with Yugoslavia. The large triangular island is Sicily.

was made by members of the Babylonian land-registry office, and it can be viewed today in the British Museum. The map includes a "salt-water river," *i.e.*, an ocean!

By the year 423 B.C., people were so familiar with maps that in one of the comedies of Aristophanes, a world map is brought onto the stage and an actor points out the location of Athens.

However, the description of the earth did not become the science of geography until the widely educated scholar Eratosthenes had written his *Geographica*. Eratosthenes was born in Cyrene around 290 B.C. A well-traveled man who studied in Athens, he was sent in 246 by Ptolemy III to Alexandria to teach the crown prince and to head the famous library there. In Alexandria he had access to the scientific material gathered during Alexander's expedition to India, as well as the records of the seafarer Pytheas of Masilia. Naturally, most of Eratosthenes' work constitutes mere hearsay and is not accurate. However, Eratosthenes did not simply record what he had heard and learned. He also engaged in critical reflection, which is more important than simply measuring or recording.

Philosophers and conquerors

Eratosthenes attacked the problems involved in geography with almost incredible brilliance. At that time no astronomical technique had been invented to determine degrees of latitude. Since he did not know the exact location of various regions and nations, he compared reports concerning their climate and plant life and arranged them in zones. For example, he placed Carthage and Alexandria at the same elevation, or at the same degree of latitude, as we would say today. He traced another "degree of latitude" from the southern tip of Spain to the southern tip of the boot of Italy, to the tip of Greece, then across Rhodes to Asia Minor, and finally to the upper course of the Ganges. All in all, he did not do a bad job. He also invented the first climatic map of the earth. Later when Columbus sought a sea route from Spain to India, he would have had no trouble if he had followed Eratosthenes' map, for there are ways to travel around the land masses on the map.

Eratosthenes is famous chiefly for having measured the circumference of the earth, which he believed to be a sphere. At noon of the summer solstice, the sun stood directly above Syene, in Aswan, which was, he thought, directly south of Alexandria. At the same time a stick in Alexandria cast a shadow whose angle measured one-fiftieth of a circle (7° 12′). Since the distance between Syene and Alexandria was then measured at five hundred stadia, Eratosthenes concluded that the circumference of the ball-shaped earth must be five hundred times fifty, or 25,000 stadia. We do not know what distance a "stadium" entailed, and thus scholars disagree about the accuracy of Eratosthenes' calculations. Some mathematicians believe that his results were correct to within a few miles. However, these results may have been off by several hundred miles, for Eratosthenes' basic assumption was false: Syene is not located where he believed it was. However, in the final analysis this is unimportant. The significant fact is that Eratosthenes conceived the earth to be a sphere, a concept which is more important than any measurement.

The next great geographer was Strabo, of Amaseia. Born in 64 or 63 B.C., Strabo was a wealthy, well educated man of noble family who arrived in Alexandria in the year 25 B.C. He left us a description of the city and the harbor, including accounts of the great lighthouse and the buildings built by Mark Antony and Cleopatra VI. He was a precise observer, and wherever he traveled—to the border of Ethiopia, to the Red Sea, to Syria, Rome, and Corinth—he discovered, compared, and wrote new things. However, he was a man of few ideas, and he did not improve the existing maps of the world. Roman maps which have come down to us, maps made around 100 B.C., are highly inaccurate. Perhaps they were merely intended to guide soldiers marching from one place to another, for places and distances are represented with considerable accuracy. However, mountains appear as tiny chains of hills and seas as a couple of thin strips of water.

Knowledge of geography continued to go downhill. Einhard (770-840 A.D.), the friend and biographer of Charlemagne, tells us that the great ruler possessed three "maps":

- the "whole world," divided into three continents
- a city plan of Rome
- a city plan of Constantinople

The fact that the "maps" were engraved on gold and silver plates does not change the fact that for a military commander and a conqueror, Charlemagne possessed very little in the way of maps.

Thus, it is a small wonder that by the year 1740 people knew the latitude and longitude of only about one hundred sixteen places.

The search for maps

And how much do we know today about the surface of our earth?

In 1938, when it became clear that war was imminent, military strategists everywhere began to examine all available maps. In America the results of the search were startling. Strategists could not even find maps suitable for use in waging war inside the continental United States! Military men have always been very interested in maps. At the time of the great Spanish seafarers, maps were so highly treasured for their military importance that all maps, including code books and log books, were ordered to be weighted with lead. When they were thrown overboard they would instantly sink, and thus would not fall into enemy hands. This same order applies today wherever ships are involved in war.

When World War II began in 1939, Americans searched desperately for maps. They ransacked all old and private map collections with few results. Although many maps existed, most of them were antiquated and unusable. The European nations were better off, for they still had many maps left over from World War I. But these maps also were out of date. Nevertheless, when English troops marched through northern Germany and Schleswig-Holstein in 1945, they used these antiquated maps, which contained no reference to the newer, larger, well-built streets or highways.

It would be a mistake to assume that nowadays such confusion could not arise because we possess aerial photographs of all geographical areas and on every scale. Aerial photographs are no substitute for maps. It takes considerable practice to learn to read them. They contain many irrelevant details, and it is difficult to judge heights from them. Moreover, maps, drawings, and descriptions of journeys are sometimes not available when they are needed. It is very difficult to obtain a city plan of Moscow or an ordnance-survey map (1:25,000) of your next vacation spot abroad. It is almost impossible to obtain *exact* information.

Treasure maps represent an especially appealing chapter in our survey of the surface of our earth. Probably more maps exist which show the location of stranded and sunken ships than there were ships carrying gold and silver. Still, more than enough sunken treasures remain to stir the imagination of adventures.

Hidden treasures

We know of Greek and Roman ships wrecked in the Mediterranean whose cargos must be as interesting to dealers in antiquities as they are to scientists. In addition, modern sunken treasures, as well as the wrecks of old Spanish silver ships, dot the Atlantic. We could recover many treasures if only the information given us by maps were more precise.

For 1,500 years, a treasure had been waiting for someone to come and dig it up as Schliemann found and excavated Troy. It is a treasure everyone has heard of: the Nibelung hoard. The *Nibelungenlied* was probably written in Cloister Lorsch, east of the Nibelung city of Worms. It may contain a high measure of truth. We do not know for certain who wrote it, but the author was probably familiar with the area. Kriemhild's former dowager's estate still lies within sight of the cloister.

The *Nibelungenlied* tells us exactly how and where the great treasure is hidden. Gernot suggests that it be sunk beneath the Rhine. Hagen then takes advantage of the king's absence to carry out this plan. Everyone who helps to hide the treasure must swear never to reveal its location to anyone unless all the participants agree that it should be done.

Thus, we may imagine that the treasure is hidden somewhere where it can be raised from the river again. In other words, the Nibelung hoard must be somewhere where the river (as it then was) was not too deep, where it flowed slowly, and where some landmark guaranteed that it could be found again—that is, the treasure was almost certainly concealed near a large tree or rock in a tributary of the Rhine. If we try we can imagine the method by which the "measureless hoard" was brought to the appropriate place. If a map from that time had been preserved, we could easily find the three or four places which seem to fit its terms. But, unfortunately, it is difficult to say just where the Rhine flowed in the fifth century. In 1969, a work group arrived in Mainz to search for the Nibelung treasure. The group's first task was to attempt to reconstruct the old riverbed by looking at old maps. Probably no one will succeed in this attempt. It might be better to ask a geologist to reconstruct the old riverbed, for he could learn more from observing the modern landscape than anyone could learn from old maps.

Where was Paradise?

In searching for mysterious places, we often confront the problem of determining the course of rivers centuries ago. Much time and effort have been vainly expended in searching for the biblical Paradise. The biblical description seems relatively exact:

> And a river went out of Eden to water the garden; and from thence it was parted, and became into four heads. The name of the first is Pison: that is it which compasseth the whole land of Havilah, where there is gold. And the gold of that land is good: there is bdellium and the onyx stone. And the name of the second river is Gihon: the same is it that compasseth the whole land of Ethiopia. And the name of the third river is Hiddekel: that is it which goeth toward the east of Assyria. And the fourth river is Euphrates. . . .
>
> —Genesis 2:10-14

Such a system of rivers is hardly commonplace, and we should give serious thought to its possible location. We know the course of the Euphrates. The biblical passage also refers to minerals, to gold and onyx. Finally, it mentions Assyria and Ethiopia. With this much information, it appears that scholars ought to know where Paradise was.

One of the first men to travel in search of Paradise was the Irish monk Brendan, also known as Brandon, Brandan, and St. Brendan. He lived from around 484 to 578. For some reason he believed that Paradise must be located in the Atlantic Ocean. After long travel he returned home and told people about an island of great beauty and paradisiac fertility. No one knows whether he had been on Madeira or one of the Canary Islands; but, in any case, people believed his tale. Almost twelve hundred years later, no seafarer had yet been able to find the St. Brendan Islands, and in 1759 they were finally stricken from the maps.

One of the last men to search for Paradise may have been Franz von Wendrin, an earnest student of German geography, who in 1924 tried to convince his astonished contemporaries that Paradise had been located on the border between Mecklenburg and Pomerania, and that its center was the spot now occupied by the town of Demmin!

All in all, speculations about the location of the biblical Paradise seem to have confused, rather than contributed to, what we know about geography.

Atlantis is another place which men have devoted much energy to finding. No one knows where the wealthy and legendary city may have been located. Was it north of the British Isles, near Helgoland, in the Baltic Sea, west of Gibraltar, in the Mediterranean, or north of the Bimini Islands, a group of islands to the east of Miami, Florida?

And where was Vineta, the famous Baltic trade center, which apparently still existed in the year 1100? Was it to the left or the right of the Oder estuary? Or was it near Rügen? And what of the many ghost islands reported by seafarers? Did any of them really exist? What happened to all the islands off the coast of Portugal, which maps drawn around 1350 portrayed in abundance? We are relatively certain that these islands existed, for when the old mapmakers doubted the existence of coasts and islands, they usually drew ships, mythical beasts, compasses, or allegorical figures to hide their ignorance. This was a very attractive trait compared with loquacity, the modern-day refuge of the ignorant.

Chapter Four

INVISIBLE BOUNDARIES

Alfred Wegener

ISLANDS WHICH have risen from the sea, given birth to settlements, and then disappeared again reveal the degree to which the surface of our earth is in motion: rising, becoming part of some continent, and then sinking into the depths. It is surprising and disturbing to realize how much the earth moves and to wonder just *when* its movement began. How long will the crust of the earth hold together? Is it already being destroyed?

We owe our modern view of the earth's surface to a man who was born in Berlin on November 1, 1880. We know his birthday, but we do not know the day on which he died in the eternal ice of Greenland as he was on the way to bringing aid to his friends. His name was Alfred Lothar Wegener.

Wegener left us a book entitled *The Origin of the Continents and Oceans.* This work, published in 1915, contains theories about the ocean floor, continental drift, movement at the edges of continents, the breakup of the ocean floor, and the shifting of the poles. These theories are still important today. Wegener also discussed the valuable manganese nodules on the ocean floor. He wove many facts together to form a new picture of the changes taking place on the earth's surface.

In the past people had believed that as the earth cooled, the interior contracted, and mountainous folds formed on the surface like the wrinkles which form on

the surface of an apple as it dries out and its interior
moisture is lost. Wegener replaced this view with the
picture of a primal continent breaking up, of giant drifting continental layers moving along a liquid interior.

Who was Alfred Wegener, this man who revolutionized
geological theory?

Wegener was not a geologist by trade, but a meteorolo-
gist interested in the great polar air masses which "create"
our weather. From 1906 to 1908 he took part in an expedition to eastern Greenland, that gigantic chunk of ice
which was destined to be his grave. From 1908 to 1912
he taught at the University of Marburg, in Germany, but
he was less attracted to his university career than to the
magical, silent ice of Greenland. In the winter of 1912 he
traveled to Greenland again, spent the winter there, and
in 1913 crossed the wilderness of ice.

Then World War I broke out, and Wegener became a
soldier, fell ill, and in 1919 was transferred to a navy
weather station in Grossborstel. However, by then he had
become more interested in geophysics than in meteorology, and after he went on a preliminary expedition in
1929, it seemed appropriate that he become leader of the
German Greenland Expedition of 1930. Wegener and
other scientists established stations all across the island
and prepared to spend the winter there. Then a call for
help reached him from the coast, and although it was
really too late in the year to cross the ice, Wegener set out
with a sled on his birthday, November 1, 1930. He never
reached his destination. Later his body was recovered. He
lived only a few days beyond his fiftieth birthday.

Anyone who has an atlas can see what Wegener's great
discovery was. Wegener himself once related how it all
began. He was looking at a map of the world, and he was
surprised to note how exactly the coastlines to the east
and west of the Atlantic seemed to fit together. He
thought it improbable that they had actually been part of
the same land mass until, in the autumn of 1911, he
learned about some paleontological data which he had not
been aware of until then. If the data were correct, then at
some remote time there must have been a connection, a
"land bridge," between Africa and Brazil, across which
animals and plants used to travel. And this was not the
only land bridge that had once existed! Apparently Madagascar and India had once been connected, as had

Madagascar and Australia, and Australia and Antarctica. Specialists eagerly discussed the possible existence of still other land bridges.

Wegener wondered whether it was possible that land bridges had once connected islands and continents and later sunk into the sea. For example, could the islands in the Bering Straits between Siberia and Alaska represent the remains of such a land bridge between Asia and America? Some twenty scientists, each an authority in his specialty, bitterly debated this theory. Among other evidence, the distribution of various species and families of earthworms, which could not possibly have crossed the oceans, was cited to establish the existence or non-existence of various land bridges.

The supercontinents

Wegener was not trained in all the areas his theories entailed, but he continued to think about the changes which had taken place in the earth's surface. It worked to his advantage that he did not know a great many details, for too many details can prevent one from seeing the whole picture.

At some remote time after it had cooled, the earth must have been covered by a solid crust of stone, and the stone all over the globe was covered by an ocean that may have been more than two kilometers deep. Then the stone crust began to break up, the different pieces shifted their position, folds developed, parts of the crust rose above the surface of the water, and parts of the oceans remained deep while others became relatively shallow.

Then Wegener wondered what would happen if one took an atlas and examined the areas which had formerly been connected by land bridges. He thought about it and decided that once there must have been two large, possibly mountainous, land masses, two super-continents:

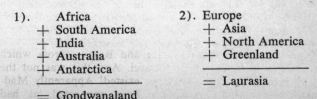

1).	Africa	2).	Europe
	+ South America		+ Asia
	+ India		+ North America
	+ Australia		+ Greenland
	+ Antarctica		————————
	————————		= Laurasia
	= Gondwanaland		

Then the two super-continents broke apart, moved across the earth riding on its interior, were cleft by fissures, and broke into smaller fragments. Afterward some of the fragments joined together again. The continents were twisted and tilted, in some cases pressed their edges together again, and tilted downward into the hot interior, where they melted. In short, they behaved like chunks of ice floating on a river. However, land bridges did not necessarily exist!

Wegener's theory has been confirmed not only by the shapes of the various land masses, but also by the similarity of mineral and stone deposits, plus plants and animals in those areas which formerly formed a single continent. Readers with a globe or an atlas can put together the pieces of the puzzle for themselves. However, one should be cautious in dealing with India. At one time this sub-continent was firmly attached to northwestern Australia, until it tore loose and began to cross the ocean at high speed, its volcanoes smoking all the way. Finally, it rammed into Asia and pushed the Himalayan Mountains toward the sky.

The time factor is exciting!

Our earth is around 4,700,000,000 years old.

Life has existed on earth for about 3,700,000,000 years.

But the land masses on earth have been crumbling for only about 300,000,000 years!

Let us try to understand the meaning of these time spans. We will designate one minute as 1,000,000 years and assume that the earth began Monday morning at O hour. By 4:30 that afternoon, living creatures would already exist. By 6:30 Thursday morning we would see something frightening. The two great land masses which have supported plant and animal life have begun to move and are apparently about to break apart! New cracks keep appearing in the land, and large chunks of it keep breaking off. The chunks slide across the surface, and the oceans which separate them become wider and wider. The fact that our lives are so short explains why we have never been aware of this disturbing spectacle.

Is the earth being destroyed?

Do these events on the earth's surface result from changes in the earth's interior which may signal the end of its existence?

Scientists do not yet know the answer to this question. Since they do not know what is inside the earth, they cannot tell us what might happen there. They cannot even give an unequivocal answer to the question of what forces in the earth's interior might have given rise to such surface phenomena. They can speculate, but they do not know.

On the other hand, we do know something of the consequences of continental drift. Almost every day we experience its effects. The fissures between the continents are continually growing wider. Even though the continents may move only a few centimeters apart, the gap between them is growing and a crack is opening up in the deep layers of the earth. When a crack cuts across the land, masses rise from the earth's interior and sometimes widen the crack. These masses may rise to the earth's surface, and then we see volcanic activity. We feel earthquakes and see hot fountains and columns of vapor rise into the air. We see volcanic ash being hurled into the sky and red-hot lava flow across the land.

When cracks in the sea floor widen, they create equally dramatic effects. A network of undersea cracks and ravines surrounds the moving layers of land, and often the temperature of the water surrounding these ravines suggests that volcanic activity is present.

The front part of a drifting land mass exerts strong pressure on whatever it encounters. Like blocks of ice, the blocks of land can raise their edges and glide *over* the land they encounter, or they can slip *under* it. One theory suggests that the first of these two processes is now occurring in Chile. As South America moves westward, Chile is pressing down on the floor of the Pacific. Presumably the sea floor is melting at this point. Each year some ten centimeters of the Pacific floor disappear into the depths of the earth. However, the coast of Chile is suffering, too. It is forced to bend, is being torn open by fissures, and has to "digest" the water pressed beneath it.

As a result, the Chilean Andes are riddled with smoking volcanoes, and earthquakes are an everyday occurence.

To be sure, scientists had known about the Chilean volcanoes for a long time, and they had been recording devastating earthquakes for decades before they developed the theory that these phenomena were caused by a layer of earth bending over and melting away. The presence of volcanoes and earthquakes actually gave rise to the theory and did not merely confirm it.

Scientists have devoted special attention to the fissure between Europe and Africa in the east and North and South America in the west, the great fissure filled by the Atlantic Ocean. Here the interior of the earth presses upward. It raises the floor in the middle of the ocean, curving it upward until the stone bursts. A deep ravine clearly marks the fissure. We can measure the heat of the earth's interior on the floor of the ravine. Moreover, viscous masses of rock press upward here. Analysis has shown that the "freshest" rock, or the rock which is leached to the least degree by the sea, is located in the middle of the Atlantic, in the ravine and along its borders. The farther we move east or west from this point, the older the rock becomes and the longer it has been weathered by the sea. Thus, the sea floor between the continents is "new" ground! In places where the masses of rock are raised above the surface of the sea, we find is-

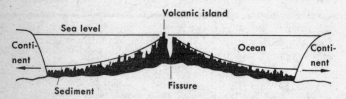

The sea floor splits open between the continents—for example, between Africa and South America. Lava presses upward through the fissure and forces the continents apart. The newly formed sea floor is covered by a layer of sediment, and the older this region of the sea floor is, the thicker the sediment becomes. Thus, the sediment layer is thickest close to the continents. The most active volcanoes are those in the immediate vicinity of the fissures. Here volcanoes rise to sea level and form volcanic islands.

lands: the Azores, the St. Paul Islands, Ascensión, and deep in the south, Tristan da Cunha. What we regard as "islands" are really the tips of the tallest mountain range on earth!

Lava flows out of the sea floor, cools and hardens, and pushes the continents farther and farther apart. Moreover, volcanic activity on land is much less extensive and dramatic than it is beneath the quiet vastness of the oceans. Once again, the time factor seems crucial. The oldest rocks in the Atlantic are scarcely more than 150,000,000 years old. This means that 150,000,000 years ago, the four great land masses of Europe, Africa, North America, and South America were still at peace and formed a single continent. Apparently the earth was in a state of rest, and volcanic forces had not yet caused it to burst apart.

Let us return to the time scale we used earlier, according to which one minute represents 1,000,000 years. On this scale, 150,000,000 years would correspond to two and a half hours. This seems a very short time. However, just two *minutes* ago a crack opened up which will soon separate Africa from Asia and make Africa into an island: the Red Sea.

Africa will be an island

In 1966, geologists established an astonishing fact: the floor of the Red Sea is hotter than its surface! Deep ravines on the sea floor have the incredible temperature of 56.5°C. Is this possible? If the water were this hot, wouldn't it be forced to rise to the surface? Investigation revealed an even more startling phenomenon. What exists down below is not a "Red Sea," not water like that which the ships are crossing up above. Down below there is a thick layer of brine! This brine contains metals vital to industry. Swiftly the news traveled around the globe: the depths of the Red Sea are a storehouse of inconceivable mineral wealth.

An initial estimate made in 1968 revealed that a layer of Red Sea brine ten meters thick contained zinc, lead, silver, and gold valued at $2,400,000,000, not to mention the less valuable metals!

In 1972, while mining companies were beginning to struggle over mining rights, scientists took the temperature of the Red Sea and discovered another amazing fact. In the place which had had a temperature of 56.5° C. in 1966, the temperature had now risen to 59.2° C. Fantastic as it sounds, somewhere in the depths of the sea there flowed a stream of hot water with a temperature of 104° C. Under normal pressure on the earth's surface, this water would instantly evaporate! Doubtless it is this water which dissolves metal salts in hidden zones of the earth's crust and allows them to form a heavy, hot layer of salty broth beneath the waters of the Red Sea.

An ocean is being born in the Red Sea

But what will happen when the temperatures in the Red Sea get even hotter? If Asia is separating from Africa at this point, it will be the site of a vast geological upheaval. A boiling sea more than 6,000 feet in depth will come into being, and perhaps a gigantic fissure will open from which volcanoes of mud, then hot gases, and finally streams of lava will burst forth. There will be massive earthquakes, the Red Sea will burst open along the Suez Canal, a ravine will form near the Dead Sea, and at last a new, deep indentation will be driven into the earth's surface near Africa. When this happens, we may have access to new minerals in the form of beds of mineral salts. Moreover, the new fissure may open up fresh oil fields. Then the sea may suddenly be covered with oil, which will have devastating effects on plants, wildlife, and shipping.

Does this description represent mere fantasy? Certainly not. And like the Red Sea, the Gulf of Aden constitutes a great fissure between Arabia and Somalia. Many signs, including mountainous structures and volcanic activity, indicate that a crack will open near Djibouti. Things look just as grim at the other end of the Red Sea. Since the beginning of recorded history, volcanic activity has existed at the northern end of the sea. The entire continent of Africa is shifting away from Asia and will be pushed up against, perhaps even beneath, Europe.

Without a doubt the Red Sea offers a splendid modern example of the continental drift postulated by Wegener. This area deserves to be studied.

The puzzle of Europe

The old continent of Europe experienced similar cataclysmic events, although long ago. The Mediterranean formed, the Bay of Biscay burst open, and England freed itself from France and turned thirty degrees clockwise. (Europe has turned fifty degrees in relation to North America.)

If we look at a globe, we can make out a puzzle of Europe. To fit the pieces of the puzzle together, first we bend Spain's northern coast to the north, and then move London to where it really belongs, namely, somewhere near Orléans. Then we must compress Italy, Sardinia, and Corisca and move them to the west, just south of France. (The region around Corsica and Sardinia turned counterclockwise for around 6,000,000 years. However, for the past 6,000,000 years, it has apparently been at rest.)

If we wish, we may speculate about whether and how the Arctic islands to the west of Greenland could be reunited to form a single land mass. These islands look as if they had been driven apart and toward the northwest by the crash of the giant meteorite which formed the crater of Hudson Bay. Scientists can make few measurements in the icy wilderness of the Arctic islands, and thus there is room for speculation about how they may once have fit together.

Greenland is one of those regions which appears to fit into a larger puzzle. It must once have been part of the supercontinent of Laurasia and probably "broke off" from North America some 60,000,000 to 70,000,000 years ago.

But theories involving continental drift are still tentative. For example, as late as 1967 scientists disagreed as to whether America and Europe had moved close together again after the two continents split apart. Some scientists believe that they may have crashed together again, remained "stuck together" for a time, and finally separated again, leaving parts of each continent glued to the other.

Are the Canary Islands part of South America?

People who vacation on the Canary Islands may wonder whether these islands were once part of Africa or South America or whether they were never part of any continent. They may have been formed by volcanoes rising out of a crack in the sea floor. However, it is also possible that they broke off the South American continent and remained behind when South America broke away from Africa and started to move westward. Or do the Canary Islands represent the tips of the sunken Atlas Mountains of northern Africa? The petrified shells of ostrich eggs can be used to substantiate these theories. Ostriches cannot possibly have crossed the sea to the newborn islands, for Africa and the Canary Islands are more than sixty miles apart! It is more reasonable to assume that the birds witnessed the separation of the islands from Africa.

Recently geologists have been attempting to prove that the eastern Canary Islands once belonged to the African or South American continent, whereas the western islands are volcanic in origin.

Most of the land masses which have broken away from larger masses have moved to the west. We do not know how fast they have traveled. Probably their speed fluctuated from time to time. When India broke away from Australia and crashed into Asia, it was probably traveling very fast. It is estimated that South America is drifting at a rate of less than one inch a year. All countries along the equator are probably moving at the same speed. In zones where there is more movement, land travels at a faster rate. Thus, every year the Red Sea appears to become three quarters of an inch wider, and in the same amount of time the coasts of the Pacific Ocean pull apart as much as two inches.

The true boundaries on earth are not the boundaries between nations, not rivers or high mountains, and not even the coasts of the oceans. The real boundaries are the deep fissures and ravines which separate the drifting continents. For example, the boundary between Europe and North America is invisible to us. It lies deep in the center of the Atlantic Ocean. Only in Iceland can we see a small piece of the boundary. Geologically speaking, Iceland is a divided island, half of which forms part of America and half part of Europe.

Scientists cannot explain exactly why the earth is constantly reshaping itself, but they continue to come up with new theories. For example, they suggest that a gigantic meteorite bombardment created many craters in the earth so that it resembled the moon. The instability of the earth's axis caused changes in climate and the formation of huge masses of ice. According to this theory, the Sahara Desert and all of North Africa were covered with ice. Huge masses of ice at the South Pole disturbed the earth's equilibrium and triggered the breaking up and drifting of the continents.

Other theories suggest just the opposite explanation: because the land masses were changing, the climate of many regions changed, too. This view appears to have some merit in the case of Australia, which apparently wandered across the South Pole twice.

In the spring of 1973 scientists struggled to find the correct explanation for geological events which had taken place in Egypt. The men who built the Great Pyramid of Giza 4,500 years ago tried to build it along a line that ran exactly from north to south (or as we might interpret it, from east to west). Since then it has stood in the desert, unmoved and unmoving. However, eventually scientists discovered that its builders did not pay as much attention to the direction along which the structure had been built as had once been assumed. Had the architects made a mistake? Some geophysicists believe that they did not, and that all of Africa may have turned and shifted position. But what caused it to do so? Naturally, it could have been continental drift, but in this case Giza must have been moving in the direction opposite to what scientists believe it did. Or did an earthquake in the year 908 B.C. shift the position of Giza? Did melting ice in Greenland and Antarctica change the position of Africa and thus of the pyramids? No one knows the answer.

The phenomenon of paleomagnetism further complicates these mysterious events.

Where the North Pole was

To tell the truth, we do not even know the source of the earth's magnetic field, which causes the earth to have a magnetic North Pole and South Pole. The theory that the interior of the earth contains a mass of magnetic iron is as false as it is old. This theory assumes that the earth's interior is extremely hot; but experiments show that the magnetic properties of iron disappear at a temperature of 770° C. Thus, the theory cannot be correct. Nor can "magnetic storms" be the cause of the earth's magnetism. Another untenable theory is that the earth's rotation triggers electrical current in the atmosphere, and the current creates the magnetic field.

Is it possible that the interior of the earth contains something like a gigantic dynamo? For decades many scientists have been playing with this possibility; but they cannot prove their theory. Nevertheless, strange as the theory sounds, it is the most credible to date.

But no matter what creates the earth's magnetism, the magnetic field has existed for millions of years. For example, when a volcano erupts and molten lava flows down the mountainside, the magnetic field leaves its mark on the lava as it cools. The iron minerals in the lava arrange themselves so that they point from north to south. (Lava contains large quantities of iron. For example, if you take a pocket magnet to Mount Etna, you can easily find pounds of magnetic sand and dust.) In the same way, when the dust of magnetic minerals is deposited on the ocean floor, the magnetic particles behave like little magnetic needles and all align themselves so that they point from north to south. However, in old lava beds and old ocean deposits, the magnetic particles are not aligned in accord with our modern magnetic field! Thus, the poles were once aligned in another direction.

In a short time scientists developed four or five more or less complex theories to explain these strange findings. In some cases the theories seem quite convincing. They enable us to understand how, depending on their location and the way they turn, the drifting continents assumed various positions in relation to the North Pole. If we trace the various points where the North Pole appears to have been located, we will be able to derive a curve

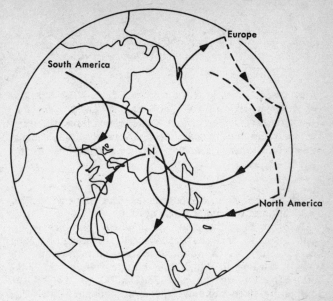

Curves marking the wandering of the poles. The earth's magnetic North Pole is located and has always been located at the letter N. However, in the past the land masses of Europe, South America, and North America were in different locations, and if we trace the past location of the direction north in relation to these land masses, the result is the curves depicted in the diagram. The diagram indicates that Europe followed a twisted course on the globe. This course leaves us with the impression that the North Pole was once located in California and at another time south of the equator. In reality, compass needles "frozen" in ancient rocks point to the points which make up the curve.

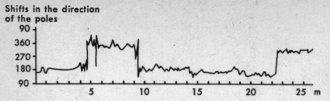

Fluctuations of the earth's magnetic field. Measurements of a twenty-six-meter-long drill sample taken from the southern part of the Indian Ocean show three reversals of the magnetic poles. (A simplified version of the diagram found in *Earth and Planetary Science Letters,* Vol. 20, p. 315)

for each of the various land masses. The curve will end at the location of our modern North Pole.

Unfortunately, the study of magnetic particles in ancient lava and deep-sea deposits tells us something else. Let us return for a moment to our quick-motion time scale, according to which one minute stands for 1,000-000 years. During the past 76,000,000 years—just one hour and sixteen minutes—the earth's magnetic field has reversed itself one hundred seventy-one times. At one point only 50,000 years passed between two reversals of the poles. Our modern magnetic field is long overdue for reversal!

What would happen if the magnetic field were to reverse in our time?

We know nothing about what would happen. We cannot even say for certain whether a reversal of the poles occurs instantaneously or takes several centuries. For some time people have been afraid that a reversal of the poles might also alter the direction of the earth's rotation. This fear is probably not justified. However, if the earth suddenly stopped turning and then began to turn again in the opposite direction, it would mean the end of our world. The sun would now rise in the West and set in the East, and devastation would overtake most of the plants and animals on earth and human civilization would be destroyed.

If such a catastrophic event had taken place on earth again and again, we would long ago have found the geological records to prove it. Instead, the reversal of the magnetic field probably takes place relatively slowly and without influencing the earth's rotation. There may be a few major earthquakes and tidal waves, but most living creatures are unharmed. However, despite the fact that this is the age of science *par excellence,* we know almost nothing about what takes place during a reversal of the poles, and most scientific theories are sheer speculation.

Chapter Five

FIRES IN THE DEPTHS

Mere theory?

As FAR as we know, the interior of the earth is hot or at least warm. But why should it be hot? The sun warms up its outer shell. And floating as it is in the coldness of the universe, shouldn't the earth have cooled off long ago? Anyone who asks this question assumes something which has not been proven. He assumes that the earth was hot in the beginning. He believes the theory that the earth was formed from a white-hot ball of glowing gas. In reality, we do not know how the earth was formed. Possibly it may have derived from a ball of glowing gas, as elementary schoolbooks often tell us it did; but scientists do not know for sure. However, we do know that heat increases as we go deeper into the earth. Volcanoes, geysers, and cracks in the ocean floor testify to the presence of seemingly inexhaustible quantities of heat. Does this heat derive from chemical oxidation, from chemical processes corresponding to the burning of coal with air? Chemists can easily conceive of several hundred reactions which might be taking place inside the earth, but they cannot prove that they are.

Scientists became familiar with the element radium around the turn of the century. Shortly thereafter someone composed this verse:

What does radium do?
It gives off heat, dear public,
so that soon the world can do without the men
who bring us coal and coke.

(*Jahrbuch der Naturkunde*, 1905)

Scientists immediately began to wonder whether radium or other radioactive substances might be responsible for the earth's interior heat. To put the question in modern terms: Does the decay of radioactive isotopes of uranium, thorium, radium, and potassium create the energy inside the earth? Unfortunately, a number of factors seemed to disprove the theory. For example, the earth's core is assumed to consist of nickel and iron; but iron and nickel have no isotopes to decay. Thus, an iron-and-nickel core could not help to create heat. Moreover, volcanic eruptions have contained no substances which support the theory of radioactive isotopes in the core. We know of a few radioactive thermal springs, but these do not support the theory, either, for in order to create heat by radioactive decay, the waters would have to be much more radioactive than they are. Thus, for the time being, we must simply be patient while scientists attempt to find new arguments in support of their theories.

However, it would not be too surprising if we suddenly found a solution to the problem, for in 1972 scientists discovered something which until then had seemed unthinkable.

A vague possibility

However, first let us return to the year 1939. On March 10 of that year Otto Hahn and Fritz Strassmann, two chemists from the Kaiser Wilhelm Institute in Berlin-Dahlem, published their final evidence demonstrating the possibility of the nuclear fission of uranium. They published their article in the periodical *Die Naturwissenschaften*. Without realizing it, they thereby laid the foundations of the world in which we must live today, a world in which all the major powers possess the atomic bomb.

Almost three months after Hahn and Strassmann published their article, a physicist from the same institute, S. Flügge, published a long essay in the same periodical. The article treated the possibilities of creating energy by nuclear fission. Could man find technological outlets for the energy content of atomic nuclei?

Hahn and Strassmann startled other scientists, but Flügge's essay attracted the attention of economists and military men. We are concerned with several sentences near the end of the essay which treat the existence of fissionable materials on earth. Among other things Flügge says:

> In general we can say that an explosion in nature is a very improbable event, for we never encounter sufficiently powerful concentrations in conjunction with the sufficient absence of substances which strongly absorb neutrons. . . . However, naturally it is quite possible that such processes do occasionally occur and that they may have a certain interest for geologists because of their relationship to volcanic phenomena.

These are the limits of the situation as viewed by a learned, imaginative man in 1939. In this essay he not only made public the possibilities inherent in nuclear fission, but also influenced the history of the war which was to break out a few months later; for he contributed to the fear that Germany would create a super-weapon, an atomic bomb.

The war came and went, mankind in the East and the West learned to live with the bomb, large beds of uranium were discovered and exploited, and nuclear power plants began to supply electricity for a new technological age. Flügge's essay had become scientific history, and now no one paid much attention to what it said.

Then in 1972 people heard of a discovery so strange and incredible that it seemed to have come out of a science-fiction novel. Because it seemed so incredible, at first no one paid much attention. This strange discovery was the fact that nature can build atomic reactors. Events confirmed Flügge's suggestion: a nuclear reactor that had been created by nature was actually discovered in Gabon, West Africa.

The triumph of nature

French scientists at the Pierrelatte atomic research center proved that a natural atomic reactor could exist. Uranium as it occurs in nature contains only .72% of the truly valuable form of uranium, uranium 235. First we must mine the uranium beds, which are often difficult to reach, then separate the uranium ore from the surrounding stone, then clean and work the ore and use expensive new technological processes to get at the uranium metal. Finally the uranium 235 must be concentrated, for nuclear power plants cannot be run profitably unless the concentration of uranium 235 is higher than .72%

One thing seemed clear: uranium everywhere would contain .72% of uranium 235. This seemed a factor to be reckoned with, until—until June 15, 1972, when a routine investigation in Pierrelatte disclosed an anomaly. Of two samples, one contained only .44% and the other only .59% of uranium 235! Had some error occurred? Had a previously "burned-out" sample been found in the reactor?

No. The reactor contained fresh uranium from valuable ore which came from Gabon, West Africa. But how could the percentage of uranium 235 contained in the samples be so low? As a rule, such low percentages occurred only in uranium that had been "burned out" in a reactor. If a mineral contains "burned-out" uranium, a nuclear reaction must have taken place. If a nuclear reaction had occurred in Gabon, this presupposed that originally the uranium 235 content of the ore contained in the two samples must have been *higher* than the normal .72%, for otherwise the natural reactor could not have gone "critical." Moreover, something must have damped the nuclear reactions (in our reactors we generally use graphite or heavy water) and something must have cooled the reactor, for otherwise the uranium would have gone past the "critical point" and everything would have exploded like an atomic bomb. Moreover, for the reactor to function, something even more improbable must have occurred. As Flügge stated, there could be no substances present which absorbed neutrons. Anyone who knows how difficult it is to fulfill this condition in our own reactors would consider it impossible for a "fossil nuclear fission reactor" to exist in nature.

Moreover, if atomic fission took place in the uranium bed in Gabon, it must have created the usual products of fission. Plutonium and neptunium must have been formed, and in this case they would no longer be considered "artificially created" chemical elements, but would have to be counted among the natural elements.

I will not go into all the "if's" and "but's." Suffice it to say that all the evidence proved that a natural nuclear reactor had in fact existed in Gabon. Moreover, the products of the radioactive nuclear processes established that the reactor had been in operation 1,700,000,000 years ago and that it was fueled by uranium containing three percent uranium 235.

The uranium was contained in a porous, sloping layer of sandstone located just beneath a layer of very pure clay. To a large extent the clay prevented the sandstone from being polluted by neutron-absorbing substances. When water ran down through the sandstone, it damped the neutrons formed by the decay of uranium 235 and thus enabled them to trigger a chain reaction. The chain reaction created higher temperatures which evaporated the water in the sandstone and stopped the reaction. The next time there was a sufficient amount of rain, the water percolated into the sandstone again, and the reactor reached the critical point and produced another nuclear reaction.

Did many such reactors once exist on or inside the earth, and did they help to heat up our planet? No one knows.

We must marvel at the fact that human inventiveness and technical skill cannot create anything which nature itself did not create long ago. Perhaps, since we humans form a part of nature, we cannot surpass nature and must accept our natural limitations.

However, leaving behind such philosophical questions, let us ask instead how nature can have created uranium ore so rich in uranium 235 as the ore in Gabon. Were processes at work there that we humans cannot duplicate, that we have not yet discovered? Or does a uranium 235 content of 3% represent the norm, while the .72% we are accustomed to finding is abnormal? We can ask questions, but we do not know the answers.

It is fascinating to realize that radioactive processes are still creating new elements and minerals. By no means has our earth achieved its final state. Even after 4,700,000,-000 years, the earth is still changing. But in any case, we still do not know the origin of the earth's heat. We can only note in passing the theory that its initial heat was derived from the decay of radioactive elements.

And the fire in the sky?

Perhaps this is the time to ask a question which we usually fail to ask because we are reluctant to challenge old beliefs. The sun is our most important source of heat. We tend to suppose that sunlight is a constant factor—that although the sun may be gradually cooling, it always shines with equal brightness. Is this true?

I will not describe in detail the nuclear fusion processes which we believe create the sun's energy. Unquestionably the concept of the fusion of hydrogen atoms into helium atoms represents a brilliant piece of astrophysical speculation. However, the theory requires that neutrinos (the smallest elementary particles) be created in the process. We ought to be able to find neutrinos on earth, but we have not been able to do so. It is questionable whether the sun is "burning" at all, and not simply radiating heat. Do the hydrogen fusion processes in the sun pulsate so that the sun's energy production fluctuates periodically? If this is true, it is possible that the sun's radiant energy is relatively weak in our time, but that in several million years its energy production will increase and the earth will be heated to higher temperatures again. Can changes in the earth's climate be understood in relation to fluctuations in the sun's energy production? Do these fluctuations contribute to the formation of deserts and periodical ice ages on earth?

In any case, we should beware of assuming that events on earth always pursue a constant course. The fluctuation or pulsation we observe in the tides and the seasons may also characterize the earth's climate and other phenomena.

The brevity of the time in which man has observed scientific phenomena may explain our tendency to regard evolution as a steady, uninterrupted flow. We should never forget that only three hundred fifty years have passed since men began to study the heavens with the aid of the first primitive telescopes. And we have only been aware of the existence of distant galaxies for fifty years. We are only beginning to know the true significance of exact science. No wonder we continually have to revise our theories about the world.

Mysterious hot spots

As the continental layers move across the earth and break apart, hot material rises from the interior of the earth and flows out through cracks and ravines. Volcanic activity occurs near fissures, regardless of whether they are located on land or in an undersea basin.

Another form of volcanic activity connected with continental drift is the phenomenon of "hot spots." We know little about them, but they appear to testify to the molten, liquid nature of the earth's interior. The name "hot spots" is well chosen. Apparently places exist beneath the wandering continents where hot, liquid masses rise up-

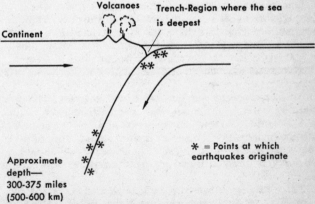

Volcanoes

Trench-Region where the sea is deepest

Continent

** **

Approximate depth— 300-375 miles (500-600 km)

* = Points at which earthquakes originate

The sea floor pushing itself under the land. Parts of the land are pushed downward, and so a "trench" is formed parallel to the coast. Earthquake and volcanic activity develop in this zone. At a great depth (around five to six hundred kilometers beneath the sea), major earthquakes are triggered where the two land blocks meet and clash.

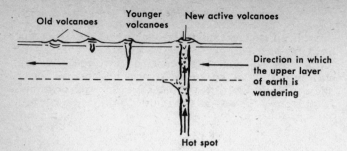

Old volcanoes   Younger volcanoes   New active volcanoes

Direction in which the upper layer of earth is wandering

Hot spot

Illustration of the hot-spot theory. A layer of earth drifts over an area where hot lava is rising from the depths of the earth. The lava periodically perforates the layer which is drifting above it and raises volcanoes on the land. As soon as the volcanoes are pushed past the hot spot, they become extinct. Compare the text concerning hot-spot lines in the earth's crust.

ward. Like cutting torches, these hot masses melt their way through the eighteen or twenty miles of continent above them and then through the overlying sediments until they reach the earth's surface.

One of these hot spots is located in a place where no one would expect it: in the middle of Europe! While the continent of Europe drifted across it, it acted like a blowtorch, cutting a mark from the Carpathian Mountains to the Eifel region of Germany. It would not be surprising if a volcano soon developed somewhere west of the Eifel region.

In fact, we can predict what will happen. The first warning will be earthquakes in the Ardennes of France and Belgium. A few small peaks around two hundred meters in height will rise from the ground, and some of them will emit volcanic ash. Finally, lava will flow out. For several decades eruptions of ash and lava will continue.

To some degree we can predict when these events will take place, for we can clearly see the history of the hot spot. A line of volcanoes extends from the northwestern corner of the Carpathians across the Riesen Mountains, the Erz Mountains, the Fichtel Mountains, the Rhön Mountains, the Vogelsberg, the Westerwald, and the Sieben Mountains. These volcanoes outline the path of the continent passing over the blowtorch of the hot spot, which melted its way upward to create the series of volcanic smokestacks.

The oldest of the volcanoes is about 30,000 years old. The youngest volcanoes are the ones in the Eifel region of West Germany. Around 12,000 years ago, these volcanoes were still active. They hurled ash, clouds of dust, pumice-stone, and probably hot-water vapor into the surrounding landscape. Europe moves one inch a year relative to the hot spot. But this figure tells us little about the probable location of the next volcanic eruption. We can't be more precise than to say a region up to three hundred miles west of the Eifel is in danger! People who live in this region may console themselves with the thought that the theory of the European hot spot is pure speculation. However, geological fate is relentless, and man cannot influence the energy of a hot spot.

Series of blisters

We can trace the paths of other hot spots along the earth's crust. I have already mentioned the movement of the British Isles, their special continental drift, and the fact that they turned to one side. The British Isles also crossed a hot spot. It burned its volcanoes along a line that begins south of Belfast, Ireland, and crosses northern Ireland, the isle of Aran, the large island of Mull, the island of Rhum, and reaches at least as far as the island of Skye. In other words, the line extends around two hundred miles. The oldest volcanoes along the line are around 75,000,000 years old.

Scientists consider it possible that the line of volcanoes continues northwest across the Faroe Islands to Iceland. If their theories are correct, then the hot spot is now located beneath Iceland. Perhaps it was this hot spot which formed the island of Surtsey on November 14, 1963, and which in the spring of 1973 covered large areas of the port of Heimaey with ashes and then flooded the town with lava. None of the existing evidence contradicts this theory. On the contrary, the traces left by hot spots correspond to what we now know about the movements of land masses involved in Wegener's continental drift.

There may be a hot spot in Hawaii, too. If we look at a map of the Pacific, we see a chain of islands running northwest from Hawaii. The Midway Islands form the end-point of the chain. At this point an undersea mountain chain, the Emperor Seamounts, stretches off to the north. The mountains in this chain are several thousand meters tall, but not so tall that their tips appear as islands on our map. What happened here ?

The Pacific sea floor glided across the Hawaii hot spot. At one time the northernmost of the Emperor Seamounts was located over this hot spot. Then the floor of the Pacific drifted northward, and the hot spot burned a line into the sea floor. Volcanoes erupted. When the Midway Islands lay above the hot spot, the sea floor changed direction and began to drift less toward the north and more toward the west. New islands rose to the surface and drifted westward until finally the Hawaiian islands had taken on the shape we know today.

Should the results of the drifting of land masses over hot spots be compared with the effects that a blowtorch has on a steel plate, or with a row of blisters? Probably it does not matter which simile we choose. But clearly the creation of "blisters" is not yet at an end. New volcanic mountains will develop in the earth's crust to replace the Hawaiian islands as they continue to drift to the north-west.

One rather speculative question remains unanswered: Are "atomic reactors" still burning in the hot spots deep in the earth? Are radioactive elements still decaying there? If not, what is the source of the vast quantities of energy which melt the continents and drive volcanic smokestacks up through the ocean waters?

We do not know the answers to these questions. We know nothing about the inner structure of the earth and know next to nothing about how it produces heat. When we search for answers, we only discover new and mysterious phenomena. Can we glean some knowledge from the handful of mysteries we have discovered? We must believe that we can, for otherwise our search would have no meaning.

The ice beneath the lava

Travel folders always depict Hawaii as a tropical isle filled with sunshine, palm trees, sand, and places to swim in. Hawaii is, in fact, an island paradise. The active volcanoes, which sometimes overflow with lava, are located in the southeastern area of the islands and serve as a tourist attraction.

But Hawaii is also filled with mysteries, mysteries so inexplicable that scientists at the Geophysical Institute of Hawaii, in Honolulu, can hardly believe their own measurements. The island contains ancient ice! Beneath the lava flows of Mauna Kea, a "dormant" volcano two miles in height, lies a mass of ice several miles wide and some thirty-two feet thick. The ice is riddled with hardened lava. It is so old that the tritium clock has stopped running and cannot be used to tell its age. All the tritium the ice contained has long since undergone radioactive decay. All one sees is ice—clear, bright ice that contains no air bubbles but does contain insect remains!

Who can solve the riddle of the ice? What is concealed in the depths of the island?

Traveling with Jules Verne

It is understandable that when volcanoes are inactive, they are covered with snow and ice. Many volcanoes rise out of "the eternal ice." One of the tallest volcanoes in the world is Mount Rainier, in Washington, in the northwestern United States. This mountain, which lies south of the port of Seattle, is 14,000 feet high, and naturally the top of it is covered with ice. However, there is something strange about this ice. If Jules Verne had known about Mount Rainier, he would have made it the place where the travelers entered the earth in his science-fiction novel *Journey to the Center of the Earth*. In this mountain, volcanic forces struggle with the eternal ice, and the result is a phenomenon unique on this earth.

For a hundred years people had heard that the ice cap of Mount Rainier concealed a secret, a maze of corridors and caves. But not until 1970 did scientists begin a systematic investigation. It was necessary for them to do so, for shortly before, seismographs had recorded violent earthquakes in the gigantic crater of Mount Rainier, and indications were that the heat in the cone was increasing. The danger was obvious. If the ice melted, some 4,000,000 cubic yards of water would flow down the slopes from each of the two craters at the top of Mount Rainier. The water would tear stones, rocks, pebbles, and mud from the mountainside, trigger landslides, fill up the valleys, melt glaciers, and in general threaten everyone who lived nearby.

In August, 1970, an expedition climbed to the top of the easternmost of the two craters. When they arrived, instead of the crater they saw a round hole one thousand feet wide and five hundred feet deep, filled with snow and ice. In the white mass they found three large holes sloping downward from the inner wall of the crater. The holes sloped downward at an angle of between thirty-five and forty degrees.

The descent was difficult and dangerous. Deep in the crater there were corridors in the ice, some of them as much as thirty feet wide and almost fifteen feet in height. The members of the expedition took the danger in stride and continued to descend. The adventure led them into a tangle of large and small corridors, some of which branched off and then met again at some other point. It was less like a maze than a system of tunnels. Some corridors led directly to the center of the crater; other dark passages led to dead ends. At a certain depth the explorers found a broad "highway" which sometimes widened into a hall and which followed the circumference of the crater wall. This "highway" alone was over a half-mile in length! For the most part, the floor of the passages was damp, muddy, and strewn with broken rock.

The riddle of the red glove

The system of tunnels was filled with strange and threatening noises. Hot steam piped, gurgled, and hissed from hundreds of places in the ground, carving its way through mud and potholes and melting the ice on the walls and ceilings, which dripped continously onto the ground. At other points there were streams of foul-smelling, poisonous sulfurous gases. In many places the path was not only dark but shrouded in clouds of vapor which concealed everything from view. All the moisture the crater contained rained down into the depths. Apparently a pond or a lake is located somewhere deep inside this underworld.

A warm draft was blowing even at the tunnel entrances, more than 13,000 feet high in the crater wall. The tem-

perature here was 4° C. But on top of everything else.
it was hot inside the tunnel system! The steam in the corridors was as hot as 56° C, and at one point the temperature of the rocky floor was 86° C.

Struggling against the heat, vapor, water, and gas, the
geologists recorded, measured, and made charts of what
they found. They marveled at the steep descents and at the
cathedral-like grottoes which had been melted out of the
ice. At one point, when the ice above them was four hundred fifty feet thick, they made two amazing discoveries.
On the ground before them lay the remains of a bird
which as a rule inhabits the coast sixty miles away. And
above them in the icy ceiling of the corridor they found a
red woolen glove!

Mysterious discoveries ought to occur in an adventure,
and this adventure had its share. Up above, at the edge of
the crater, the explorers found the remains of another bird.
Could a storm carry birds as high as the top of the crater?
And how did the first dead bird make its way deep into
the heart of the crater? Perhaps, like the glove, it was
brought there by some mountain-climber of long ago. Or
perhaps the bird and the glove once lay on top of the
crater ice, until snow covered them and the heat of the
crater melted the ice, allowing both objects to slowly sink
into the depths, covered with new layers of snow and ice.
This may well be the case. However, no one doubts that
Mount Rainier still contains many secrets and that there
may be other explanations for the presence of the glove
and the bird.

Still another mystery of Mount Rainier is the question
of what happens to all the water that continually streams
into the depths of the crater.

". . . and Moses went up"

It is easy to understand why volcanoes, "the mountains
that spit fire," have always appealed to the imagination.
One of the earliest descriptions of a volcanic eruption
comes from the Old Testament; but despite its age, we can
date it fairly exactly. The eruption took place on Mount
Sinai, on the Gulf of Suez. The nineteenth chapter of Exodus is a clear, factual account, and it shows that Moses
was an amateur volcanologist.

When the mountain became active, the Israelites were camped near Sinai:

> And it came to pass on the third day in the morning, that there were thunders and lightnings, and a thick cloud upon the mount, and the voice of the trumpet exceedingly loud; so that all the people that were in the camp trembled.
>
> —Exodus 19:16

The "thick cloud" is undoubtedly a cloud of volcanic ash or dust that has been hurled from the crater. Many photographs have shown that frictional electricity discharges itself in such clouds in the form of long streaks of lightning accompanied by thunder. We can also take the "voice of the trumpet" literally, for when quantities of gas are freed from the earth, they make a roaring and whistling sound through the cracks, fissures, and smokestacks opening up inside the crater.

The eruption rose straight up into the sky. Moses observes:

> And Mount Sinai was altogether on a smoke, because the Lord descended upon it in fire: and the smoke thereof ascended as the smoke of a furnace, and the whole mount quaked greatly. . . .
>
> —Exodus 19:18

> And when the voice of the trumpet sounded long and waxed louder and louder . . .
>
> —Exodus 19:19

> . . . and Moses went up.
>
> —Exodus 19:20

Who could have resisted the temptation to observe such a spectacle from close at hand?

The war fleet goes to Vesuvius

The fleet commander Pliny the Elder was less fortunate than Moses in his attempt to observe a volcanic eruption from close at hand. His nephew Pliny the Younger described what happened when Vesuvius erupted in 79 A.D. The squadron of Roman ships commanded by Pliny the Elder lay in the port of Misenum, almost exactly thirty kilometers west of the volcanic crater. In fact, the fleet was anchored at an old volcanic crater that had filled up with water. The whole area around Naples is still riddled with volcanic activity. For example, in this region we find the volcanic island of Ischia, the Campi Flegrei ("Burning Fields"), the hot springs of Baia, the vapor caves of Solfatara, and the "New Mountain" (Monte Nuovo), a mountain one thousand feet in height which developed over a period of a few days in 1538. Another example is the city of Pozzuoli, which continually rises and sinks.

Pliny describes the eruption of Vesuvius as seen by his uncle, who was fifty-six at the time:

On August 23 at around one o'clock in the afternoon, my mother drew his attention to an extraordinary cloud. In form it was only comparable to a tree, a stone pine. It rose up straight and smooth like the trunk of a tree and then divided into several branches. In places it appeared completely white, but in other places, where it cast up earth and stone, it was dark and spotted.

At this moment no one knew that at least three villages and countless human beings would be the victims of this eruption. The people who lived in this area thought no more of the danger than people who now build their homes in the Campi Flegrei or on the isle of Ischia or at the foot of the modern Vesuvius. One is tempted to think that the citizens of Herculaneum should have been on their guard, for just seventeen years before, most of their town and its 5,000 inhabitants had been annihilated by a volcanic earthquake. By 79 A.D., the town had not yet succeeded in eliminating all signs of the disaster. However, anyone who knows the area will recall that almost six miles separate Herculaneum from Vesuvius. The townspeople could not imagine that they were in danger. And an even greater distance separates Pompeii from the volcano.

Thus, Pliny had no fear of observing the volcanic phenomena from nearby. Apart from personal courage and a sense of responsibility, it was primarily curiosity which made him give the command: "Prepare fast ships. I want to see this more closely."

Pliny the Younger continues:

Ashes were already falling on the ships, and the nearer the ships sailed, the hotter and denser the ashes became. Soon the ashes were followed by pumice and by black stones that had split open from the heat. But then the ships came into shallow water, and the debris from the mountain made it impossible to reach the shore.

But the Roman commander was not afraid: "Fortune favors the brave. Travel on, Pomponiamus!"

The helmsman obeyed him and landed in Stabiae, the village which lay closest to the erupting volcano. Even today it is still covered by lava and debris.

An exemplary officer, Pliny calmed his retinue, took a bath, had food prepared, ate in good spirits, and serenely watched the flames and the eruptions which lit up the night. He even went to sleep. No one dared to wake him until the yard beside his room was piled so high with volcanic ash that they were afraid that soon they would be unable to open the door.

Pliny and his men talked things over. Should they stay in the house, which had begun to be shaken by earthquakes, or should they go outside and brave the ceaseless rain of bits of pumice stone?

They knew that it must be morning, but dust and ashes darkened the sky, so the men had to light torches.

Could they travel back across the sea? Binding cloths and padding around their heads to protect themselves from the ashes and pumice, they walked to the sea; but the waves were high and the wind was blowing in the wrong direction. Pliny stopped to rest, camping on a cloth he had brought with him, and refreshed himself with fresh water. Then a suffocating cloud of sulfurous gas drove the men apart. Pliny rose, supported by two servants, then suddenly collapsed and died.

The world had lost one of its greatest scientists, an outstanding scientific author who, among other things, wrote thirty-six comprehensive volumes of natural history, and the Roman Empire had lost a faithful officer.

The eruption of Vesuvius must have looked about the

same to the citizens of Pompeii as it did to Pliny. Archaeologists have excavated large portions of the city, which is located on an old river of lava overlooking the fertile fields. To do so they had to remove earth, ashes, and light pumice stones no larger than finger joints. Probably no one in the city recognized that this rain of pumice betokened deadly danger—until the sulfurous vapors suddenly cut off their breathing. The dead people, whose forms were imprinted in the layers of dust and ash, died with their mouths wide open, struggling for air. A dog whose shape was imprinted in the ashes is showing his teeth in a vain attempt to swallow breathable air.

Dust and water

But Vesuvius had not finished erupting. Pliny the Younger tells us that the sea floor rose and that sea creatures lay upon the dry land. He also says that flames shot up from Vesuvius and that clouds of dust and ashes poured over the Gulf of Naples. Capri disappeared beneath the dark clouds, and soon the clouds rolled on to the Roman port of Misenum. Here, too, the sky grew dark, and the populace fled in panic, covered with ashes. The earth quaked so violently that the fleeing people fell down and even wagons were overturned.

Pompeii vanished beneath a layer of ashes and pumice fifteen feet thick. Herculaneum suffered even more, although no one was there to be killed. Herculaneum was located on lower ground than Pompeii and lay at the edge of the sea. (Now it is some distance from the sea, for the sea floor has risen and the coastline now runs farther toward the west.) Herculaneum was flooded. Vast quantities of water poured down the slopes of Vesuvius, tore loose huge expanses of ash, flooded the fields, tore away rock debris, dashed against the houses, flowed through the streets and into cellars, rooms and courtyards, and finally ran gurgling into the raging sea. Walls were crushed, roofs flooded, and timbers carried away by the flood. When it was all over, the city was covered by a layer of mud, ash, and stone that in some places was thirty feet high.

It is no wonder that for centuries people forgot that Herculaneum had once been the site of a prosperous city. When Vesuvius erupted again in 1632, flooding the

Herculaneum. This is how the excavated portions of the city look to modern visitors. The sea coast once lay where the photographer stood to take this picture. The mud from the eruption of Vesuvius covered the buildings to a level twice as high as the mud which can be seen at the upper right-hand corner of the picture. (The roofs of the buildings are modern additions.) (Photograph by F. Boschke)

region with molten lava, Herculaneum had been forgotten. No one knew that beneath the layer of lava there lay a paradise for treasure-hunters, amateur archaeologists, historians, and art historians. It was not until one hundred years later that the first tentative excavations were begun in the ancient port.

Only a small portion of the region around Herculaneum has been uncovered. This is true partly because the ruins of the medieval city of Resina and the buildings of the modern city by the same name are located above Herculaneum. To be sure, whole streets are now being torn down, but only so that new apartment buildings can be built in their place. How often must the city be destroyed before people understand that the forces of nature are stronger than the works of man and that although volcanoes may sleep, they are bound to erupt again and again?

Excavations have shown that Herculaneum was a city with narrow streets running southward. The houses had high ceilings and beautiful square inner courtyards, gardens, rows of columns, colorful mosaics, an abundance of art objects made of bronze and other materials, and bright wall paintings. There were public baths, shops, and places where people practiced trades. Archaeologists found everything which people leave behind when they flee in panic. And all the citizens fled in time. Until now not a single victim has been discovered in the city. No dead lay in the impressive houses of the wealthy or in the narrow rooms beside them which were rented out.

Part of the old Roman city still rests beneath its two layers of lava, ash, and pumice. No one knows when Vesuvius will deposit another layer of mud, ash, lava, or pumice on top of the town. But the day will come.

The eternal fire in Sicily

We sorely need to undertake an extensive study of volcanoes. Because we know so little about the interior of our planet, we do not know the source of volcanic forces.

Tourists climbing Mount Etna. (Photograph by F. Rajah, Taormina)

However, we should at least be able to find out when and how, or at least where, a volcano will erupt. Volcanic eruptions should no longer come as a surprise. This is especially true because large areas of Europe, Asia, and Africa live under the threat of a major eruption: the eruption of Mount Etna, in Sicily.

The history of the Mount Etna volcano is a history of ceaseless catastrophe. In historical times alone, Etna has erupted some one hundred forty times. At some point, on the spot where there now stands a mountain 10,000 feet high, a crack or hole opened in the earth, and gas, cinders, and ash, and perhaps molten lava, poured out of it. The expelled material formed a circle, a high wall, around the place of the eruption. In the center was a crater. At first all this did not amount to much; but the second eruption spewed more rocks over the crater wall and covered everything with lava.

The process continued for hundreds and thousands of years. Finally, although gas pressing up from the interior was still able to force its way up to the crater and drive stones and ashes along with it, the viscous stone inside the earth could no longer raise the heavy cone of the mountain above it.

However, the gas had to get out from time to time, and thus more and more often the side of the mountain was torn open and lava flowed out and down its slopes. The most violent eruption of this kind occurred in 1669. The mountainside split open for a distance of nine miles! Lava flowed out, destroyed a dozen villages, reached the port of Catania, and then poured out into the sea. Today the glass-hard, blue-black stone, twisted in bizarre shapes, stands as an image of the power of nature. At the same time that the lava poured out, thirteen gorges in the mountainside expelled stone, ashes, and sand, which piled up and formed a mountain seven hundred fifty feet high.

Where do the gases, the stones, ashes, lava, and the fury of the volcano come from? We do not know and can only guess. Because we can only theorize about the causes of volcanic activity, we cannot predict for certain when future eruptions will occur. Only one thing is certain: Etna is not yet extinct, but is still an active volcano. Those who live at the foot of the mountain can see a cloud of smoke by day and see the lava glowing red at night, and they know that the volcano is still active.

Mount Etna erupts. The slag wall left by a river of lava encloses a house.

On March 20, 1971, a local guide noticed that the snow was melting at one point at the top of the Etna crater and that heat was being emitted from the inside of the mountain. However, it was not until the morning of April 5 that two fissures opened at a height of 9,000 feet and then grew until they were two hundred, then three hundred, yards long. Ashes and sand were emitted at two points until they formed a heap one hundred fifty feet high. Finally, on April 12, glowing lava poured out of the crater. Then the pace of the eruption accelerated. Soon the lava reached and swamped the observatory, smashing first one wall and then the entire building. The strength of the eruptions fluctuated. Deep lava flowed down the mountain and into villages and fields, sometimes following the course of valleys and ravines, and frequently changing direction.

Thousands of observers arrived from half of Europe. They enjoyed watching the destruction, the spectacle of the annihilation of fields, plantations, buildings, and streets, plus the adventure of not knowing what was going to happen next.

It was fascinating to watch the wall of stone pushing forward, glowing bright red for an instant here and there, and to see the leaves on the trees dry up, the branches smoke, and the trunks flare up and crumble away. The lava rolled over everything like a tank.

There are always a few clever natives who know how to make money from the eruptions. They would scoop up a little lava from the glowing river with a long pole, press a coin into the lava, let it cool, and then sell it as a souvenir. More ambitious "entrepreneurs" poured the lava into rough molds and made something they generously call "ashtrays." Anyone who has taken home one of these ashtrays may irreverently wonder what Moses brought back with him from Mount Sinai.

What will happen next? The spectators of the volcano do not know, and even experts cannot tell for sure. However, people know from experience that a sluggish mass of lava does not instantaneously begin to spatter or change into freely flowing liquid. Thus, the spectators are not in any immediate danger.

As a rule, less than one cubic kilometer of lava flows from Mount Etna during each eruption. When lava flowed from the side of Etna in 1971, spectators watched a molten river ten meters high move toward three villages and destroy streets, bridges, and fruit plantations. However, only around 4,000,000 cubic yards of lava flowed from the volcano each day.

An average day on Stromboli

Other volcanoes behave differently. But wherever a volcano is located, the inhabitants are used to earthquakes, the noise of thunder, columns of smoke, and violent eruptions. The island of Stromboli is nothing but a round, central cone rising steeply out of the Mediterranean. The people who live on the island worry only when they see *no* eruptions occur. When this happens, one of them may climb the nine hundred eighteen meters to the top of the mountain to see whether "the holes" are stopped up. As long as the mountain is letting off pressure through minor eruptions, the people feel safe. But if the chimneys are stopped up, they worry that a major eruption may occur and that they will be in genuine danger. They remember the year 1930, when, after a period of relative peace, the crater suddenly hurled out chunks of rock weighing as much as thirty tons. The rocks damaged houses, bright lava cinders filled the air, and a hot avalanche of lava flowed down the hill and killed four people. The mountain did not quiet down again until great quantities of lava had flowed into the sea.

Anyone who visits Stromboli today is guaranteed the pleasure of seeing a volcano in action. But when he sees how loosely the great fields of ash are attached to the cliffs above, and when he sees how hot, glowing chunks of rock continually roll down the two-thousand-feet-long "fire chute" to the waves below, he knows that on Stromboli living creatures are always in danger. He will be glad when the steamboat that runs from Messina to Naples arrives several days later and he can leave the island.

He will remember the sight of the vast cone of ash, the abandoned homes, the ravaged gardens, and the oppressive poverty of the few old people who remain on the island. Stromboli is no place for tourists to vacation. Despite the fascinating spectacle of the volcano and despite the luxuriant and colorful vegetation on the lower slopes of the mountain, Stromboli is a highly uncertain place. It is a lottery in which only the lucky survive. We know too little to predict what will happen today or tomorrow on Stromboli or in any other place where volcanoes are active.

The tourist guide's trick

Not all volcanic phenomena are as depressing as a visit to Stromboli. Anyone who wishes may visit the Campi Flegrei, near Naples, in the company of a tourist guide who will show him how to trigger the "Solfatara" phenomenon. The word "phenomenon" suggests that although scientists know about the occurrence, they cannot really explain it. Tourist guides begin their presentation by standing on the flat floor of the crater, which is filled with hollow echoes, near a hole in which some blue-gray mud is boiling away. Then the guide points to one slope of the mountain that is made of speckled white pumice. At one thousand foot intervals, small clouds of black vapor, little "fumaroles," rise from the pumice. The tourist sees, as well as smells, the vapor. (Be careful: it destroys nylon.) Then the guide asks for a cigarette, lights it, and bends down to a little hole in the ground that is no more than a quarter of an inch in diameter. He holds the cigarette near the hole and the distant fumaroles send out thick clouds of vapor!

The trick can be repeated over and over, and the guide will receive generous tips from all the tourists if he allows them to perform it themselves.

Scientists have attempted to explain this phenomenon by saying that the fire of the cigarette ionizes the air or that the cigarette smoke provides nuclei around which the water-saturated air can condense. However, no one knows why the cigarette affects the fumaroles from such a distance away or only affects them when it is held close to the tiny hole in the ground.

Guides who work at Vesuvius and in the Campi Flegrei have known this trick for decades. However, in other places it is a novelty, and people who travel, for example, to Volcano Island, can make quite a hit with it. There are no guides on Volcano; thus, vacationers are completely taken aback when someone uses the Solfatara phenomenon to make vapor rise from the beach where they were swimming. If you don't have a cigarette, a bit of burning paper or wood or even a match will do.

Chapter Six

THE BURNING EARTH

The gate of hell

ALTHOUGH HUMAN beings have always been familiar with volcanoes, we are still fascinated by them. Let us take a look at Iceland, this island which seems to be one single giant volcanic mountain.

A chronicle about the volcano Hekla reports not only that it became active again in 1104, but also describes it as the gate to hell! In 1675 the Frenchman de la Martinière wrote of his travels, in which he explained why Hekla was the gate to hell. He said that sometimes the Devil removed the souls of the damned from the fires of the volcano and cooled them on the ice—presumably so that they could be burned and purified better later on.

Since 1104, Hekla has erupted at least fifteen times, the last time in 1970. During its last eruption its hellish maw disgorged gases containing fluoride which killed around 100,000 sheep. The Icelanders are no strangers to volcanoes. Nevertheless, some eruptions surprise even them.

It was 6:30 A.M. on the morning of November 14, 1963. The men of the fishing boat *Isleifur II,* which was traveling about thirty kilometers south of the coast of Iceland, entered the cabin to warm themselves with a cup of coffee. Shortly before 7:00, one of them climbed up on deck and smelled a strange odor. The man was a machinist, and so he thought of the possibility that one of his machines had been damaged and checked the oily waste water. No, it was not the waste water. At 7:30 the cook woke up the captain to tell him that the boat was rolling strangely. But there was nothing special to be seen from the deck. The dawn air was somewhat overcast toward the southeast, rather as if a ship were burning there. However, the radio reported no news of any trouble. Then the men noticed that a dark cloud of ashes was hanging over the sea. A volcanic crater had erupted beneath the sea! Unfortunately, the curious captain could not steer straight for the point of eruption, but at 8:00 the crew pinpointed the location of a column of ashes one hundred eighty feet high. The next day, in a place where the sea had been four hundred feet deep, they found an island thirty feet high. After one more day the island was already one hundred twenty feet high and one thousand feet long, and it was still growing.

Ashes, mud, and giant clouds of smoke and vapor were hurled miles high; glowing rock erupted from the crater; and finally lava flowed out and into the sea. The ashes were borne to the neighboring island of Heimaey and settled in a dark layer on the roofs of Vestmannaeyjar—a warning that was not heeded.

The new island was dubbed Surtsey, after the Norse fire-god Surtur. On June 5, 1967, after three and a half years, the eruptions ceased. At this point Surtsey was around one square mile in size, a dismal heap of ashes and lava on which there was no living thing but algae. Later moss and dune grass would grow on Surtsey, and gulls and other birds now come there to rest. The world has gained an island.

The island that is part of two continents

If we draw a line between the island of Surtsey and the Hekla volcano, the island of Heimaey lies somewhat to the east of this line. Then if we extend the line southward, it runs into the great fissure in the middle of the Atlantic, along which the earth has been pushing upward ever since North and South America separated from Europe and Africa. In Iceland the forces at work in the depths have raised the fissure above the sea. Iceland is an object lesson in Wegener's theory of continental drift. If you fly over the island in an airplane, you will see beneath you a ravine that is miles long. If you look at a map, you will read the words "Thingvellir trench" and see America on the left and Europe on the right. Iceland is an island which forms part of two continents!

Since the continents are still pulling apart, Iceland will continue to grow wider. One day it may be divided into an American and a European half. Volcanic activity will continue for some time, and whatever lies near the fissure is in danger.

In the region of the fissure where Surtsey and Hekla are located is the island of Heimaey. Its inhabitants saw the clouds rise from Surtsey, but their own volcano, Helgafell, the "Holy Mountain," had been extinct for 7,000 years. Seven thousand years is an eternity for human beings, but not for a volcano.

A fissure opens up

On January 22, 1973, seismographs in southern Iceland recorded a series of rapid earth tremors. The tremors followed each other so quickly that seismographers could not agree whether one hundred twenty or one hundred thirty tiny earthquakes had taken place. In any case, the tremors seemed slight and were probably not important. Then thirteen hours later, at two o'clock in the morning, a fissure opened on the eastern slope of Heimaey's Holy Mountain. The fissure grew until it was a mile long. Then fifteen or twenty smokestacks began to emit ashes and fiery cinders. Within five minutes the "extinct" volcano had turned into a sea of flames. Flames shot out of the crater and climbed nine hundred feet into the sky.

Two men who were wandering around during the night gave an eyewitness account of what happened next. If their account is accurate (and there is no reason to believe that it is not), everything happened without warning. The two men suddenly stopped in their tracks and stared at something they simply did not comprehend: the bright glow of a fire appeared very close to them. Was the town burning, or had the Holy Mountain exploded? When they understood what was happening, they ran to wake up the women and children. Other sleepers were awakened by the glow of the fire, threw on their clothes, and gathered up their money and personal possessions. A few quickly telephoned friends and acquaintances in Reykjavik, the capital of Iceland, and told them:

"The volcano is erupting!"

"Don't play jokes in the middle of the night."

"It's no joke! It's erupting right in front of us! We're leaving home now!"

"Are you drunk?"

Outside, firemen and police officers ran through the streets, the sirens howled, and finally the noise woke up the last of the sleepers. Everyone decided to evacuate the city and went down to the harbor, and the radio signaled Mayday.

An hour after the eruption began, the first airplane landed on a runway that was already covered with rock debris from the erupting volcano. Transport planes flew out the old and the sick and the hospital was evacuated. Women and children were evacuated by ship.

Meanwhile, the lava burst out of the crater and flowed, smoking and hissing, into the sea. The first narrow fissure

The excavation of Heimaey. This photograph, taken in 1974, shows how people have shoveled the debris from the tops of the houses. (Photograph by H. Kunert, Bammental)

became a broad crevasse that ran down into the sea. After one month what some geologists had predicted actually came to pass. One whole side of the crater broke off and huge masses of rock plunged downward until they reached the fishing port of Vestmannaeyjar, which had been covered with ashes ever since the eruption began and which now was threatened by flowing lava.

The sea floor began to move, a reef rose up beneath the water, and it became progressively more difficult to navigate through the narrow passage into the harbor. Now the roofs of the houses began to collapse beneath the weight of the rain of ash, and the more than 5,000 inhabitants of Vestmannaeyjar were evacuated. Then several buildings burst into flame, and the people gave up the harbor buildings for lost. The village seemed doomed.

In March, 1973, policemen, firemen, and workmen made a desperate attempt to cool the advancing lava with water so that the front of it would harden and compel the river of lava behind it to flow in a new direction. Then poisonous gases containing fluoride streamed out of the cracks in the earth, and many people collapsed. The village, a center of the fishing industry, was abandoned.

Six months later the town was covered with a sheet of black ashes, but the people began to hope again. The eruption had slackened, and the inhabitants began to think of rebuilding. They started to dig out the parts of the town that had not been burned to a crisp and unearthed some of the topsy-turvy houses, with their bright red, green, and blue corrugated-iron roofs.

Each year Iceland becomes about an inch wider, the distance by which North America drifts away from Europe. This is a tiny distance compared with the size of the earth, but still this tiny span is enough to set loose powerful volcanic forces from the earth's interior.

We do not know where the next volcanic catastrophe may take place. Perhaps volcanic forces have spent themselves in Iceland for the span of one human generation, and the next volcanic reaction will take place toward the south of the mid-Atlantic ridge, in the Azores, where the last eruption took place in 1957, or on Tristan da Cunha, where the last eruption was in 1961, or on Tenerife or one of the other Canary Islands.

We are still blind victims of the forces of nature. When a journalist on the island of Heimaey asked Icelandic geologist Sirgurdur Thorarinsson how long the eruption would last, Thorarinsson replied, "When the volcano has stopped erupting, then I will predict that the eruptions have stopped." This may have represented the brusque reply of an exhausted man, but no scientist could have answered the question more precisely.

Habit and custom

It is fascinating to witness the unexpected birth of a volcano. We have an eyewitness account of the birth of the volcano Paracutin, in Mexico, in 1943. An Indian was plowing his corn field, trying to loosen the soil. Then smoke began to rise from the furrow he had just plowed. Soon the smoke grew thicker all along the furrow, and then a crack opened in the earth. The crack became longer and wider, the earth trembled and rose up, and sand flew into the air. In just one day a mountain forty-five feet high had risen in the middle of the corn field. In six months the mountain had developed into an active volcano.

Anyone who sees the birth of a volcano will be afraid and run away. When a volcano spits out the interior of the earth, we see clouds of vapor, smoke, dust, ash, cooling bits of lava, molten lava, showers of rocks and round "bombs," black, yellow, red, and gray rocks, rivulets of water, mist, mud floods, loose pumice or solid material, cinders as hard as glass or soft gravel, stinking gases, numbing vapors, and suffocating sulfurous gas. Although it is dangerous to become habituated to the threat of natural disaster, this is just the reaction of inhabitants of volcanic regions. They watch what is going on, but they do not flee. As if they were hypnotized, they wait to see what will happen next. Their inexplicable, irrational behavior seems to be part of the natural phenomenon that is taking place.

The most extreme example of this irrational behavior took place in St. Pierre when Mount Pelée erupted in the first days of May, 1902. Typically, all the inhabitants stayed in the city for weeks without feeling afraid.

The timetable of death

St Pierre, a city of around 30,000 inhabitants, was the social and economic center of the island of Martinique, one of the many islands belonging to the Lesser Antilles, which form a semicircular island group that extends from Trinidad to Puerto Rico. This island chain leads across Puerto Rico, Haiti, Cuba, and the Bahamas to Florida. Washed by the Atlantic on the east and by the Caribbean on the west, the islands are miracles of tropical beauty. All of them are volcanic. Like those of its island neighbors, Martinique's economy is based on the export of sugarcane and rum.

In the beginning of March, 1902, visitors at Mount Pelée were sitting at the edge of the crater and gazing into its watery depths, and children were playing nearby. Then people saw a curl of smoke in an inlet of the crater. Finally, a fountain rose from the water and subsided again. It had a pungent smell that made people cough, and then it was gone. Mount Pelée, the "Bare Mountain," had been dormant for fifty-one years.

April passed and nothing unusual was to be seen on the mountain. But on May 2 it became active. Its volcanic activity increased, one might say, systematically.

May 2,	morning:	Gray dust flows from the crater.
	forenoon:	Flames emerge from the tip of the mountain.
	noon:	A small channel of lava appears at the peak of the mountain, and gray ashes fall on the city.
	afternoon:	Holes and cracks open briefly in the slope of the mountain.
	evening:	The volcano "hums," and the ground vibrates.
May 3,	morning:	Mud flows down the mountain slope, and the water level is high in rivers and streams.
	noon:	Violent earth tremors occur. People remain undisturbed. In fact, an "excursion" to Mount

Pelée is planned for May 6. A committee announces that there is no cause for concern!

evening: The excursion is [temporarily] canceled. The glowing of the mountain peak is recorded as "a spectacle of great beauty."

May 4, morning: A slight fall of ashes occurs. There are lightning, purple clouds, and fireworks on the mountain, accompanied by loud crashing sounds. For some ten minutes, a rain of small bits of hot pumice pelts the city.

noon: Fissures open along the mountain slope and lava flows out. The botanical garden is destroyed by falling ashes. Poisonous gases kill birds. Clouds of black smoke are seen at the peak of the mountain.

evening: Some two hundred people have died; however, the official report is that the eruption seems to be dying away.

May 5, morning: Water levels are still high in rivers and streams. Everything is covered by ashes and dust. A wave of mud covers a factory and kills one hundred fifty-nine people.

noon: A giant tidal wave some forty-five feet high rises from the sea and destroys the harbor.

evening: The island has run out of coffins.

May 6, morning: Ashes rain down on the sea for a distance of several hundred miles. The city is shrouded in darkness, lit up by lightning.

noon: The authorities state that there is no immediate danger.

evening: A major eruption of lava occurs at the peak of the moun-

	tain and is accompanied by a frightening noise.
May 7, morning:	Part of the crater collapses, and lava is hurled out to the accompaniment of noisy explosions. Molten lava flows downward and stops only a few hundred meters before it reaches St. Pierre. Houses burn at the edge of the city.
noon:	The harbor is filled with debris. One ship puts out to sea prematurely.
evening:	A tropical rainfall hits the ash-covered city. Some citizens of St. Pierre plan to hold a ball!
May 8, morning:	5:00: The volcano awakens again.

5:30: The thunder grows louder and masses of smoke pour from the top of the mountain.

8:00: A "cloud of fire" emerges from the crater and moves toward St. Pierre.

8:03: The wave of fire reaches the city. Twenty-nine thousand, nine hundred thirty-three people die. A prison inmate and a cobbler survive. The city burns and glowing ashes cover the ruins.

| May 9 and on several days thereafter: | Further eruptions occur. |

On May 7, the crater La Soufrière erupted on the neighboring island of St. Vincent and cost 1,565 people their lives. This crater has become active countless times. The last eruption occurred only a few years ago. The first people to observe it were some tourists who climbed the mountain on October 17, 1971. They saw a vast crater lake which smoked a little and smelled somewhat of sulfur. All this impressed them so little that they told no one what they had seen. None of them suspected that things were not as they should have been. They did not learn until later that the water level in the crater had risen forty feet higher than normal!

On November 3, 1971, the water in the crater lake was eighty feet higher than normal and was mustard-colored instead of dark blue. Smoke filled the mouth of the crater. On November 20 a lava island began to rise from the water, and every day its height increased by many feet. Would there be a major eruption? Earth tremors shook the ground and fumaroles hissed everywhere.

Then the eruption stopped, and until now St. Vincent's volcano has been at peace. But 96,000 people are wondering what may happen in the future. They have not forgotten the fiery cloud that decimated St. Pierre.

La Soufrière has given notice of its intentions, but once again the people will wait to see what and whether something will happen, and once again they may wait too long.

Kitsch in lava

A "cloud of fire," a burning cloud of gas, has never again fallen upon a city as it fell on St. Pierre. We will never know what gas composed the cloud, although it may have been hydrogen or carbon monoxide. However, a volcanic eruption does not always result in death and destruction. A volcanic eruption, a river of lava on the island of Lanzarote, created one of the most amazing natural wonders on earth.

What actually happens when molten lava flows downhill? It flows out of a hole, fissure, or crack in the volcano and cools and hardens where it comes in contact with the ground and the air. A "skin" of dark slag forms around the lava flow, but inside the lava is still hot and liquid. As new layers of lava press down on the old lava, new fissures open in the deepest parts of the flow. Lava flows out of the fissures, cools underneath, at the sides, and at the top, where it hardly flows at all. Then it forms a new crust of slag, and the whole process repeats itself. The lava continues to flow downhill, filling up hollows, forming lakes on level ground, and branching out in new directions. It flows long after lava has ceased to flow from

Three types of volcanic eruptions:
1). Peak eruptions. A cloud of steam, stones, sand, and dust shoots high from the peak of the volcano, and large stones and lava fall back to the earth close to the peak. Dust and pumice stones "rain" down at a distance of as much as several kilometers away. Fine dust spreads far across the landscape. 2). A crack or a crater develops on the side of the mountain. Dust and pumice are hurled high into the air. Molten lava may flow from the crack, as it did in Heimaey. Eruptions of gas are also normal. (Poisonous gases containing fluorine are common in eruptions in Iceland. The "cloud of fire" which struck St. Pierre also belongs in this group.) 3). Nothing but masses of stone rise from the interior of the crater.

the volcano itself. What remains is a tunnel or tube made of slag.

As a rule, this tunnel of lava slag collapses, and later geologists find nothing but two parallel walls of slag which at one time were the side walls of the tunnel. The thin ceiling of the tunnel has collapsed between them.

However, sometimes the temperature in the tunnel is so hot that its walls melt and form a firm, vitreous crust. For example, this happens when hot gases hiss through the tunnel after the lava has ceased flowing. In rare cases a second stream of lava flows along the same path as a tunnel and fills it halfway full.

A lava tunnel like this exists on one of the Canary Islands, Lanzarote. The piece of lava which normally closes off a tunnel is missing here, and a man can climb into the tunnel through the opening. Moving slowly, he

A scientist photographs a wave of molten lava as it rolls toward him. (Photographed in Hawaii by H. U. Schmincke, Bochum)

goes through a corridor which is sometimes wide, sometimes narrow and crooked, until he reaches a giant tunnel. In places the tunnel is ninety feet in height and width.

The walls are black, grayish-brown, or reddish-brown and encrusted with yellow and white mineral deposits. In some places they are smooth, in others full of ledges, sharp projections and fissures, and covered with blisters.

Here and there are dollops of stone hanging from the ceiling that have melted and hardened to a smooth surface. At one time molten lava dripped from these stones onto the floor of the tunnel. In many places the ceiling and walls of the tunnel are covered by smooth hollows many square yards in size. Along the side walls at a height of around twelve feet are overhanging, yellowish-brown projections. These are the remains of the second lava flow which passed through the tunnel, remains which have been baked onto the side walls. In places the upper surface of this second lava flow has been preserved. One can climb up to it, walk along it, and look down through the holes at the floor of the big tunnel below.

At other points one walks along a sort of gallery halfway between the floor and the ceiling. It is an adventure to squeeze through the sometimes narrow passages, and some places are so low that one has to crawl through them. Then again there are places where the passage expands to form a hall so wide that in the darkness one can scarcely tell where the walls are. At some points part of the ceiling has collapsed. At one narrow place a massive rock hangs down between the banks of the second lava flow. Apparently it broke off from the ceiling of the tunnel, was carried along a short distance by the second lava flow, and was finally squeezed into its present position—spanning the walls of the tunnel like a bridge. However, one does not have to bend down to get under it, for there is thirty feet of open space to walk through.

At one point where the river of lava once made a turn, the tunnel widens to form a hall. A conductor's podium stands in the hall. The acoustics are supposed to be very good, and there is room for an audience of 1,000 people.

A few hundred yards beyond, the visitor finds himself in a chaotic, rocky landscape which stretches deep into the dark recesses of the tunnel. The lamp cannot light up the end of it. This part of the lava tunnel is in its original condition, for up to now we have visited only the front portion, which has been more or less "tidied up." We have already walked over a mile into the tunnel, but three more miles remain before we reach the original source of the lava. In times of trouble, early humans lived in this tunnel. Moreover, in more recent times the inhabitants of the island took refuge here from pirates and plunderers.

Perhaps we will not find anything comparable to this tunnel except on the moon. The famous "channels" on the moon, which have not yet been explained, may possibly be collapsed lava tunnels.

When mountains disappear

We speak of eruptions like that of Vesuvius in 79 A.D. or the disastrous eruption on St. Pierre as "major" or "violent" eruptions. However, we do not have words to describe some eruptions in which whole mountains are hurled into the air.

During the eruption of Krakatoa on November 1, 1883, a mountain two thousand four hundred feet high flew into the air along with a piece of the island seventy feet square. It is reported that debris was hurled eighteen miles into the sky, and fragments of rock flew as far as one thousand miles away. The thunder of the eruption was heard three thousand miles away, and fluctuations in atmospheric pressure were recorded around the world.

The eruption of the volcano of Santorin must have been an even more cataclysmic event. Today the Mediterranean is the site of an island group which represents the remains of the lower slopes of what was once a volcanic crater. The rest of the land was blown into the air. We may assume that the eruption took place around 1,400 B.C., and the earthquakes and seaquakes which accompanied the eruption probably destroyed the civilization of Crete.

The sky was darkened by the dust clouds of the erupting volcano, and the clouds created three days of "Egyptian darkness" in Egypt that may have been the reason for the exodus of the Jews. Calculations suggest that ten cubic miles of stone may have been hurled into the air with a force comparable to that of 1,000 hydrogen bombs.

We do not know when and how such eruptions occur, eruptions which destroy the volcanic mountain itself. For example, at the moment Mount Etna seems quite harmless; but no one knows whether it might not someday share the fate of Santorin and leave nothing behind it but a big round crater filled with the waters of the Mediterranean.

Poverty and danger

Early in history human beings who lived in volcanic regions accepted their fate without question. They clung to a few rules of thumb about volcanoes which bordered on superstition. Earth tremors and prolonged quakes were warnings which they often heeded too late. Even today people who live on Stromboli say things like this: "When the mountain is quiet, it's dangerous." Or they may say just the opposite: "We just had an eruption, so next year the volcano will be peaceful."

Sometimes scientists cannot make more accurate predictions than these. However, some useful methods of measurement do exist. For example, scientists can test the temperature of the ground, record almost undetectible quakes, measure the movement of the land, and take infrared photographs of the slopes of craters to detect the development of hot areas. However, all these techniques cost money, and it seems especially tragic that people in volcanic areas are often very poor. They need the aid of generous people so that they can afford the scientific measures which can help to ensure their survival.

Chapter Seven

THE WATER PLANET

Twenty-nine percent geography

IN THE past we believed that we had no more pressing task than the investigation of the earth's land masses, but in investigating the land we have shamefully neglected the oceans. Scarcely one-third of our planet is land, and clearly we cannot compose a comprehensive picture of the earth if we take only the land into account.

Around twenty-nine percent of the earth is land with an average height of seven hundred fifty feet, whereas seventy-one percent is ocean with an average depth of 10,000 feet. In short, our earth is a water planet. The biological constitution of man, who is a land dweller, has made us overestimate the extent and importance of the earth's land masses. If we had gills instead of lungs and lived in the water instead of the air, we would have a completely different notion of the world than we have now, and our science would be very different. If we were sea creatures, probably we would just now be beginning to investigate the insignificant twenty-nine percent of dry land which we had hitherto forgotten. To our surprise we would discover that volcanic activity existed on land, as well as in the sea, as do hot springs, gas eruptions, and quakes; we would study high and low tides as phenomena related to land masses; we would have to struggle against the unfiltered radiation of the sun; we would be forced to acknowledge how dangerous was the sea of air above us; and probably we would marvel at the diversity of species in the insect kingdom.

However, as things stand we can only answer questions about the earth in terms of that part of the earth which is not covered by water. To be sure, we know in what areas the sea is especially deep and where sand or rock covers the ocean floor, but the pirate captains of old knew just as much. Until a few years ago we had only a twenty-nine-percent geography.

We have come closer to the bottom of the sea, but we do not yet understand it. We enter the water, feel ourselves become almost weightless, observe unfamiliar plants and fish, see sand, stones, basins, and slopes beneath us—and swim past them. We are on friendly terms with water. Anyone who dives or spends a seaside vacation with goggles and a snorkel feels comfortable in the water; but we do not come into contact with the sea floor. We may sometimes pick up a stone from the sea floor or let white, glittering sand run through our fingers, but basically we are not interested in the floor of the sea. It is the sea, the water itself, which interests us. The bottom of the sea seems as insignificant as its surface.

Only one phenomenon really stirs our imagination and awakens our interest in the ocean floor: the fact that gas bubbles rise from it! All fishermen and boat captains are familiar with this phenomenon: "Look, bubbles are rising to the surface!" And anyone who has ever gone swimming along the beach of a volcanic island will remember how bubbles rose to the surface at some points and how tempted he was to dive beneath the water and see where the bubbles were coming from.

Where does the land end?

Given the biological constitution of man, it is no wonder that we waited so long to begin serious investigation of the ocean floor. Successful attempts were made to drill along the coasts for minerals, especially petroleum and natural gas, but also coal, iron, and sulfur. This drilling led to a conflict over mineral rights and caused a body of water as large as the North Sea to be divided up among various countries. Fishing rights and territorial water boundaries (three, eight, twelve, fifty miles from the coast) remained unchanged. What was regulated was not the use of water, but the use of land, which led to the curious phenomenon that legal rights were obtained over horizontal stretches of land rather than vertical ones. In any case, the regions which were divided among the various countries were, strictly speaking, not at the bottom of the sea at all. Instead, they were areas where the sea was relatively shallow, areas along the "shelf," or those parts of the continental layer which in our time happen to be covered with water. If the oceans were lower, we would see land here, land which would stretch some distance until it reached the true edge of the continent. At this point, where the oceans really begin, there is a steep drop into the sea.

Here we are touching on the questions of whether the oceans are rising or falling and of how long they have remained at their present level. One thing is certain: during the last ice age, vast quantities of water which now fill the oceans lay on the land in the form of ice. Scientists have calculated that at that time the water level of the oceans was three hundred feet lower than it is today. An estimated 4,000,000 cubic miles of ice remain on the continents. If they were to melt, the oceans would rise another one hundred fifty feet.

By looking in an atlas the reader can determine whether this rise in sea level would endanger his home. Vast areas, including whole countries, would become uninhabitable. Given the catastrophic effects of a marked rise in sea level, it is especially important that scientists be able to answer the question of whether the oceans are rising. This is no purely academic question. The last remains of Ice Age ice melted around 9,000 years ago. If in another 10,000 years the sea rises three hundred feet, this would mean that in just one hundred years it will rise three feet, and some of us may expect to live that long. Three additional feet of water would make many coastlines uninhabitable.

Could the world's dikes be raised another yard to accommodate the change in sea level? Or would people have to leave countries like the Netherlands that already lie far below sea level? Experts reassure us by saying that the sea appears to be rising only .039 inches a year, or three inches every century. However, they also say that the accuracy of their predictions is limited, for seasonal snowfalls and thaws disturb their calculations. Thus, they can be certain only of what will happen within a five-year period. Perhaps the best course would be to prepare for the worst.

Danger for Holland

Unfortunately, many of the regions which would be endangered by a rise in sea level, such as the German and Netherlands coast of the North Sea, are also threatened by something else. Experiences in the Ruhr district have taught Germans that shafts dug by miners sometimes collapse beneath the weight of the overlying stone. The damage then becomes visible on the earth's surface, where cracks develop in the walls of houses, buildings tilt and become uninhabitable, and hollows and craters appear in the ground. Natural gas is tapped from layers beneath the North Sea coast. This process weakens the load capacity of the overlying rock, and eventually the ground is bound to sink. Calculations indicate that by the year 2050, the North Sea island of Borkum will have sunk about eight inches. To be sure, this is only a rough estimate.

In any case, regardless of whether the water which covers the edges of the continents rises or recedes, we cannot regard the land it covers as the bottom of the sea. Only the ground at the bottom of deep-sea regions can be regarded as the bottom of the sea. What do we know about these regions, and is it worthwhile to try to find out more?

Growing oceans

Let us recall how the sea floor was born and how it continues growing. Viscous material flows out between the continents, appearing to make the earth larger and forming new, virgin ground. If it were possible to reverse this process, the oceans would become narrower and finally disappear. In fact, one theory suggests that 3,500,000,000 years ago there were no oceans. At that time the earth was correspondingly smaller, possessing only about half its present diameter, and completely covered by a firm crust. Scientists believe that they have found pieces of this most ancient earth rock. For example, in Greenland they have discovered granite-like minerals around 4,000,000,-000 years old. They have found even older, blackish chunks of rock on the tiny island of St. Paul, in the middle of the Atlantic, slightly north of the equator. The edge of this rock is estimated as 4,500,000,000 years old.

The way in which oceans grow indicates that the closer the sea floor lies to the continental shelves, the older it is, and the farther it is from land, the younger it is. In the past, sailing-ship captains used to plumb the oceans with sounding leads, and they could tell by the material brought up on their plumb line what the sea floor beneath their ships was made of. If they were near the coast, the sample would be mud, and farther out to sea it would be sand or rock. To be sure, these test samples were taken only in shallow waters. However, eventually scientists succeeded in taking samples of the ocean floor in deep-sea regions, and the samples confirmed that mud and sand cover the sea floor close to the continents, whereas farther out to sea the sea floor is rocky and "cleaner," and thus probably is newer.

The land beneath the water

Research institutions and industry became very busy in the 1960s, when engineers had begun to devise the technological means of working minerals on the ocean floor. In 1876 the British research ship *Challenger,* a three-masted sailing ship, had brought up a strange mineral from the deep-sea floor. However, so many rare and novel things were brought back from this expedition that the few knobby rocks seemed a matter of curiosity rather than of importance. However, scientists then discovered two things about these "manganese nodules." First, they not only contained manganese, which is necessary in the production of quality steel, but also nickel, cobalt, copper, and zinc, all of which are in short supply on the world market. Second, vast regions of deep-sea floor are virtually covered with manganese nodules. The supply seems inexhaustible, and apparently we can overcome the technological problems involved in working the metal. In 1966 a "manganese road" was discovered off the coast of

Florida, and scientists traveled along it in a research submarine.

Unfortunately, we know very little about what creates the manganese nodules, some of which have a diameter of up to ten inches. The nodules sometimes contain fish bones, shark teeth, and the like. We also know that the round nodules usually grow very slowly and in thin layers. As a rule they grow only about one-tenth of an inch every 1,000 years. On the other hand, surprisingly enough, maganese nodules also exist outside the deep-sea levels—for example, in the Baltic Sea, Lake Michigan, and the Scottish lochs. Even more amazing is the fact that a British ship pulled up a nodule weighing nearly eighteen hundred pounds that had fastened itself to a cable.

The seeing sound

Exciting discoveries like that of the manganese nodules stimulated scientists to develop a more imaginative technology and contributed to deep-sea research. Such discoveries advanced the art of deep-sea photography so that photographs could be taken at a depth of more than 15,000 feet. But, at the time, it was only possible to investigate small sample patches of the sea floor. Scientists had to develop a better, faster method of investigating the vast reaches of the ocean, and they succeeded in adapting a technique which had existed for decades: sonar or "seeing sound."

For decades ships' captains had used echo-sounding apparatus to measure the depth of the water beneath their keels. Then herring fishermen improved the apparatus so that it could be used to track schools of fish. The technique was increasingly refined and finally became "Asdic," the weapon with which the British Navy tracked submarines. Precision instruments were used to "see" foreign objects, whether they were swimming or lying on the ground, moving or at rest. Instruments for creating sound waves of all kinds and energies already existed, as did various kinds of "firecrackers" and instruments for producing wire and gas explosions. The apparatus for receiving the reflected echo had to be improved and adapted to scientific needs.

Soon instruments which had been more or less designed to measure the depth of the ocean basins began to yield more information than scientists had expected, and they proved to be among the most productive pieces of scientific apparatus in the world. The sea floor sent back emitted sound waves and supplied scientists with facts about the deep-sea world. Moreover, depending on the energy and wave length of the sound waves, some of them entered deeper layers of the ocean floor. The waves penetrated through layers of sand and mud, and when they encountered a solid layer, some of the sound energy was reflected back. Sometimes the instruments not only recorded the fact that there were five or ten solid layers in the sea floor, but also recorded the intervals between the layers. Thus, the instruments produced a profile of the layers which covered the sea floor.

Among the most striking discoveries made with the aid of the new instruments was the discovery that the Mississippi, the Ganges, the Indus, the Congo, the Amazon, and other large rivers empty sand, mud, and rock fragments hundred of kilometers out into the oceans. In fact, these rivers have dug their riverbeds wide and deep beneath the surface of the sea. Ravines, valleys, and basins on the original sea floor have long since been filled with material which rainstorms washed into the rivers and thence into the sea.

However, we should not imagine that all this material

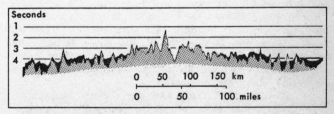

When we cross the Atlantic at 44° north latitude (for example, if we go from Bordeaux to Boston), we cross this profile of undersea mountains. The darkened areas are ravines and valleys filled with sediment. The scale on the left-hand side of the diagram shows the time it takes sound to be reflected back from the ocean floor. (*The Sea*, Vol. 4, I; Wiley, 1970)

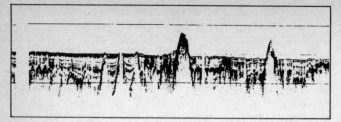

Layers of sediment in the Canary sea basin west of Africa.

lies spread out in well-sorted horizontal layers. Earthquakes have displaced the layers, undersea currents have washed some material away and deposited it to form new layers somewhere else, and raging floods have created steep inclines.

The desire to "see" all this more clearly gave birth to a new instrument: "side-looking sonar." This instrument not only sends and receives sound waves vertically, but its sound reflectors can also be directed to the side. What we "see" with this instrument is fantastic. The sound waves reveal the waves of petrified fields of lava, the flanks of mountain slopes, the jutting edges of rocky ravines, and even isolated fragments of rock.

It may sound incredible, but whereas we who live on the solid ground cannot say with any certainty what layers exist in the one hundred fifty feet of earth beneath our feet, we do know what layers compose the land covered by the ocean waves. For example, we have devoted enormous effort to learning how deep are the layers of rock, gravel, and sand which fill the Rhine trench, and yet we still do not know all there is to know about it. On the other hand, we quickly and easily obtained exact information about the mountains, abysses, and ravines between the Spanish Sahara and the Canary Islands, including the extent and depth of the sediments it contains. We also know how many of these sediments, which sometimes are six hundred feet thick, are composed of hard or soft materials, and even what foreign matter exists in the different layers.

It is not my intention to discuss the military significance of the new sonar techniques. However, this significance is clear: nothing, including submarines, tank installations, secret supply depots, or atomic installations, can any longer be concealed beneath the sea.

$$2H_2 + O_2 \rightarrow 2H_2O$$

If our speculations about the origin of the earth are valid, then at some time early in its life the earth must have lost its atmosphere, or at least the lighter gases in its atmosphere. Hydrogen, the lightest gas, must have flown away into outer space. If that happened, then we must wonder where the hydrogen contained in all the earth's water came from. The earth should have been as dry, lifeless, and naked as the moon. Properly speaking, water ought not to exist on earth. Naturally, scientists have something to say about this matter, but instead of answers they can only offer suggestions as to how water came to exist here. I will mention two of these suggestions:

1). Hydrogen rose out of the depths of the earth, and water developed from it.

2). The atomic nuclei of hydrogen, protons which we call the "solar wind," were blown from the sun to the earth and converted into water.

We do not know the true explanation. Perhaps one day an even more amazing theory may be proved the correct one.

The dirty bathtub

In legends, frightening adventures and terrible deeds take place in bodies of water, for often human beings regard water as an enemy. The seas and oceans still remind us of brave seafarers, daring men who entrusted themselves to the waves. The Mediterranean, and especially the Greek islands, have earned a prominent place among the legends of the sea, and anyone who has seen the chains of Greek islands understands that they irresistibly lure us to pass from one island to the next, seeking adventure. The adventures of Odysseus exemplify the lure of the Mediterranean isles. However, although man may have known the Mediterranean longest, it is still the most mysterious, enigmatic body of water on earth.

Wherever in the Mediterranean we sail or swim, whether along the steep coasts of Spain or near the sandy beaches of Cyprus, we are surrounded by water of a magnificent blue. Parts of the Mediterranean are as deep as 16,800 feet, and we may regard it as a huge bathtub 900,000 miles square filled with 700,000 cubic miles of water.

The floor of the Mediterranean is covered with "dirt" which geologists call "sediment": rock, sand, clay, volcanic ash, and organic waste. Every 1,000 years the layer of sediment grows one to two inches, and in the area of the Balearic Islands (Mallorca, Ibiza, etc.) it grows fourteen inches every 1,000 years. Probably nowhere in the giant bathtub is the layer of sediment higher than one half-mile. In any case, sonar reveals layer upon layer of sediment in the Mediterranean. But there is a riddle in these waters: What are the layers composed of, and how did they come to exist? We have known for several years that the layers of sediment tell us of a geological catastrophe of incredible proportions.

Before turning to the newest discoveries and interpretations, I should mention that sonar has revealed that the Mediterranean is divided into three parts. Thus, it is not *one* sea, as we imagined it to be for thousands of years, but consists of three separate formations. The western part is a basin with a well-rounded floor which extends as far as Corsica and Sardinia. The middle portion, which extends between Corsica and Sardinia on the one hand and Italy and Sicily on the other, is full of steeply rising volcanoes. Two rough mountain chains extend through the middle of the third part. One chain begins at the sole of the Italian boot and curves like a dragon's tail until it reaches Cyprus. A second chain, parallel to the first, runs from the heel of the Italian boot past Greece to the southwestern tip of Turkey. Crete and Rhodes are visible parts of this mountain chain.

Salt beneath the Mediterranean

It was the smooth floor of the western Mediterranean that posed riddles. Its sedimentary layers were broken by high mountains made of *salt,* mountains which do not reflect sound. Salt beds are by no means a geological rarity, for vast salt beds containing salts of potassium and sodium, as well as calcium sulphate and anhydrite, exist beneath northern Germany, in the Rhine trench, in Spain, in northwest Africa, in Sicily, and in many other areas. However, it seemed incredible that the floor of a sea could be covered with water-soluble salts.

A description of the input and evaporation of water in the Mediterranean makes it clear why this idea seemed incredible:

Every year	900 cubic miles evaporate
Rain and snow supply	250 cubic miles
Rivers supply	40 cubic miles
Total annual water supplied	290 cubic miles
Annual loss of water from the Mediterranean	610 cubic miles
Water content of the Mediterranean	700,000 cubic miles

Thus, if we could close the Straits of Gibraltar, the Mediterranean would dry up in around 1,000 years. All that would remain would be a layer of salt around sixty feet high. And this is *much too little* to explain the salt mountains on the floor of the Mediterranean, which may be one to two *miles* thick.

Scientists were relatively content as long as they merely suspected the existence of these mountains of salt, and for a time they thought that the sonar pictures of the layering of the sea floor might be interpreted in a way which would not indicate the presence of salt. But then engineers drilled deep into the Mediterranean floor and found salt. However, the salts were of a kind formed only when seawater evaporates from a desert!

Swinging door at Gibraltar

We have no choice but to accept the amazing theories which scientists have developed about the Mediterranean salts. They theorize that at first the Straits of Gibraltar were closed off by a mountain chain. Thus, between Europe and Africa, in the location of the present-day Mediterranean, there stretched a dry ravine 6,000 to 12,000 feet deep, a valley of death. The water of the rivers which flowed into the ravine cut deep channels at its edge (these channels do, in fact, exist!), but the water did not flow into the ravine, for it all evaporated too quickly. (See table showing the quantities of water evaporated from the Mediterranean annually, p. 143.)

Then the Straits of Gibraltar opened wide, and a huge wave, a gigantic waterfall—the Atlantic—rushed into the ravine. Then the Straits of Gibraltar closed again, and after around 1,000 years the Mediterranean dried up. Salts were deposited, and everything was dead and lifeless —until the devastating flood poured in again! The whole process must have been repeated eight or ten times.

We may well wonder whether there are not more sensible explanations for the presence of salt mountains on the floor of the Mediterranean. Scientists admit that their theory sounds strained. However, they point out that the plant and animal remains found in the salt are Atlantic organisms which lived in cold waters!

But what mechanism caused the mountains in the Straits of Gibraltar to rise and sink? Was it a giant meteor or an asteroid whose orbit frequently brought it close to the earth? Or was it forces inside the earth? And what created the Mediterranean ravine in the first place?

We can ask questions, but we have no answers. Perhaps someone in the world can think of a better explanation than the one I proposed above. The explanation must take into account the formation of mountainous salt beds containing organic remains.

Does the legend of the great Flood describe the last flood of the Mediterranean? At least we have an answer to this question: no. The salt in the Mediterranean desert was formed very recently, only 5,500,000 to 6,000,000 years ago. However, man and his primitive ancestors did not appear on earth until 2,000,000 years ago. They can have no memory of the events which shaped the Mediterranean.

If all the land goes under

The deposits of sediment, rock debris, suspended matter, plant and animal remains, and waste material have altered the coastlines of the continents as much as the destructive power of the sea. A river like the Po, the Amazon, or the Mississippi may build a large delta, while elsewhere water cuts fissures into the land, forms islands, and then finally covers the islands, too. We are familiar with the actions of water, and, like many scientists, we may sometimes wonder whether the water is winning out over the land. If the mountains were to fall into the sea and all the land were flat, the sea would soon cover the entire surface of the earth.

Are the land masses growing today, or is the sea increasing? Once again we have asked a question so simple that we cannot answer it.

The salt beds of northern Europe prove that large, flat sea basins existed in earlier epochs of the earth's history. At such times water must have covered large areas of the earth.

Professor R. L. Grasty, a physicist at the University of Toronto, has an interesting theory about how water distribution on the earth has shifted. His theory is based on a fact discovered by geologists, the fact that 60,000,000 years ago, during the Cretaceous era, the sea withdrew from the large land masses. Grasty thought about what other events had taken place around that time, and he realized that this was when the subcontinent of India, which had originally been wedged between Africa and Australia, crashed into the Eurasion continent. We can imagine how India, like a giant steamship with its smoking volcanoes, glided across a region which was later to be the Pacific at a speed of three to six inches a year. When India finally crashed into Eurasia, all Asia trembled and the Himalayas were formed at the point of impact. It is easy to understand that this compression of land masses to form a mountain range would create flatlands which would fill up with water. When this happened, the water would have to drain somewhere. Grasty calculated that when India joined Asia, the level of the oceans must have fallen thirty meters.

But does the quantity of water on earth remain constant? This question demands an answer, but once again we can only guess. A new, complex measurement of the comparative quantities of oxygen isotopes in old minerals and modern seawater indicates that water is lost from the surface of the earth and enters the interior. When continental layers like South America are pressed downward, they carry water with them into the earth's mantle. But now let us forget the question of how much water exists in relation to the land and ask a more basic question: How did the earth look at the beginning of creation?

We do not know the answer, but the following picture is a plausible one.

A dry earth containing no water, gray like the moon, with a surface scarred by meteorites, barely half its present size, rotates at high speed as it orbits the sun. Then by the time the earth is somewhat more than 1,000,000,-000 years old, the oceans begin to form.

Will the earth in its final stages be completely covered by water? Indications are that this may be the case. No dramatic forces are needed to bring this about. Every year rivers transport two cubic miles of solid matter into the oceans. The total volume of the land above the sea is 26,000,000 cubic miles. This means that in the brief period of 10,800,000 years, all the earth's land masses could be covered by water! Given these figures, we may wonder how it is that continents still exist on our planet. Shouldn't they have long since disappeared?

Do continents still exist because violent forces inside the earth continually push up the continents? Someday we will know more about this subject.

Chapter Eight

"ALL THE FOUNTAINS OF THE GREAT DEEP"

Boiling columns of water

IT IS said that in 1847, a North American hunter found a region which seemed to him like the gates of hell. What made this brave man tremble is now regarded as one of the great natural wonders of the United States: the geysers of Yellowstone National Park. Here, hot, stinking vapor hisses its way out of cracks and holes; over there, jets of water stream upward; roaring, boiling columns of water up to one hundred eighty feet high erupt from giant conduits; and holes full of mud bubble in the ground. The poor hunter who discovered this place had probably never heard about volcanoes, fumaroles, or the geysers of Iceland, and he had a perfect right to think he had discovered the entrance to hell.

Today tourists from all over the world visit the geysers of Yellowstone, and visitors are never disappointed. For example, approximately every fifty minutes the Old Faithful geyser "faithfully" hurls a boiling column of water one hundred feet into the air. Why does this happen? Since 1870 scientists have been trying to find the answer.

In 1935 scientists succeeded in sinking a thermometer one hundred twenty feet down into the seething pipe of the geyser, but the experiment was unsuccessful. In 1968

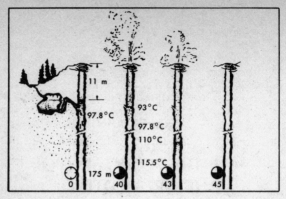

This fantastic mechanism was one suggested explanation of the time mechanism of the Old Faithful geyser: 1). filling and heating of the geyser; 2). eruption; 3). concluding eruption (steam); 4). the pipe is empty for twenty minutes.

modern instruments of measurement were lowered into the geyser, this time with better results. Ninety feet down, the instruments recorded a strange fluctuation of temperature. During the first eruption the water was 110° C, and three minutes later it was only 93° C. Then the temperature wavered between 93° C and 105° C until the next eruption, when it rose to 112° C. The geyser conduit, or pipe, appears to be more than five hundred feet deep. In its deeper parts the temperature remains more constant, but even here enormous jumps in temperature sometimes occur.

The region where Old Faithful is located lies 7,230 feet above sea level. Water, which boils at 100° C at the surface of the sea, should boil at only 93° C where Old Faithful is because of the low atmospheric pressure in the mountains. If the water in the conduit of the geyser heats up to temperatures higher than 100° C, this means that it must be under great pressure—the pressure of the column of water above it. But this cannot be the only reason for the bizarre fluctuations of temperature inside the conduit. Assuming that the water deep down in the conduit is heated to a constant temperature by volcanic action, in addition some mysterious mechanism must exist which pulsates like the motor of a washing machine. Does some kind of gear shift program the eruption of the geyser?

It seems impossible to understand the phenomenon of Old Faithful. Some scientists believe that an underground system of pipes, cracks, or fissures functions as follows: cold water from the surface seeps down into a hollow in the ground. When the water in the hollow has reached a certain level, it travels through a system of siphons and pipes down into the conduit of the geyser. Hot water already exists in the depths of the conduit. Now the cold water comes down on top of the hot and mixes with it until the steam pressure in the conduit is strong enough to raise the water it contains and hurl it out of the vent.

This theory seems to consist mainly of "if's" and "but's," and we may well wonder whether it is correct. However, scientists seem to think it may be, and as yet they have come up with no better explanation.

A lava hot plate

If nature can create hundreds or even thousands of geysers, it should be possible for human beings to create something similar. This happened, quite by accident, fifteen years ago. In Oregon, engineers bored through a layer of water and formed a pipe in hardened lava that was four inches wide and one hundred feet deep. They intended to utilize the volcanic heat of the earth, its geothermal energy. Instead, they created a geyser which erupted every eight to ten hours, shooting a column of water sixty to one hundred feet into the air!

Several minutes after each eruption, a second and sometimes a third eruption occurred. Scientists knew that the conduit of this geyser was a simple vertical pipe. Nevertheless, they ran into grave difficulties when they attempted to measure temperatures in the pipe and record scientific data about the geyser. Finally, they had to admit that they were stumped. The Crump Well geyser will not betray its secret.

Scientists simply do not know much about geysers. A comprehensive geophysical dictionary published in 1971 does not mention geysers at all. Things which we cannot understand annoy us, and so we are happy to forget them. Meteorites once provoked the same reaction: they simply did not fit into the prevailing scientific image of the world. As recently as 1803, at a time when craftsmen had been working meteorite iron for centuries and when many private collectors had set up their own meteorite museums, the highly respected French Academy of Sciences denied the existence of meteorites. Why did it happen? The fact that chunks of stone and iron were falling from the sky could not be explained in terms of the currently recognized laws of nature, and thus scientists regarded the phenomenon as impossible, or at least incredible.

The same now holds true for geysers. Although scientists may be unable to explain them, applied scientists such as engineers have been utilizing the heat energy of hot springs for a long time, whether or not these hot springs periodically spew out steam and water. In Iceland, Italy, New Zealand, Japan, the Soviet Union, Mexico, and the United States, volcanic or "geothermal" energy has long been used to create heat.

An adventure began in 1904 when Italian engineers dared to drill in a smoking field of fumaroles near Larderello, southwest of Florence. Fumaroles are places where hot steam is emitted from the earth with a whistling sound. Just how risky this undertaking was became clear when the same thing was tried in the United States. After the American engineers had begun drilling, 3,000 tons of rock, mixed with hot steam and boiling water, were hurled out of the hole with a roaring sound. No matter what they did, the Americans could not close up the hole again. In Larderello, a smoking, stinking plain, the engineers were lucky. They immediately hooked up a small turbine to the steam source where they had drilled. By the beginning of World War II they had built a geothermal plant with a capacity of 135,000 kilowatts, enough energy to run the equivalent of three large ships run on atomic energy. Then the plant was destroyed by bombs. However, the Italians rebuilt and expanded it to more than 300,000 kilowatts.

The Icelanders have also had good experiences with geothermal energy sources. The capital of Iceland, Reykjavik, is heated with hot volcanic spring water, and in other places this water is used for climate control in greenhouses. Naturally, the Icelanders bathe in the hot springs, as people have done in the Mediterranean since the days of the Roman Empire, and the springs are sometimes used as health spas.

In the 1950s the people of New Zealand foresaw that they were soon going to suffer an energy crisis and began to utilize the great geyser region of Wairakei as an energy source. Soon they had built a plant with a capacity of 200,000 kilowatts.

People in the U.S.S.R. have great plans. Soviet geologists believe that they have located a region in Siberia east of the Ural Mountains which is larger than the Mediterranean and which contains vast quantities of hot springs with temperatures between 60° and 160° C. They speak of a "hot-water ocean," which is also supposed to contain a quantity of valuable dissolved minerals.

No one knows where these vast quantities of thermal waters come from. In any case, Soviet scientists are happy that the hot springs will enable them to heat not only hothouses, but entire cities. They have devised a special technique to achieve this. Instead of bringing the hot water to the surface, they will lower gigantic boilers to depths of six miles into the "hot-water ocean." The steam created in these kettles will then be used to run turbines and generators. This plan is advantageous because the plants will have access to the pure, mineral-free water they need to run properly.

Large numbers of hot springs exist in the area around San Francisco and Los Angeles. Unfortunately, until 1970 American scientists did not make much progress in utilizing this energy source. Laws prevented them from doing so. Quarrels occurred about profits from the enterprise, profits in which the U.S. government wished to share. Nothing could be done until the question of taxes was cleared up. The dispute centered around the question of whether hot springs were a limited and exhaustible source of fuel, like petroleum and minerals, or whether they were inexhaustible, like other bodies of water such as lakes, ponds, and rivers.

In December, 1970, the Geothermal Steam Act was finally passed and opened the way for Americans to utilize the earth's heat energy. A plan called The Geysers can already supply half the electricity used in San Francisco. The prices charged by this plant are lower than those charged by petroleum and nuclear power plants.

A similar plant near the extinct volcano of Cerro Prieto will contribute to satisfying the energy needs of Mexico.

If world interest in the phenomenon of hot springs continues to grow, perhaps scientists will devote more time to studying them. So far, geophysicists, physicians, and chemists have not been able to answer our questions about them.

On the island of Lanzarote we may see a devoted conservationist pour water into an iron pipe and rejoice when the volcanic temperatures cause it to blow out in the form of steam. His gentle, embarrassed laughter when we ask him about the phenomenon is at least more honest than the hemming and hawing of many scientists on the subject of hot springs.

Scientists do not even know enough to explain the game which visitors to Lanzarote play with the geysers there. If someone throws some soap or detergent into the mouth of the geyser, the result is an especially violent eruption in which the water shoots very high. Scientists attempt to explain this phenomenon by saying that the soap reduces the surface tension of the water. This explanation may be worth no more than that of children who say, "It doesn't like the taste of the soap." Tourists have fed so much soap into the great geyser of Iceland that it has "lost the beat" and sometimes fails to erupt when it should.

Tides

What we should realize is that scientists today have scarcely begun to learn about the largest bodies of water, the oceans. For example, there is the phenomenon of the tides.

The earliest inhabitants of the North Sea coast, the English Channel, and the Atlantic coasts of Spain and Portugal must have observed the rising and falling of the tides. But early scientists who lived in the Mediterranean area did not become aware of the tides until Alexander the Great's classic India campaign. The tides exist in the Mediterranean to only a slight degree so when Alexander's soldiers reached the Indian Ocean in 320 B.C., they must have been amazed to see its tides rising and sinking every twelve hours.

Besides Alexander's soldiers, another man reported the strange phenomenon of the tides. He was a merchant from Marseille named Pytheas, and when he returned from a trip around Britain he told people about the rising and falling of the sea. He even suspected that the phenomenon must somehow be related to the moon. Around one hundred years later (Eratosthenes, circa 273-192 B.C.), it was recognized that high and low tides occur approximately twice every twenty-four hours. In those days it was often merchants and soldier-adventurers who increased our knowledge about the natural world, and thus it is a pity that Alexander did not travel a little farther into India. If he had done so, he would have arrived at the Harappa civilization in the Indus Valley, and the people there could have told Alexander's soldiers the meaning of the tides and the practical uses they could be put to. For around 2,000 years the Harappans had been a seafaring people who knew the ocean well. Since 2,500 B.C. they had not only known about the monsoon winds, but had known how to use them to sail ships!

The most amazing thing we know about the people of Harappa is that they used the tides in a giant dry dock near Lothal. First they hollowed out a dock seven hundred feet long and one hundred feet wide. The walls, which were thirteen feet high, were built of baked tiles. A canal twenty-five feet wide enabled them to pass ships into the dock at high tide. At low tide the dock was dry, the canal was closed, and men could repair the ships and get them ready for travel.

Around 2,000 B.C. the sea receded and the entrance to the dock was left dry, but the ancient Indian engineers did not despair. They built a new canal a mile long so that they could use their dock again. Today all that is left in Lothal is impressive ruins. If the dock still existed, it would not suffer by comparison with the modern Indian docks in Bombay and Visakhapatnam.

Two mountains above the earth

It was not for another 3,700 years, until the year 1700, that Europeans decided to devote serious study to the tides. Beginning in June, 1711, Frenchmen in several French ports precisely recorded the times the tides occurred and then turned over their data to the French Academy of Sciences in Paris. They continued to measure the tides for five years, until 1716.

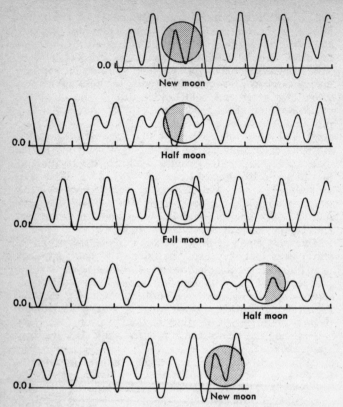

Heights of the tides during May, 1973, along the Pacific coast of California. The month begins with the new moon, and the two daily tides vary markedly in height. On May 9 the moon is waxing, and, as is to be expected, the two daily tides are uniformly high. On May 16 there is a full moon, and once again the tides vary markedly in height. As the moon wanes they become more uniform again, and only at the end of the month, when there is a new moon, do they differ sharply once more. Again the level of the lunar tide rises slowly.

The data they gathered accomplished little or nothing. Their best measurements, those made at the Atlantic port of Brest, "disappeared" until 1781, and even when found the data proved incomplete. Also, the people who observed the times of the tides were not always reliable; they always recorded the tides in local time; and sometimes they failed to record the times correctly.

The scientists compared the erroneous data and made computations, and seventy-four years later, in 1790, they used the data to prove that the moon must possess 1/59 of the mass of the earth. There was no end to their speculations. They continued to compute on the basis of the old data and finally more than a century later, in 1824, they decided that the moon's mass was 1/75 the mass of the earth. Actually this was not such a bad guess. We now know that the moon possesses 1/81.3 the mass of the earth.

We now possess accurate tables which tell us the times the tides will occur in any place, port, river mouth, or canal. We can also predict with a high measure of accuracy how high the water will rise, information which is beneficial to shipping. And now every schoolboy knows that the moon controls the tides. (The sun also contributes slightly to the phenomenon, especially to the "springtide.") Gravity, the reciprocal attraction between the masses of the earth and the moon, is clearly revealed in the tides. The attraction is strongest at the point where the earth and the moon are closest. Thus, a mountain of water rises on the side of the earth which is turned toward the moon, and the earth rotates under this mountain once every twenty-four hours. We might expect tides to occur every twenty-four hours, but, in fact, a tide occurs every twelve hours, or, more precisely, every twelve hours and twenty-five minutes.

If the earth had two moons which stood opposite each other, with the earth in the middle, we would not wonder why a tide occurs every twelve hours; then it would seem logical that gravity would compel the waters of the earth to form into two mountains. However, since the earth has only one moon, the explanation is not so simple. Scientists have devised the strangest "explanations" for the presence of a second tide. For example, they have suggested that on the side of the earth which is turned toward the moon, everything is strongly attracted by the moon and therefore the water runs together and forms a mountain. On the side of the earth turned away from the moon, the moon's attraction is weaker, so the water there forms a second mountain. What a strange theory: on one side of the earth a tide forms because the gravitational attraction of the moon is very strong, and on the other side because the moon's attraction is weak? If the ocean waters form a tide which rises toward the moon, shouldn't there be a perpetual low tide on the opposite side of the earth?

Anyone who wants to accept this simple theory must also accept the fact that the mutual attraction of the earth and the moon will make them fall on each other. As we know, this does not happen, and we all know why. Centrifugal force compensates for the gravitational attraction between the earth and the moon. The rotating system of the earth and the moon has a common center of gravity, and any forces operating within the system act upon this common center.

The common center of gravity in this system lies a distance from the earth's center of about 1/80 the distance from the earth to the moon. In other words, the center of gravity is not the center of the earth, but a place removed from this point by a distance of three-quarters of the earth's radius. The line leading from the moon to the center of the system's gravity and thence to the center of the earth leads to the point on the earth where the second tide is located. At this point gravitational attraction is so strong that a second tide *must* exist.

The situation is different at the poles. Here gravity and centrifugal force more or less cancel each other out, and all that remains is a slight gravitational attraction to the center of the earth.

Naturally, the tides are a somewhat more complex phenomenon than I have described, for the sun also plays a role in them, and the earth's axis of rotation is not perpendicular to the plane of the earth's orbit. However, this is an accurate description of why both a high tide and a low tide must occur twice every twenty-four hours.

The earth rotates beneath the two tides. Once every twenty-four hours, every place on the earth's surface (except the polar regions, where there logically can be no true high and low tide) lies at the point closest to the moon, and once every twenty-four hours it lies at the point opposite the moon. If water exists at this place, it is raised into a "high tide." If there is land at this point, it is raised about one foot. Then comes "low tide," and the water or the land sinks again.

The continents resist high tide. They allow the tides to thunder against their coasts and force masses of water into bays, where the water piles up. In Canada's Bay of Fundy the tide sometimes rises nearly seventy feet. The changing distance between the earth and the moon, the position of the sun, winds, the varying depths of the sea, and many other factors make it difficult for us to precisely predict the behavior of high and low tides. No one can do more than approximate the time when the tide will reach a certain level at any given place.

Waves

The rising of the tide is always a fascinating sight. Wave after wave rolls toward us, wetting down the sand and the rocks higher and higher on the beach. As we stand there we count whether it is every seventh or every twelfth wave that rolls especially high and breaks into surging foam. The sea is a magnificent, eternal spectacle which makes us daydream and feel we are on vacation. Yet a question shimmers up at us from the waves: Where do they really come from?

Be happy if there is no one around of whom you can ask this question, or if you know someone who will quickly invent a pseudo-satisfactory answer. Even if you listened patiently to a scientist for hours, he could tell you no more than this: "We have not yet formed a satisfactory explanation of the mechanism which creates waves." This statement is clear and honest and serves much better than a jumble of concepts and definitions or mathematical depictions like this one describing the group velocity of waves:

$$cg = \frac{c}{2} \cdot \left(1 + \frac{4\,\pi\,h}{\lambda \sin(4\pi h/\lambda)} \right)$$

It is simpler and more pleasant if we just go on counting the waves and wait until the wind makes the next high wave rise toward us!

Still, it is critical for thousands or millions of human beings that we find out more about the origin, growth, diffusion, and energy of waves. Many in the long list of disastrous floods could have been avoided or been much less serious if we had known more about waves. Water is not only a substance necessary to our lives, but it can also be one of our bitterest enemies.

The Great Floods

Aside from the many great floods in which the sea has invaded and devastated large parts of Europe, we know of many floods which took place early in history and which taught men to fear the waves.

Let us return to 6,000 B.C. At that time many regions in the modern North Sea were bog and swampland which had not yet been covered by the sea. People went hunting in places which today lie beneath sea waters. Peat was found on the sea floor thirty miles from the coast. The formation of peat occurs when the ground level of water is high and the water is slack. Records document the following figures:

6,000 B.C. The ocean rises; large regions of the North and Baltic Seas which had hitherto been dry are flooded.

5,500 B.C. Peat is formed up to a point which is now seventy feet beneath the sea. The sea continues its swift ascent.

4,000 B.C. Land which in modern times lies thirty feet beneath the sea is still dry at this time.

3,000 B.C. The sea rises more slowly. The surface of the sea is ten feet lower than it is now.

1,300 B.C. The sea is still six feet below its present level.

Meanwhile, the people who lived along the coast were forced to build their homes on artificial hillocks. These

When the dikes break

The more protective dikes men build, the more land they create which lies *deeper* than the sea outside the dikes. Thus, when dikes break today, it is usually too late to remedy. On the Sunday morning of January 31, 1953, a violent storm and a high tide sent *one* especially high wave crashing against the dikes of Holland. Almost simultaneously, more than fifty sections of the dike broke apart, and a wave rolled in to cover the low-lying land. Three thousand houses were torn away, 40,000 buildings were damaged, 72,000 people were left homeless, and 1,835 people drowned at almost the same moment.

It is easy to accuse the people who seem responsible for the disaster and to ask why they did not take proper measures to prevent it. Why were no rescue plans made, and why were the dikes not built high and strong enough to withstand the highest tides? It would be more helpful if we wondered about the scientific causes of the disaster. What factors control the height and strength of waves? And why do we know so little about ocean phenomena, which shape our life and our death? Why do we know so many unrelated facts about the ocean and yet have so little genuine knowledge about it?

The great rain

When speaking of floods, we should not forget the floods which have afflicted the interiors of the continents. During periods of heavy rainfall the great rivers of North America, among them the Mississippi, have caused devastating floods. However, these disasters are overshadowed by the floods which have terrorized China for 4,000 years: the floods and changes in the course of the Huang Ho, the Yellow River.

The very name Yellow River makes it clear that the waters of the river are filled with dirt and mud. It has been estimated that in one year the Huang Ho washed away six times as much soil and other solid material as engineers had to move in building the Panama Canal. And since the first maps of the river were drawn, it has changed its course by hundreds of kilometers eight times!

It probably has claimed more human lives than any other river in the world. In the fall of 1887 it rose more than sixty feet, flooded three hundred villages, made 2,000,000 people homeless, and drowned another 1,000,000.

Natural catastrophes of this kind remind us of the biblical deluge. It has been proved that this was an actual historical event. While excavating Ur in Iraq, archaeologists found a layer of mud more than nine feet thick which was left by the great flood. The people who lived in that area must have felt that the flood was indeed the end of the world.

The myths of almost all peoples contain references to great floods. Depending on regional conditions, the cause of the floods is recorded as rain, a storm, the waves of the sea, or a melting glacier. We do not know what may have caused the flood recorded in the Old Testament. The Bible does not give an exact account of the event. In Genesis 6:17 God states: "And behold, I, even I, do bring a flood of waters upon the earth." It would have been better if the passage read: "I do bring a flood of waters *from the sea*." In this case the passage would mean that the biblical flood was really caused by a storm or an earthquake which raised the waters of the Persian Gulf and sent them across the flatlands.

Another passage suggests that an earthquake was the cause of the flood. Genesis 7:11 states that "the same day were all the fountains of the great deep broken up." This sudden rising and falling of the water level typically occurs during earthquakes. There may also have been a heavy rainfall. However, rain alone could not have caused a deluge on the scale described in the Bible. Probably no more than twenty-four inches of rain have ever fallen anywhere in a twenty-four-hour period. (The town of New Smyrna, Florida, holds this record.) At a rate of twenty-four inches a day, eighty feet of water could accumulate in "forty days and forty nights"; but it would accumulate only if no water ran off. The mountains of Ararat, which rise to 16,900 feet, would scarcely have gotten their feet wet. Probably the great flood was merely a local flood along the lower Euphrates, whose cause was an earthquake in the Persian Gulf.

Tsunamis

The biblical flood could hardly have earned much attention in Japan. However, in the Japanese islands, where the Pacific sea floor layer meets the continental layer of Asia, many earthquakes occur, and these quakes in turn sometimes cause seaquakes. Naturally, we have even more difficulty predicting seaquakes than earthquakes, for we do not have the technological means of monitoring activities on the ocean floor.

On September 1, 1923, rock layers were displaced in the depths of Sagami Bay, south of Tokyo. It was later learned that the ocean floor had risen up seven hundred feet, in some places, and in other places it had sunk as much as one thousand feet. The tidal wave triggered by these motions raced toward the Japanese coast. Fifteen to thirty feet high, the wave struck the beach, climbed up it, wiped out several villages and small cities, and, among other things, grabbed hold of a train carrying two hundred passengers which had just arrived in the railway station at Nebukawa. The wave, which had created a river of mud forty-five feet deep, sucked the train back into the bay along with the village. Later on, no one could even find the remnants of the train, the station, or the village. Tidal waves of this type are known by the Japanese name "tsunamis." There is virtually no protection against tsunamis because far too little is known about them.

However, usually nature does give warning that such a tidal wave is coming. People on beaches or in harbors struck by tsunamis report that a few minutes before the tidal wave arrived, the water suddenly ebbed drastically! No one can tell us why this happens. For no apparent reason there is an unexpected low tide. When this happens, the important thing is to get as far away from the shore as one can, for tsunamis reportedly reach speeds of up to five-hundred miles an hour.

Even if you succeed in getting away from the shore, you have a chance to survive only if the tsunami is a small one. If the wall of water attains a height of two hundred feet, like the tsunami which crossed Cape Lopatka and struck the peninsula of Kamchatka, in Siberia, on October 6, 1737, perhaps the best course is simply to wait and hope for a miracle.

People living in Hawaii and along the West Coast of the United States were lucky in May, 1960, because they were warned by a series of violent earthquakes in Chile. When the warning came that tsunamis were approaching, the Hawaiians had five hours to prepare for the disaster. Television and radio broadcasts directed the people to leave the shore and travel into the mountains in cars and buses. As expected, the waters withdrew from the shore and then returned to crash down on the islands. There was massive damage to harbors and property, but only a few people were hurt.

However, things turned out much worse for the people caught in what may have been the worst flood disaster of this century, the flood of East Pakistan in November, 1970. Without warning, a hurricane drove a tidal wave eighteen feet high onto the flat land in the Ganges and Brahmaputra deltas. Three hundred thousand people were killed and millions were left homeless.

Chapter Nine

WHEN THE ELEMENTS RAGE

Crazy experiments

No ONE knows how many medieval bell-ringers were struck by lightning because they believed the inscription on their bells: FULGURA FRANGO—"I break lightning." However, there must have been quite a number, because until the year 1750, no one understood anything more about thunderstorms than the fact that they were somehow dangerous. Until 1750, the ancient Germanic belief that lightning was caused by Donar throwing down his hammer was as correct as any of the current scientific explanations. Now, more than two hundred years later, what have we learned about thunderstorms and their causes?

In June, 1752, a Philadelphian who was a writer, statesman, scientist, and the fifteenth child of a soap-boiler and maker of tallow candles set out on a suicidal mission. His name was Benjamin Franklin, and he was forty-eight years old. He knew little more about electricity than the fact that the tips of wires would give off sparks if they were brought into contact with frictional electricity. The electricity could be created by rubbing a piece of brimstone.

A man who thought in practical terms, Franklin drew the following conclusion about electricity: if one placed a rod on the roof of a house, lightning would flow out of it, and the house would be spared. In short, he had discovered the principle of the lightning rod. However, the lightning rod was first tested in France, and not by Benjamin Franklin. Franklin had dreamed up an insane experiment which other people should take care not to duplicate. When a storm approached, he quickly fabricated a kite out of two sticks and a thin silk handkerchief and sent it into the sky. He fastened a key at the bottom. As soon as the rain had dampened the kite and the cord so that they could conduct the "electrical fire" more easily, Franklin said that a man could move his knuckles close to the kite, and the "fire" would stream out abundantly.

In this experiment Franklin may not have had more luck than brains, but he certainly had more luck than knowledge. In the same year a Frenchman, the Prior de Marly, was not so lucky. He erected an iron pole fifteen meters long "in the middle of a beautiful field," and when a storm broke, he quickly ran to the pole to perform various experiments. First "a small ray of blue fire that smelled of sulfur sprang from the pole." The brave man repeated the experiment six times (!) and then received a shock which affected his arm "as if someone had struck my bare skin with wires."

In 1753 another "electrifier" learned what electricity was like. G. W. Richmann, the son of a Swedish captain, was at that time a professor of physics in Petersburg. He wanted to know exactly what electricity was all about. In an act of heroic madness he conducted his lightning rod into his laboratory. Curious to see what would happen, he summoned a sketch artist, the counterpart of the modern photo journalist, to keep him company.

Then the inevitable happened. The artist saw a blue ball of fire the size of a fist travel to the professor's head. Then something began to smoke, and the artist fainted. Richmann was beyond help. A red spot on the dead man's forehead was bleeding and there was a blue patch on his foot. His left shoe was burned. A contemporary dryly remarked that it was not given to every electrifier to die in so praiseworthy a manner as the envied Richmann. The man who said this was Joseph Priestley, a free-thinking English theologian who was also a splendid chemist and who, threatened by the mob, had to travel to the New World, where he became a farmer and died in 1804, a bitter and ruined man.

What remains interesting about Richmann's experiment is the artist's comment about the ball of blue fire. If only the man had not fainted so quickly! Today he could be the star witness in a bitter scientific debate. He could bear witness to the fact that ball lightning exists.

Does ball lightning exist?

There are a few questions about which modern scientists disagree more violently than they do about the question of whether there is such a thing as ball lightning. Actually, there is no longer any question that the phenomenon exists. We have reliable and credible descriptions of ball lightning which go back for thousands of years. These descriptions tell of bright bluish or reddish balls of fire as large as a football which move slowly, soundlessly, and with a flowing motion. Finally, the balls of fire disappear almost without a sound.

The oldest witness to the existence of ball lightning is Posidonius, "the man from Rhodes," a Greek philosopher who was born in Syria around 135 B.C. He traveled widely and founded a philosophical school which held that the entire cosmos is alive, including stones, plants, animals, men, and heavenly bodies. His school also recognized that the moon caused the tides. Posidonius died in Rome at a ripe old age.

Another scientist worthy of mention in this context is Lord Rayleigh (November 12, 1842-June 30, 1919), a great English physicist and discoverer of the gas argon, who investigated the question of what caused ball lightning.

Once again we encounter a curious circumstance: when there are several things which scientists do not understand, they link them together just so that they can arrive at a plausible-sounding theory. In the nineteenth century they theorized that ball lightning had something to do with meteorites, with "thunder stones." This theory cleared the way for even bolder speculations, culminating in the theory that ball lightning did not exist at all.

We should take into account the fact that as long as scientists have no photographic proof of the existence of a phenomenon, they are not likely to believe verbal descriptions, no matter who it is who claims to have seen it. And even when someone succeeds in photographing ball lightning, scientists still try to interpret the picture as a picture of something else—because they do not know what ball lightning is. Ball lightning does not fit into their image of the world, and so they deny its existence, just as, until the year 1803, they denied that rocks could fall from the sky.

Let us examine issues of the English periodical *Nature* over a two-year period to see how modern scientists disagree over the question of ball lightning.

March, 1971:
   1). Ball lightning is an optical illusion.
   2). Is ball lightning formed from antimatter?

April, 1971:
   3). Along with others, I saw ball lightning while traveling in an airplane, and I did not drink any alcohol. Also, I do not believe in the antimatter theory.
   4). Why should ball lightning be an optical illusion? People both smell and hear it, as well as see it!
   5). Do people see ball lightning, or do they just see sparks in front of their eyes?

October, 1972:
   6). I believe that ball lightning originates in the same way as the energy of a laser impulse causes evaporation to occur from a solid surface.
   7). Cosmic radiation or antimatter may cause ball lightning.

November, 1972:
   8). The famous photograph of ball lightning taken by R. C. Jennings in 1962 does not really show ball lightning. Instead, it is probably the photograph of a street lamp.

Thus, scientists are divided into two camps: some of them believe in the existence of ball lightning and are making a desperate effort to explain the phenomenon; others simply deny that ball lightning exists. However, the descriptions of the many people who claim to have seen ball lightning agree in so many respects that it is difficult to believe that they were the victims of optical illusions or overly active imaginations.

Thunder and lightning

What is known about thunderstorms and storm-related phenomena? In 1971 a work was published describing what may be a new species of lightning, the crown flash. This kind of lightning begins with a bright discharge inside a cloud. Then the lightning rises to the top of the cloud and surrounds its peak like a crown. But does this crown represent an electrical discharge? Is it caused by glowing ice crystals? Is it nothing but what for decades has been known as sheet lightning? Or is it something like the St. Elmo's fire which used to burn on the mastheads of sailing ships and which superstitious sailors believed heralded disaster to their ship? Physicists have explained St. Elmo's fire as a relatively harmless spark discharge.

How do thunderstorms come about, and what creates thunder and lightning?

We know that lightning is a giant electrical spark. Thunder is a kind of supersonic explosion, and without a special type of cloud, the cauliflower-like cumulo-nimbus clouds, a "normal" thunderstorm cannot take place. (I have already mentioned instances in which lightning appears in a clear sky.) But beyond this, scientists are in disagreement. There are various theories as to how the clouds come to be electrically charged, but these theories are so many and so diverse that one would need a book to describe all of them properly.

Do ice crystals rub together and break, creating static electricity? Do raindrops produce the electrical charges? What do they create them from? When and how does summer heat influence the formation of thunderstorms? But, after all, storms occur during the winter, too!

Even attempts to use a computer to elucidate the factors which play a role in thunderstorms have produced no results. Scientists have many theories, but none of them can say for certain which theory is correct.

We do have one account of what goes on inside a storm cloud, from U.S. Air Force jet pilot W. Rankin. In 1959 he was forced to bail out of a plane flying inside or just above a cumulo-nimbus cloud eight miles above the ground. At a height of 11,000 feet his parachute should have opened, and thirteen minutes later he should have been on the ground. However, it was almost forty-five minutes before he came down. Air currents in the cloud raised and lowered him as if he were in an elevator. Although he was wearing a thick helmet, the thunder deafened him. Blue shafts of lightning forty inches thick shot through the air around him, and he could feel the changes in atmospheric pressure. It was pouring rain, so he held his breath for fear that he would drown in the air. The storm tossed his body around with such violence that once the wet, dripping silk of his parachute wrapped itself around him and he feared that the parachute would not open and he would finally crash to the earth.

The land of fairy tales?

This must have been a terrifying and beautiful experience, but what does it prove? Like every thunderstorm, it proves that we can scarcely conceive of the energies which rage inside a cumulo-nimbus cloud. We do not know much more than this. Even the many strange tales about flashes of lightning do not tell us any more:

• Crusaders who left Rhodes on January 1, 1523, left gunpowder mines behind them, and in 1856 lightning set fire to the mines, which exploded, leveling the fortress and many surrounding streets to the ground.

• A flash of lightning tore the clothes from the bodies of two girls but did not harm them.

• A flash of lightning twisted the prongs of a hay fork into corkscrews but did not harm the farmer who held it.

• A flash of lightning struck a bird in flight, and when it fell to the ground it was fully roasted.

It is not clear what these stories are—legends, fairy tales, or half-truths. In any case, scientists have devised a number of interesting projects relating to thunderstorms. I will mention only two of them. First, scientists are wondering whether thunderstorms, which are admittedly dangerous, can be "tamed." Can we prevent Donar from hurling down his hammer?

In principle the theory is simple. Clearly, lightning occurs only when the tension in the electrical field becomes so great that a spark discharge, the flash of lightning which we see, can flash into being. Thus, the question is this: How does one prevent the development of electrical tension? If the electrical field contained conductive particles, the electricity would drain off instead of increase.

It proved very easy to solve the problem. First scientists introduced fine metallic particles into a highly charged electrical field, and then what they had hoped would happen actually did. Spark discharges occurred at the corners of the metallic particles, and these discharges supplied charged gas particles, ions, which enabled the electrical tension to drain.

Amazingly, this laboratory experiment could be repeated outside the laboratory! An airplane sowed a million fine aluminum strips, which all together weighed no more than one hundred grams, beneath a group of storm clouds. Within eight minutes the potential voltage of the electrical field sank from 300,000 volts to 30,000 volts. To be sure, this does not prove that man can "neutralize" thunderclouds, but the possibility exists.

A second research project closely related to the first is now under way. Scientists wondered how the electrical field of a thunderstorm altered when lightning flashed through it. Strange as it seems, until 1973 they had never investigated this particular problem. Like all flowing current, the electrical current which is lightning creates an electromagnetic field in the electrical field of the thunderstorm. If the lightning travels from the cloud to the earth, it then reverses direction and the current flows backward. Various electrical fields interpenetrate, and no one can say what a multitude of things may take place in fractions of a second. But scientists *can* detect the changes which a flash of lightning produces in the electrical field from a distance of sixty miles away!

Around 16,000,000 thunderstorms take place every year, yet we do not even know why thunder thunders the way it does. This fact should spur scientists on to learn more about the subject. Perhaps it is more important that we learn what kind of world we are living in than that we spend our time here as pleasurably as possible.

Prognosis for the fourth dimension

Like thunderstorms and rainstorms, other kinds of storms are striking exhibitions of the forces of nature. If the earth were covered solely by water or land and if it did not rotate, the situation would be simple: warm air would rise from the equator and stream toward the cooler poles, and cold air would flow from the poles back to the equator. The oblique angle of the earth's axis would produce seasonal changes in accordance with the earth's position in its circuit around the sun; but, in general, the weather on the earth would tend to be uniform. However, the earth's surface is not at all uniform. Thus, for example, during the day the air above the land warms up more quickly than the air above the sea, and the air above the land streams upward. Cooler air blows in from the sea. At night the land cools more quickly than the water, and the winds blow in the opposite direction.

Wind and clouds, rain and snow, all meteorological phenomena influence each other. This mutual influence causes the weather to be very different at different atmospheric heights.

Even computers cannot cope with the three-dimensional aspect of our weather. Thus, despite all the data they have stored up and despite all their experience, meteorologists cannot forecast the weather more than twenty-four or forty-eight hours in advance; and, like all scientific predictions, even these forecasts often prove incorrect. Scientists still have a great deal to learn before they can forecast the weather three or four weeks in advance, yet weather forecasting is among the oldest sciences of man.

The best way to forecast the weather is to determine the location of high- and low-pressure systems and then to decide how these systems will behave. In other words, the idea is to decide where the wind will be blowing from and what kind of weather it will bring with it. It is difficult to analyze the idiosyncrasies of sea and land masses, and we must also take into account a number of other factors, such as the rotation of the earth. Light and mobile as the air seems to us, it actually represents an enormous mass. If we could weigh the earth's atmosphere, it would weigh 57,000,000,000,000 tons!

Let us try to picture what this weight means. We can do so by imagining how large a box filled with water must be to produce the same weight. The box would be 600 miles long, 600 miles wide, and one hundred ninety feet high! If we represented the weight of the earth's atmosphere in granite blocks, we could build a giant monument which would dwarf all the other buildings on earth. It would be 600 miles long, 600 miles wide, and 12 miles high. We could easily fit the state of Texas beneath this gravestone, with plenty of room left over.

When masses of air move slowly on hot summer days, we are satisfied with the way the wind is behaving. However, if air storms along in a hurricane, nothing can resist its strength. In 1945 the crew of the heavy cruiser *Pittsburgh,* which was traveling near Okinawa, learned that a storm can even destroy objects made of solid steel. The storm and the high waves it created literally twisted off the bow of the warship as far back as the forward gun turret. Such events may seem incredible, but photographs prove that they actually happened.

Storm

On September 2, 1935, a hurricane struck Florida. Wind velocities of over two hundred miles an hour were recorded. In some areas nothing was left standing. The storm drove sand against objects with such force that it took the paint off automobiles. Moreover, some dead people were found whom the sandstorm had stripped of all their clothing, including thick leather belts and shoes. Besides that, the sand had stripped away their skin. They had been flayed to death.

There is no point in speculating as to which kind of storms are the most dangerous or how to tell the different types apart: hurricanes, gales, cyclones, typhoons, spring storms, mistrals, boras, tornadoes, etc. It is more important to know how human beings can protect themselves from these storms. For example, in the poorer regions of the southern United States, where some people live in flimsy wooden houses, they must take refuge in cellars. Houses without cellars are usually equipped with holes in the yard which are known as tornado cellars. Nevertheless, no one can say how many deaths were caused by storms in the last few decades in the southern United States alone. Hurricanes have caused more damage in the United States than any other kind of natural catastrophe. It is difficult to judge how much energy a hurricane possesses. In 1961 Hurricane Carla supposedly had the force of ninety fifty-megaton bombs. In any case, such storms are far more powerful than the usual type of atomic bombs.

During World War II meteorologists began to name hurricanes after women. They did this simply because often a number of hurricanes occur in rapid succession and it is easier for news reporters to refer to each one by a proper name. The first hurricane of the year is always given a name beginning with "A," and the hope is that no more than twenty-six will occur in any given year. (The twenty-sixth would, of course, begin with "Z.") So far no more than eleven hurricanes have occurred in any year. To avoid misunderstandings, no name is used more than once every ten years, and the year of the storm always accompanies the name. Pacific typhoons also receive one of a list of eighty-four women's names.

People sucked into the air

Like hurricanes and typhoons, tornadoes and the related cyclones and water spouts are storms which we can explain but cannot really comprehend. No one knows the cause of tornadoes. We cannot even answer the question of why tornadoes, which are a rare phenomenon elsewhere on earth, occur so frequently in North America. Tornadoes are incredible things. Can you believe that a storm could whirl over a farmyard and:

- tear the feathers from chickens?
- pluck the wool from sheep, leaving them bare?
- lift off a church roof and set it down twenty kilometers away?
- lift a cow, a horse, a bison, and a car?
- suck people high into the air and set them down again without hurting them?
- lift a man, carry him over the trees, and set him down thirty-seven feet away?
- lift a train from the tracks and set it down again several yards from the tracks?

Witnesses testify that all these events really happened. There is an old story that an entire herd of Kansas cows "flew through the air like birds" during a tornado. Scientists agree that such occurrences are possible.

In 1967, nine hundred twenty-eight tornadoes were recorded in the United States alone. If tornadoes did not occur so frequently, no one would imagine that such whirlwinds could really exist. A gray, brown, or sandy-colored cloud floats on the earth, and a dark cloud floats in the sky. In between there is something that thunders and howls and looks like a curving, rotating rope, and which in reality is a funnel of air rotating at uncanny speeds. The funnel may be small, no more than six or nine feet in diameter, but it may also be a half-mile wide. Sometimes it exists for only a few seconds, but some tornadoes have spent hours plowing a trail of terror across the land. The path of the tornado may be only a few feet wide, but it can be three hundred miles long, and the funnel can travel at up to fifty miles an hour. However, the bizarre thing about tornadoes is that although the funnel may easily rip trees out of the ground and break boards into splinters, twenty or thirty yards away everything is perfectly still. Air inside a tornado rotates very swiftly. For example, it has repeatedly been demonstrated that wisps of damp straw which are caught up in the funnel can be driven like bullets deep into wood, and splinters of wood can pierce an iron plate half an inch thick. And yet, directly beside the tornado, nothing is touched!

Many books have been written about the origins, causes and dispersals of tornadoes, but we have very little solid information about them. Somehow atmospheric moisture, high temperatures, layered air masses, level land, and other geographical features interact to create tornadoes. This all sounds fairly credible, but then so did the story we heard in our nurseries that thunder is caused by two clouds crashing together. People who live in tornado country are in desperate need of more accurate information on the subject.

The fire storm

Germans have known that rising, hot masses of air are a decisive factor in the creation of tornadoes ever since the night of July 27-28, 1943, when the United States Air Force dropped so many incendiary bombs on the city of Hamburg that finally the entire city was in flames. The temperature was 800° to 1,000° C, and people were being burned to a crisp both outside and inside. What people called a "fire storm" became an artificial tornado! Trees were twisted out of the ground and shot into the sky like flaming torches, the storm tore the clothing from the bodies of people who attempted to flee, and vehicles turned over and were whirled around in the air. It was said that fire was flowing upward a distance of four miles like air up a chimney, and the air streamed up to follow it. Far outside Hamburg the storm was measured as having an intensity of seven.

The atomic bomb dropped on Hiroshima also triggered a tornado.

The survivors of Hamburg and Hiroshima could easily believe the account of Ezekiel, who may have seen a tornado six hundred years before Christ was born:

And I looked, and behold, a whirlwind came out of the north, a great cloud, and a fire enfolding itself, and a brightness was about it, and out of the midst thereof as the color of amber, out of the midst of the fire.

—Ezekiel 1:4

Apparently this is the same thing a common farmer saw when he looked out of his open tornado cellar into the interior of a funnel directly above him: the "eye" of the tornado is a tunnel shot through with lightning.

Waterspouts

Waterspouts, which occur at sea, are related to the tornadoes which occur on land. A tornado was observed to change into a waterspout when it left the land and entered the water; and when it reached the opposite bank, it changed into a tornado again. Just as a tornado lifts up sand, stones, timber, and anything else it encounters, a waterspout can lift fish and drop them down somewhere else. Obviously, airplanes which travel through tornadoes can be destroyed, just as ships can when they encounter waterspouts. When we realize that these whirlwinds are not at all uncommon, we can understand the unexplained disappearance of many ships and planes.

The secret of the zeppelins

The various kinds of storms, caused by differences in air pressure, are magnificent spectacles of nature at work. They also reveal the fact that many natural phenomena are in need of further study. The discovery of the "jet stream" indicates what surprises may still lie in store for us.

We have known about jet streams since 1930. A German meteorologists in Hamburg, H. Seilkopf, was the first to observe and understand them and gave them the name "jet streams." However, at first no one knew about the discovery. Seilkopf, who was also an excellent ornithologist, was entrusted with the task of plotting a course for the zeppelins which were then attracting so much attention.

At that time people were amazed by the fact that the German zeppelin, a gigantic pod full of gas equipped with a few weak motors that were used to steer, accomplished its flights in record time—much faster, in fact, than its motors should have permitted. People admired the Germans' skill in air flight. It would have been more appropriate if they had admired German meteorology; but the secret of Seilkopf's discovery of the jet streams was closely guarded. At a great height the Germans were able to introduce a zeppelin into a jet stream around two hundred fifty miles wide so that it could fly at unparalleled speeds to its destination. In their flights to Russia or the United States, zeppelins usually arrived hours earlier than expected.

The secret of the jet streams was not revealed until 1940, when the United States was fighting a war in the Pacific. To their horror, U.S. bomber pilots discovered that at some points their planes did not move forward, but appeared to be immobilized in the air. They had encountered a jet stream, a sort of horizontal whirlwind, which prevented them from moving. At the same time the Japanese were using the jet streams to carry balloons filled with explosives across the Pacific into the United States.

Today it is routine for pilots to read maps to determine the location of the jet streams, and when passengers are requested to fasten their safety belts, it often means that the pilot wants to pass close to the turbulent borders of a jet stream.

Storms or phenomena resembling storms occur even at altitudes above the usual air-traffic routes, altitudes where the air is so thin that we can scarcely measure its motion. However, foil released by rockets at an altitude of sixty miles has enabled scientists to record gales traveling at speeds over two hundred miles an hour. As a rule, air does not travel at such speeds close to the ground. Sometimes vertical currents of "air" were observed in these "storms" which hurled the foil upward again.

Traitorous trails in the sky

I have mentioned that research into jet streams was kept secret for some time. Another phenomenon which was secretly investigated during World War II was the formation of vapor trails which betrayed the location of high-flying bombers and scout planes. The delicate white vapor trails were more effective indicators than radar of the presence and flight direction of planes. But what could be done to prevent vapor trails from forming? First scientists had to find out what they were and how they were formed.

It was easy to say what vapor trails were: they were made of ice crystals, the frozen water formed when motor fuel burned. The trails also contained frozen moisture which had condensed around the exhaust fumes from the motors. It appeared that it would not be too difficult to understand vapor trails and to find some way of keeping them from forming.

In their first experiment scientists attempted to capture the ice crystals which formed vapor trails. The crew of one plane took air samples from the vapor trail of the airplane preceding it. But scientists found it difficult to interpret the samples. Were the samples a species of snow or hail, or merely a kind of mist? Or were they all three? Later the plane which took the vapor samples was equipped with flat plates covered with soft paste. The theory was that the snow or hail crystals would leave impressions in the paste. However, the experiments proved fruitless.

As yet no one knows exactly how the sparkling snow crystals we admire each winter are formed and grow or when they acquire their symmetrical, hexagonal crystalline forms. One new theory suggests that a snowflake begins as a tiny ice-crystal disk which develops ice whiskers, or delicate, hair-thin needles of ice. The ice needles then absorb water vapor, which freezes, forming the six crystalline arms of the normal snow crystal. This theory is less a theory than an observation, and it tells us little more than Kepler's work, *Concerning Hexagonal Snow,* which was written in 1611.

Chapter Ten

CHANGING ENVIRONMENTS

Why ice ages?

THE GREAT physicist Georg Gamow, who taught for many years at the University of Colorado, used to say that several centuries ago astrologers had taken a step forward and had become astronomers, so it was high time that meteorologists become meteroronomers. Clearly, more research is needed in the field of meteorology. Perhaps one day it will be possible to forecast the weather not just for the next couple of days, but for weeks ahead of time, or even to do something more important—to discover how and why we experience fluctuations in climate.

Meteorological research might even give us a clue to the mystery of the Ice Age. We know only that ice ages have occurred recently in geological history. But no one knows *why* they occurred. For countless thousands of years, vast areas of the earth were covered with glaciers, with mountains of ice. During this time life was at a standstill and animal and plant species perished. Yet we possess nothing but vague hypotheses concerning the causes of these phenomena. We cannot even answer the question of whether the climate on earth is slowly growing warmer or whether we are now entering a new ice age.

When we think about climatic changes, we are bound to wonder how warm or cold our planet was when life on earth first began. Our ancestors, the first primitive organ-

isms, were born when the earth was around 1,200,000,
000 years old. We do not know for certain, but we
believe that at that time the temperature on this planet
was around room temperature, or 20° C. Later, during
the 3,500,000,000 years life has been evolving, there
were certainly times when and places where the earth
and the atmosphere were hotter or colder. In part, we
humans owe our existence on earth to fluctuations in
climate. Periods of drought and heat and ice ages with
snowfall, hail, and frost may have robbed many of our
competitors of the highest rank in the animal kingdom.
Today we see that the development of the various human
races is dependent on climatic conditions.

But what is the situation today? Is the ice on earth
growing? Measurements and calculations indicate that
around ten percent of the earth's surface is covered with
ice. Nine percent of these ice masses lie at the North
Pole, one percent is scattered over the earth in the form
of glaciers, and ninety percent of the ice is in Antarctica,
at the South Pole.

These are amazing figures. One might have imagined
that the earth's ice supply would be divided equally between the North and South poles. In any case, we may
well wonder whether the ice, especially the giant masses
of ice in Antarctica, is increasing or whether it is slowly
melting and threatening to drown mankind. Scientists do
not know everything about this subject, but they believe
that the ice is growing and the oceans are sinking. However, in recent years there has been some question about
Greenland, where some measurements indicate that the
ice is growing and others indicate that it is melting. In
any case, we do not know enough to rest assured that
we are safe.

When it is 4° C colder than it is now

When the temperature averages 4° C lower than it
does now, the life-style of people in Central Europe will
change radically. The glaciers of Sweden and the Alps
will grow in size, and people will have to use vast
amounts of fuel and capital to heat their houses and to
keep the roads open to traffic. To cite just one example,
the farmers in Holstein who now raise cattle will probably

keep reindeer instead. Moreover, Central Europeans will have to accommodate millions of refugees from the more northerly countries.

The countries along the equator will suffer even more. When the temperature grows colder and the quantities of ice and snow in the polar zones increase, less water will be available to fall on the equatorial countries in the form of rain. Drought will ensue, resulting in the death of livestock, bad harvests, widespread famine, and the extinction of all life over wide areas. Will the future be as bleak as this? Scientists who met at a special conference in 1972 to discuss the problem think that these disastrous events may well take place. They recall that around 4,000 years ago, flourishing cultures in Egypt, Mesopotamia, and the Indus Valley perished because of insufficient rainfall. The rock paintings of the Sahara, which depict a wealth of animals which once lived in the area, testify to the importance of adequate rainfall for all life. Finally, let us remember the dead cities of the Mayas, which apparently had to be abandoned because the water supply became insufficient around 770 B.C.

How close are we to another ice age? Some experts believe that the optimum temperatures for human beings prevailed around 6,000 years ago. Since that time the temperature had fluctuated, growing periodically warmer and colder, and around the tenth and eleventh centuries there was a warmer period when the Vikings were able to farm Greenland (hence, the name Greenland). However, in general, the movement of animals into warmer zones proves that we are in for a cold spell. These animals resemble the semitropical species which were the contemporaries of our Stone Age ancestors, and they show that at least in England and Germany, the periods between ice ages commonly last only 10,000 years.

It is painful to contemplate the future which may lie before us. It would be far more pleasant if we had the leisure time to make gradual preparations for the coming change in climate. However, scientists are firm in their opinion and claim to have found evidence in Greenland that in just one hundred years there will be a sharp drop in temperature which will turn gigantic forests into primitive grasslands. Moreover, these scientists remind us that the same thing happened in Greece.

They conclude that we are now at the end of a warm

epoch and that if nature proceeds on course, soon the same things will happen that happened before the last ice age (the growth of glaciers, a drop in temperatures, etc.). The change will take place in the next few centuries.

We must know more

The majority of the scientists who participated in the 1972 conference agreed on the following points: For the past few thousands of years, the climate on earth has contrasted sharply with what it has been for the last few million years. Intervals of warmth, such as that we are enjoying now, have always been of short duration. Undoubtedly, the end of the present epoch of warmth is close at hand. During the next few thousand years, and perhaps the next few hundred years, temperatures will cool and our environment will change radically. All the other changes which have taken place in recorded history will pale in comparison. This dramatic change in climate threatens man's struggle to exploit the earth's energy reserves and grow enough food to survive on. We must learn to understand changes in climate before our climate begins to change for the worse.

Thus, international and interdisciplinary research programs are sorely needed; for how little we know about the ice ages! The following is a tentative list of the possible causes of ice ages:

• The sun does not shine with uniform intensity. When its radiance dims, an ice age occurs on earth.

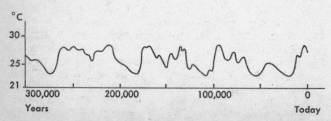

During the past 300,000 years, the temperature on earth has fluctuated in a manner corresponding to this curve. Temperatures varied locally as they do today.

• The earth travels past clouds of cosmic dust which diminish the sun's brightness.

• Periodically the earth's axis tilts, causing the sun's radiance to vary.

• The earth's magnetic field shifts, causing reactions which lead to ice ages.

• The earth's orbit around the sun alters.

• A change occurs in the relative amounts of land and water.

• Volcanic eruptions create clouds of smoke which block sunlight from the earth.

• Air and water currents change course.

• A slight lowering in temperature leads to an increase in ice and snow, and the increased ice and snow, in turn, increase reflection of the sun's light, which leads to a further reduction in temperature.

And so forth. This is by no means a complete list. However, it demonstrates the fact that scientists disagree radically and do not know anything for certain.

Meanwhile, we face an uncomfortable future, and our discomfort is all the greater because we cannot answer the question of what causes ice ages. Related to this question is the problem of whether the dinosaurs died because the earth underwent a period of cold. We have not yet solved the riddle of their disappearance. Still another question is this: What are the strange little black worms called *Mesenchytracus solifugans*, which live deep in the crystalline ice of glaciers? What do they live on, and why do they love the cold? Did they survive the last ice age buried in the ice of Alaska? Ice itself and its formation pose many riddles. To mention just one, beneath the ice of Antarctica, strange icicles more than a yard long and resembling stalactites grow down into the water at a speed of nearly an inch per minute. How do these icicles grow?

The development of a new climate

Schoolchildren learn that the Gulf Stream heats up northern Europe and that if it were not for the Gulf Stream, Great Britain, Norway, Denmark, and Sweden would be virtually uninhabitable. Science-fiction novels often tell about evil scientists who divert the Gulf Stream in order to shut off northern Europe's central heating system. Such plots exist only in our imagination. Nevertheless, it is natural for us to wonder whether human beings are capable of influencing the climate in certain areas and whether they do not in fact already do so. People concerned with the ecology believe that man is doing harm to the earth's climate. Apart from the transition from ice age to warm spell and back again, how stable is the earth's climate?

The weather has already been used as a weapon! In 1974 the U.S. Department of Defense admitted that between 1966 and 1972, American forces had created heavy artificial rainfalls in Southeast Asia to prevent North Vietnamese reinforcements from reaching the front. The Americans sowed silver iodide crystals and other chemicals at high altitudes, and raindrops condensed around them. Related to this phenomenon are the hail rockets tested in many wine-growing regions.

There is no doubt that human beings can exert a local influence on the climate. The building of large cities has not only led to air pollution, but has also influenced air currents. Every glider pilot knows that warm air rises from the houses of a city. Smoke and haze above a city testify to the fact that its climate differs from that of the surrounding land.

In the same way, man altered the climate of vast regions when he began to farm the land. Formerly forests, trees, and bushes kept the air moist, but now fields have replaced the forests, and when the wind blows across the fields, it dries them out. Moreover, at times tremendous storms carry away the soil, as they once did in the Midwest of the United States. Sometimes rain washes away the fertile topsoil, which is no longer anchored by roots and vegetation. When these events occur, the landscape changes and the climate changes with it. Knowing all this, scientists have repeatedly discussed whether human beings could not improve the climate in various regions. Would it, for example, be a good idea to irrigate the Sahara, create giant lakes in Siberia, change the courses of rivers, and melt the ice in the polar regions or close up the Bering Straits so that we could "improve" the balance between fresh water and salt water on earth?

Interesting, amusing, or exciting as such plans might

be, none of them has yet been realized, and they will not become reality during our lifetime. Or, at least, no such plan will succeed to the degree that it will substantially affect the climate. However, man has always done one thing which affects the climate. The activity which we might regard as most typical of man, an activity which differentiates him from animals, is the creation of fire, the striving to create heat and to utilize heat energy. However man creates heat, whether in home or industry, in peace or in war, with wood, coal, oil, natural gas, gunpowder, or other chemicals, by eating, working, or raising animals, he always "heats" the atmosphere.

Man has used up countries full of forests to create heat, and when he had no wood, he has used peat, lignite, and bituminous and anthracite coal. Then he discovered petroleum, then natural gas, and finally nuclear energy. One day he will probably learn to use energy created by nuclear fusion; and if all this is not enough, he will find energy sources about which we know as little today as we knew about nuclear energy fifty years ago.

Energy and heat exist in abundance

It is understandable, but unnecessary, for us to be concerned that one day we may exhaust our supplies of coal, oil, and natural gas. In the past, all predictions that energy supplies or needed raw materials would run short in a certain time span and bring about the downfall of civilization have proved unfounded, and there is no reason why they should prove more valid in the future.

How much do we artificially warm up the earth with all our energy sources?

If we designate the earth's daily input of natural heat energy, which mostly comes from the sun, as amounting to two hundred units, then the amount of heat we humans create in a day is only .03 units. Thus, our total energy consumption is quite insignificant and will not noticeably influence the earth's climate. Some people speculate that in fifty or two hundred years this will no longer be the case. They assume that the population of the world will continue to grow at a rapid rate and will consume more and more energy. However, those who predict this increase in energy consumption fail to realize that the inadequacies of the technological and industrial techniques by which we process fuel will still keep consumption relatively low.

I will cite one example of the foolishness of people who predict that we will soon run out of some necessary substance. Newspapers recently published the alarming news that if we continue to burn coal, oil, and natural gas at our present rate, we might seriously diminish the quantity of oxygen in the air. It appeared that everyone could look forward to the day when the 20.95% of oxygen in the atmosphere would be drastically diminished and we would all suffocate. Then finally someone performed the necessary computations, adding up all known supplies of coal, oil, wood, and natural gas and calculating how much carbon dioxide would be created if they were all burned up. The results were reassuring. Even if we were to burn everything burnable (which we do not need to do, and, in fact, could not do if we wanted to), we would use up only .15% of the oxygen in the atmosphere. The oxygen content of the atmosphere would sink from 20.95% to 20.8%.

The hothouse theory

It has become fashionable to make pessimistic predictions about the environment. Fortunately, we need take this fad no more seriously than we take any other. Scientists can scarcely predict what the weather is going to be like this weekend, so obviously they cannot tell what will happen five or ten years from now. The prophets who held the "hothouse theory" of the development of our earth's climate did at least have one fact at their disposal: the carbon dioxide content of the atmosphere has increased in recent decades. It is easy to understand why this is true, for with the advent of industrialization we are burning great quantities of wood, coal, and other combustible materials. In other words, in addition to water, we have been creating carbon dioxide and releasing it into the atmosphere. The carbon dioxide content of the atmosphere has increased faster in the northern than in the southern hemisphere, for there is more industry in the North. The hothouse theory states that the carbon dioxide in the air reduces the amount of heat the earth radiates into space, and that therefore the earth is going to become as warm as a hothouse. It has been claimed that many species will not be able to endure the change in climate and will become extinct, and that the "balance of nature" will be destroyed, with disastrous consequences.

One fact which contradicts this theory is that the increase of carbon dioxide in the atmosphere is so slight that we can scarcely measure it. (Carbon dioxide should not be confused with the poisonous carbon monoxide.) As a rule, the air contains three hundred twenty parts per million of carbon dioxide, meaning that there are three hundred twenty molecules of carbon dioxide for every million molecules in the air. In recent years this amount has sometimes increased by around one part per million.

If the amount of carbon dioxide in the atmosphere continues to increase at its present rate, then around the year 2000 the air on earth will actually be one-half-degree Celsius ($.5°$ C) warmer than it was before. This effect is minimal, and, for two reasons, we need not take it seriously. First, by the year 2000 we will be utilizing far less of the classic fuels which create carbon dioxide; instead, we will probably be using nuclear energy. Second, nature itself will put a mechanism into effect which will tend to balance the presence of the carbon dioxide. Higher temperatures will create more clouds in the sky, and the clouds will reduce the amount of radiation which reaches us from the sun. The reduction in radiation will slightly lower the temperature on earth.

The plants on earth would flourish if there were more carbon dioxide in the atmosphere. For optimum growth, plants need more carbon dioxide than our atmosphere contains. Today plants take over 300,000,000 tons of carbon dioxide from the atmosphere every year and produce a corresponding quantity of oxygen. Thus, here, too, there is room for nature to introduce a compensatory mechanism.

The organization of nature is not as simple as many people imagine. There is no cause without an effect, and every effect is the cause of new effects. It does not matter much what factors maintain the balance of nature, as long as one law remains valid: effect causes countereffect. This law holds true now, as it always has in the past. Finally, we must understand that man himself is a product of nature who behaves "naturally" and obeys the laws of nature even when he alters nature.

Between the years 1963 and 1970, a reduction occurred in the amount of radiation which reached us from the sun. In 1963 the volcano Mount Agung erupted and hurled dust high into the atmosphere. Not until 1970 did the air become "clean" enough so that the "normal" amount of radiation began to reach the earth again. The same thing happened when Krakatoa erupted. Industrial pollution, which has caused so much trouble locally, has never been severe enough for its presence to be recorded worldwide.

Burning forests

For millions of years vast forest and swamp fires have affected the climate in much the same way as volcanic eruptions. Forest and brush fires frequently occur in the United States and southern France, but the most devastating fire of this type occurred in July, 1972, in the Soviet Union. First Moscow newspapermen reported the presence of clouds of smoke and the smell of fire. Then satellites orbiting the earth presented the world with pictures showing that a dozen fires were burning in the Timan Mountains, more than 600 miles northeast of Moscow. The pictures showed that the wind was blowing streams of smoke more than one hundred twenty miles long away from the fires. The fires continued to burn into August, and the heat was so great that it influenced the weather. The upper levels of the atmosphere became overcast, and heavy rainfalls occurred. The rain apparently cleansed the air, so that after the fires went out, the weather was back to normal.

Planned mismanagement

The water supply is a critical factor in many communities. On the one hand, man wants to live in a dry place and does everything he can to get rid of the water which falls from the sky as quickly as possible. He straightens the courses of rivers, builds systems of canals, drains meadows and swamps, and in the winter labors to dispose

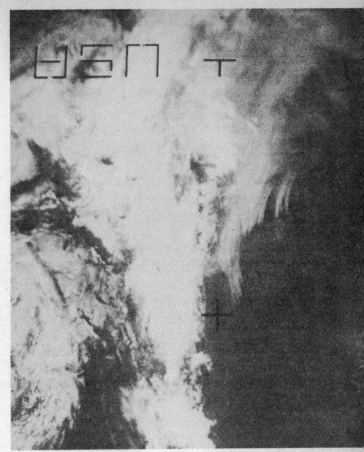

A satellite photograph shows burning forests and swamps in the U.S.S.R. (August 27, 1972). In the center of the picture are the clouds of smoke rising from individual fires. The smoke is traveling in a northerly direction. The lower right-hand corner is the northern part of the Caspian Sea. (U.S. satellite photo. Cf. *Naturwissenschaften* 59, 464 [1972])

of the snow as quickly as he can and drive the water into the sea. On the other hand, he laments when there is not enough water, builds reservoirs, and drills deeper and deeper wells. Yet during the summer drought he must drink water which other people have already drunk and in which they have bathed. This is no disaster as long as the water does not contain too much detergent or too many harmful chemicals.

Human beings are themselves responsible when they suffer from lack of water, and they are always guilty of some local mismanagement. However, something else man does has affected the earth's water supply more drastically. Man has not only drained large areas of land, but he has also irrigated large dry regions to make them suitable for farming. Some 580,000 miles of land, about the area of Alaska, have been irrigated by man. The water used in irrigation evaporates, condenses to form clouds, and certainly influences the climate more profoundly than many by-products of industry which are thought to harm the environment.

Oil dwellers

Apparently even the water which evaporates from irrigated fields does not exert a decisive influence on the climate of the world as a whole. If we have cause to worry about the earth's water supply, it is because of oil. Water and oil have been in conflict for a long time. When the chemicals were formed which became the building blocks of life (pre-biological substances like amino acids, sugars, peptides, and fats), oil products formed as waste and spread across vast regions of the water.

Oil sometimes flows out of natural oil wells in the ground. Then it flows into streams and seeps slowly into the ground and the water. It was oil wells like these, wells in the United States and Iran, which first drew men's attention to the existence of oil. Obviously, such natural oil wells exist not only on the continents, but also on the sea floor. Soviet scientists estimate that over 500,000 tons of oil pour into the oceans from oil wells every year. (American scientists believe it is possible that the figure is closer to 6,000,000 tons!) Five hundred thousand tons is approximately the same amount produced in Angola or Pakistan, an amount of considerable value to industry. This oil slowly rises from the sea, distributes itself on the surface, is forced into clumps by the wind and the waves, is chemically altered by salts and the air, becomes overgrown by certain species of algae, and finally becomes a mobile home for tiny crabs and mussels. Finally, all traces of the oil are lost.

The 500,000 tons of oil which pour into the oceans each year would not matter if man did not add to this another 4,000,000 to 10,000,000 tons of waste oil. (We do not have precise figures.) This oil could prove harmful if it were not for the small living organisms which move into the clumps of oil, multiply there, and decompose the oil until the clumps no longer float. When the used-up balls of oil sink to the ocean floor, they are no longer genuine oil but harmless organic matter.

Fortunately, man is now aware of the possible negative effects of his behavior, and this new awareness can spur him on to do research in hitherto neglected fields and force him to use fuel and chemicals sparingly and to manage natural resources with care.

Presidents Kennedy and Nixon were not the first to call attention to the need for protecting the environment. Long ago Josef Stalin created a program to promote the "improvement of nature"; but Stalin did not invent the concept. Decades before, poets, thinkers, researchers, government officials, and leaders of industry had, quietly and without fanfare, set about the task of protecting the environment.

Scientists still confront the question of whether man is capable of profoundly changing nature. Does not nature possess such an inexhaustible reservoir of methods to restore its own balance that nothing in nature can pursue an unnatural course? Perhaps in evolutionary terms, research scientists and technologists are nothing but a natural factor, a factor by which nature regulates itself on the way to some unfathomable goal.

Chapter Eleven

LIFE AND EVOLUTION

The first bird

THE FIRST evidences of evolution have been found in rocks around 3,700,000,000 years old. We know that our ancestry is as ancient as these fossils. However our ancestors managed to keep body and soul together, we must be grateful to them for having survived the struggle for existence and for having continued to evolve until they became human beings. Countless species were not so lucky and became extinct.

One of these extinct creatures is the primitive form of the bird, a creature which must have existed at one time. It was the link in the evolution of lizard-like, egg-laying reptiles into flying, fluttering, egg-laying birds. Somewhere at some time there must have been a creature which developed feathers instead of scales, which learned to fly, and which became the first bird. Probably we would know nothing about this bizarre creature if lithography had not been invented in 1793. At that time artists searched for beautiful, regularly shaped stone plates, and in the Frankish mountains of Germany they found a rock quarry dating back to Roman times which supplied them with beautiful stone plates. The stone in these plates was formed when dinosaurs lived in the area. In 1861, the imprint of a bird's feather was found on one of the plates! Thus, a primitive form of bird must have existed when the stone was formed.

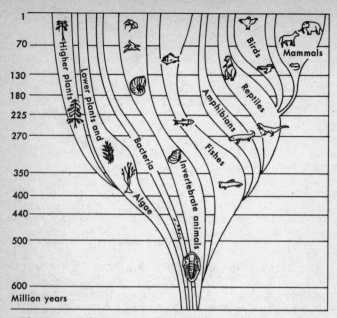

The upper right-hand corner of this genealogical tree shows the group of mammals, which evolved from the reptiles around 225,000,000 years ago. The reptiles in turn evolved from the amphibians and fish.

In the following year an almost complete primitive bird skeleton—the remains of two wings, and a long, feathered tail—was found in a layer of stone twenty meters deep. Unfortunately, the head was missing. Was this *the* first bird? As usual, scientists disagreed about what they had found. They had hoped and expected to see a feathered, lizard-like creature with scales on its body, the long tail of a lizard, claws on its wings, and teeth in an elongated mouth. Since the bird's head was missing, there was plenty of room for dispute. While German scientists were still debating, the bird skeleton was purchased by the British Museum, and the Germans saw that instead of fighting with each other, they would have done better to have found some way to hold on to their discovery. In any case, English scientists now had the opportunity to carry on the debate, and they promptly did so.

Then in 1877 a second primitive bird was found near Solnhofen. It had a head, claws, scales, and all the other physical characteristics which the scientists had hoped to see. The elongated beak-like snout contained sharp reptilian teeth.

Today we have the remains of at least four primitive birds, and in schoolbooks we see fantastic pictures in which these birds are flying around dinosaurs in a primeval landscape. Only one thing is wrong with these pictures: we still do not know whether the primitive birds could actually fly! Now, one hundred years after the first primitive bird was discovered, scientists still disagree as to whether it could fly or whether it only fluttered from branch to branch. One group of scientists claims that the bird weighed a little over a pound, that its wing span was twenty-three inches, and that the area of its wings was fifty-eight square inches. If all this is true, the bird could not have flown, for then it would have had to land at breakneck speed.

Another group of scientists claims that the bird weighed only seven ounces, that its wing area was seventy-four square inches, and that it had a long tail it could use in flight. When a computer was consulted, it said that the bird could fly and could land slowly.

A third group claims that if we compare this bird with its relative, the bony fish or teleostean, it must have weighed over a pound. However, it could fly. It would crash if it tried to land in the normal way, but it could glide into a landing, using its splendid, broad, feathered tail.

Thus, unfortunately, we still do not know whether this primitive bird was capable of flight and was, in fact, a genuine bird.

The same thing holds true of many other plants and animals which existed in the past. What we know about them is not really science, but at best a history or description of nature.

Then there is the mysterious animal whose thumb was located in a position opposite that of its usual position, an animal scientists call the "hand animal," or chirotherium. We do not know who first found the imprint of this creature's hand, the trace of fleshy paws equipped with a claw-like nail. The creature left us countless imprints of its little forehands and larger prints of its rear hands, which resemble the handprint of an adult human. But the surprising thing is that the imprint of the thumb is located where we have our little fingers. The animal, so to speak, had its right hand (or foot) on its left arm (or leg) and its left hand (or foot) on its right arm (or leg). It must have had a very strange gait.

The similarity of the hands of the chirotherium to the hands of human beings and apes is truly baffling. The chirotherium lived about 180,000,000 years ago, during the geological era when sandstone was being formed. At that time dinosaurs and other reptiles lived on earth, but there was no creature even distantly resembling a primitive man or an ape. No one knows what the creature looked like whose handprints have been preserved in the sand of the sandstone epoch. Scientists have suggested the probable size, shape, gait, and appearance of the limbs of the chirotherium, but they cannot prove their theories.

Catastrophe or evolution

Today we can easily understand the fact that new species constantly develop. We can observe and even bring about changes in genetic material by the use of chemicals and physical stimuli. A gardener can breed a number of new species from one species of flower, and all dog-breeders know how to create new breeds of dog. We can now breed plants and animals, creating new species which please us or which we deem useful. Doctors and fur-trappers sometimes intervene by exterminating whole species of living creatures. But what was it that exterminated certain species in the past? For example, why are there no more dinosaurs?

Naturally, scientists have an answer to this question. In fact, they have so many answers that one cannot choose among them!

Charles Darwin's book on the origin of species, published in 1856, forms the basis for our conception of the evolutionary process. Before 1856, scientists dismissed the question of why certain species had ceased to exist by saying that animals which had, for example, been found petrified in limestone belonged to extinct species which had been annihilated in some catastrophe. It seemed immaterial to ask what the catastrophe had been. Many people unconsciously thought of the biblical Flood, without realizing that mussels and other sea creatures should have survived this catastrophe.

L. J. R. Agassiz, an outstanding Swiss research scientist (1807-1873), was the first to recognize that the Swiss glaciers represented the remains of the ice which had covered Europe during the last ice age. He described and scientifically classified around 1,000 species of petrified fish, accomplished a great deal in the field of biological marine research in North America, and had a lecture published in the New York *Tribune*. Yet Agassiz was content with the assumption that all life on earth had died out between fifty and eighty times and each time had been created anew by God. He was bitterly opposed to Darwin's theories.

Now we do not question the validity of the theory of evolution and the theory that a logical, unbroken line of development leads from primitive unicellular organisms to man. Thus, we no longer need to assume that life was created fifty to eighty times. However, why certain species died out in the course of 3,700,000,000 years is still open to question.

Anyone who has found a petrified shell creature on a farm or in a quarry knows that once a sea or at least a beach must have been located at this place—a place which may now lie several hundred yards above sea level. Thus violent movement, the rising and falling of land masses, in short geological catastrophes, may have caused the extinction of some species. Another possible cause is the change in climate which accompanies such events.

The discovery of well-preserved mammoths in the ice of Siberia suggests that some species perished because of climatic changes. Not only were a number of mammoths found in the ice, but tons of tusks were removed from their petrified bodies and sold. The flesh inside their hairy bodies was so perfectly preserved that it was used to feed dogs. Moreover, the members of a geological congress in St. Petersburg (now Leningrad) reportedly dined on mammoth steaks. The mammoths were not the only animals native to a warm climate which were suddenly surprised by the cold of an ice age. The well-preserved, frozen body of a woolly rhinoceros has also been discovered. If these animals had not been frozen during a long cold spell, their bodies would not have been so well preserved. The catastrophe which overtook them was sudden and unexpected.

We do not know what caused the dinosaurs to become extinct. Only one thing is certain: shellfish, sea urchins, and other small marine animals which coexisted with the dinosaurs during the Jurassic age (around 150,000,000 years ago) made the transition into the Cretaceous age (around 120,000,000 years ago), but the dinosaurs and the belemnites (their remains are the so-called thunderstones) did not survive into the new age.

It may be that the dinosaurs were somehow dependent on the conifers and ferns which flourished at the same time and which were replaced by willows, poplars, oaks, and grass in the Cretaceous era. In this case the main question is: Why did these plants cease to exist? Did they succumb to a new plant disease? Or did the dinosaurs fall prey to some "dinosaur disease"? We know that later species, such as the cave bears, which lived during an ice age, were decimated by disease. But we know nothing about why the dinosaurs departed from the stage of life. Scientists keep coming up with new theories, but they are not certain whether any of these theories is correct.

For example, one theory suggests that eventually the shells of dinosaur eggs became too thin to bring forth a new generation. (Dinosaurs laid very large, round eggs which can be seen in many museums.) However, no one knows why the eggshells should have become thin.

Another theory suggests that the reactions of dinosaurs became too slow. Presumably it takes a long time for the nerves to conduct signals along a body one hundred feet long, and it might take a large dinosaur a long time to react to an attack. But if this theory is true, why did the smaller species of dinosaurs, which had shorter reaction times, also die out? Or did an extraterrestrial event cause them to become extinct? Is it possible that their genes were altered by a strong dose of cosmic radiation? Scientists have discussed this theory extensively, but they have no proof that it is true.

Another possible explanation is that a "new" species plundered the dinosaurs' nests. As long as scientists do not know the answer, anyone is welcome to come up with a new theory.

The beginning of life

Several years ago scientists found an answer to a question which has long been of the greatest concern, especially to theologians and philosophers: the question of the origin of life on earth. In less than thirty years they have made great strides toward determining the origin of life, and they have done so by means of simple experiments whose validity can be carefully tested. As soon as scientists seriously attacked the question, it became subject to an experimental approach. One is almost inclined to ask why they did not begin experimenting much sooner than they did, but this reproach would be unjust. Surprisingly, they did carry out many of the relevant experiments decades ago, but they failed to link these experiments with the question of the origin of life.

One experiment which is now regarded as classical is the experiment performed in 1953 by Stanley Miller, a young student at the University of Chicago. A simple carbon compound (CH_4) combined with water (H_2O) and ammonia (NH_3) in a hydrogen atmosphere was exposed to electrical charges (sparks), and the result was the production of small quantities of amino acids out of which we can create a "primitive" protein.

Countless researchers repeated Miller's experiment in countless variations. Miller's results proved correct and he became famous. However, his experiment was not really new, nor did the results of the experiment come as a surprise. Anyone who had looked into the *Berichte der deutschen Chemischen Gesellschaft (Reports of the German Chemistry Society)* for 1913 would have found an essay written by Walter Löb forty years before Miller performed his experiment. Like Miller, Löb exposed ammonia, water, and simple carbon compound (CO_2) to electrical charges, and he reported that he had created the amino acid glycocoll (glycine). Löb also observed the creation of sugar and formaldehyde. The latter has been of decisive importance to modern research into the origin of life.

Löb, an insignificant chemist at a Berlin hospital, was forgotten. It is to his credit that he did not forget scientists who had done groundbreaking work in the same field: two researchers at the Royal Serbian Academy of

Sciences in Belgrade, S. M. Losanitch and M. Z. Jovitschitsch. These two scientists were the first to convert elementary substances by subjecting them to a "current of sparks," and the first to call attention to the biochemical aspects of the reaction. They achieved this at the beginning of 1897. Perhaps the few lines dedicated to them in this book may call attention to these pioneers of a modern branch of research.

Löb and the two Serbian scientists could be no more than pioneers, for their experiments were not designed to explore the question of the origin of life. Instead, they were interested in biochemical processes which took place in living organisms. In 1897, scientists were not thinking in the same terms as they were in 1953. If scientists had experimented to determine the origin of life prior to 1953, they would probably not have found anyone willing to publish the results of their work, and even if they had found a publisher, they would have been laughed at or branded as heretics. Löb, Losanitch, and Jovitschitsch faced another difficulty. To some degree they were able to verify the results of the chemical reactions they affected, but they lacked the refined technical apparatus available in 1953. We can only prove what we can measure. Instruments of measurement, not intellect, set the limits of scientific research. Nowadays we can only investigate something when we can measure it. Thoughts and ideas are important and serve as the foundation of new knowledge. However, *researchers can only go where they can measure, not where logic indicates the next step lies.*

The assumption that the chemical building blocks of living cells could not have come into being in a lifeless world without the intercession of a Creator proved to be false. So did the belief that even if such building blocks and the products of their chemical reactions "accidentally" came to exist, they would immediately be destroyed and disappear. To their amazement, scientists learned that even highly complex molecular structures like the pigmentation of blood and leaves could be preserved for 1,000,000—in fact, for 1,000,000,000—years inside geological sediments.

Scientists enthusiastically created a new science, geobiochemistry. In a few years and with the aid of modern techniques, biologists, mineralogists, and chemists assembled thousands of intriguing facts. To be sure, they had to admit that many results they initially thought "surprising" were not as new as they had first supposed. For example, biochemical substances had been discovered in minerals as early as 1862.

Scientists are now trying to learn how living creatures developed from the chemical building blocks of life. They are wondering how the chemicals involved began to engage in those reactions which are the basis of all life. Slowly they are acquiring some notion of how the first cells developed from inanimate matter.

Cosmic seed

One question that confronts us is whether the transition from inanimate matter into living (and dying) organisms has taken place elsewhere in the cosmos. Is life as we know it on earth a unique phenomenon, or does life exist everywhere? Our earth is not a tiny, self-enclosed lump which has nothing to do with what happens elsewhere in the cosmos. Thus, we may well wonder whether cosmic influences have not contributed to the development of life on earth. This is an old problem in a new form, the problem of whether life is extraterrestrial in origin.

Nowhere in the vast reaches of the universe have we been able to find signs of life. However, the raw materials of life exist outside the earth, and it seems absurd to suppose that life exists on earth alone. All the substances with which Miller, Löb, and their predecessors perhaps instinctively experimented have been shown to exist in the dark clouds which fill the interstellar space.

The most exciting discovery is the fact that formaldehyde exists in the cosmic clouds. This substance paves the way to the raw materials of animal and plant protein, as well as to the sugars. As long as only small molecules composed of few atoms were known to exist in interstellar space, scientists looked on their presence as accidental. But then in 1971 the American Fred Johnson, an astronomer at California State College, made a spectroscopic analysis which revealed the presence in the constellation Orion of a form of radiation corresponding to bis-pyridylmagnesiumtetrabenzoporphine. This substance is

The largest maneuverable radiotelescope, whose swivel-mounted reflector has a diameter of one hundred meters, is located in Effelsberg, Eifel, in West Germany. Among other things, it was designed by scientists belonging to the Max Planck Society to investigate organic substances in the universe. By recording vibrations made by ancient chemical compounds, it can see 15,000,000,000 years back into the universe's past. The surface of the swivel-mounted reflector is larger than a football field, but the instrument cost less than a football stadium.

related to the pigmentation of blood and leaves! One molecule of the substance is composed of eighty-three atoms. In other words, this compound may once have formed the basis for the development of life in the remote reaches of the cosmos, or it may testify to the existence of life in the past. At the very least, it proves that the substances necessary for the growth of the more highly developed life forms can continue to exist in interstellar space. This being true, who would dare to assert that life exists only on earth?

Spectroscopic investigation is not the only technique we possess to investigate the existence of life outside the earth. Biochemical compounds exist on earth which had their origin in outer space. We can see them, investigate them, and conduct experiments on them. Like all the cosmic matter we possess, they are meteoric in origin.

The idea of investigating meteorites to find traces of extraterrestrial life is an old one. As early as 1880, a book was published in Tübingen, Germany, called *Meteorites and Their Organisms*. Author, lawyer, and amateur geologist Dr. Otto Hahn believed that he had detected a blanketing of plant life on meteorites. He believed that he had seen corals, sponges, or crinoids on them, too. Almost everything he describes is pure nonsense. However, his work deserves to be remembered as an early attempt to find traces of extraterrestrial life.

A sensation was created toward the end of 1961 when two American scientists, equipped with the latest modern equipment, reported that they had found "organized elements" in two meteorites! They demonstrated the presence of thousands of tiny round and hexagonal particles, each of them several thousandths of a millimeter in size. Immediately some scientists expressed doubts, asking how the particles could possibly represent the remains of once-existing organisms. And if the particles were biological formations, could they not have gotten onto the meteorites after they had arrived on earth? The scientific journals were flooded with arguments both pro and con, and the battle raged until 1964. No one dared to pronounce a final judgment, and no experiment provided a convincing answer. One thing was beyond doubt: meteorites bring with them out of the cosmos a number of simple and complex substances which we associate with plant life and possibly even with animal life. Perhaps these substances are merely the raw materials from which life in the universe can grow. However, possibly the meteorites also carry the remains of a heavenly body where life once dwelled, a body which now has gone down to its doom.

Thus, the conditions antecedent to the development of life do exist in the cosmos to a far greater degree than we had supposed.

The following computation shows us to what degree cosmic influences may have furthered the development of life on earth. If we assume that since the earth was formed, an equal quantity of meteorites with the same composition has been falling on the earth with equal frequency, then they must have contributed the following quantities of raw materials for the development of the first living organisms:

- 300,000,000 tons of amino acids
and
- 50,000,000 tons of formaldehyde

If we assume that this computation contains substantial errors and that the quantities involved are only half as large, or even only 1/10 or 1/100 as large, they are still sizable.

We now know that certain compounds which exist in outer space can be transported by meteorites to planets and stars. If they fall on soil that favors the development of life, these substances can become the building blocks of living organisms. If the meteorites transport amino acids to a planet, they can serve as the raw material of protein, and formaldehyde can serve as the raw material of sugars (carbohydrates).

This theory is a variation on the theory of the Swedish physicist and chemist Svante Arrhenius (1859–1927). Among other things, this world-famous scientist was director of the Nobel Institute for Physical Chemistry, in Stockholm, and he received the Nobel Prize in 1903. After 1900 he occupied himself with problems of the development and dissemination of life in the cosmos. In 1903 he published a fundamental work, *Textbook of Cosmic Physics*.

Arrhenius assumed that life in the form of spores or germ cells could cross the vast distances between the stars and thus spread through the universe. His theory was hotly debated and stimulated violent public discussions and articles by the contemporary press.

Then the discussion died down, for Arrhenius was clearly worthy of praise. For example, besides writing works on his specialty, he devised a theory about the cause of ice ages. Arrhenius reasoned that from time to time volcanoes expelled vast quantities of carbon dioxide which reduced the amount of heat radiated from the earth and warmed it up (*cf.* the hothouse theory). Then the increased plant growth produced oxygen, which had the reverse effect and finally created a cold spell. True or not, this theory attempted to explain both warm spells and cold spells.

As for Arrhenius's "pan-spermic hypothesis," we do not believe that germ cells could survive long enough in outer space to carry life from star to star. However, the notion that meteorites—and perhaps comets, as well—spread the raw materials of life throughout the cosmos no longer seems far off the mark. In 1970 it was estimated that life may exist on 300,000,000,000 to 30,000,000,-000,000 planets.

At the moment we do not know enough to answer all the questions which immediately spring to mind. I will mention only three:

1). Is life older than the earth?

2). If life has existed on other planets longer than it has existed here, how did life evolve on the other planets? Did human beings exist there, and who or what came after them?

3). Where in the universe did life develop for the first time? What is the true location of the biblical Paradise? Did Paradise exist not on earth, but in some remote area of the cosmos?

Naturally, we cannot yet attempt to answer these and many other questions. Anything we said would be sheer speculation. However, we should perhaps keep one thought in mind: life developed on earth in an incredibly short time. Only 1,500,000,000 years after our planet was formed and shortly after it had developed a relatively firm crust, it saw the development of life based on the same principle it is based on today. This means that up until the point that life began, our earth evolved at a tremendous speed, whereas evolution has been comparatively slower since that time.

Before life first began, didn't some chemical factor come to earth from outside? We are inclined to answer no. However, if we do so, we must face an unpleasant fact: if life on earth developed so quickly, then a high level of probability must exist that life will develop, the probability of an everyday event. This would mean that life is not, in fact, an extraordinary phenomenon. To some of us this thought might be painful.

Time and numbers

When we try to understand the evolutionary history of life on earth, and when we try not only to learn but to remember facts like those mentioned in this chapter, we encounter a problem: the concept of time. Our clocks show us the passage of the hours and the days, but they do not really help us to understand how quickly a day passes. The quantum of time embodied in a week is even more incomprehensible. To a schoolchild, a week is an exhausting period of study that seems to last forever. People with jobs may find that a week is far too short for them to get all their work done, and people on vacation usually feel that a week is gone before it has even begun.

We understand large numbers even less. We may vaguely grasp the meaning of one hundred or one thousand, but for most of us the only difference between 100,-000, and 1,000,000 is that the latter has an extra zero. When we are dealing with such large numbers, we can no longer picture anything very definite. Government economists and businessmen deal in figures like millions and billions, but human beings do not really understand the meaning of these numbers.

Let us construct a useful scale model for the history of the earth. We will assume that a human being reaches the age of eighty years. This means that he has lived 2,522,880,000 seconds. We can round off the number to 2,500,000,000 seconds and compare this figure with the 5,000,0000,000 years which comprise the age of our earth. Now one second of a man's lifetime corresponds to two years of earth history. We know what a second is, and we can also understand a time span involving spring, summer, fall, and winter. If we equate two years of earth history with one second of human life, we can understand evolution more clearly.

If we assume that the first life developed on earth when our planet was around 1,500,000,000 years old, our human observer would be 23.7 years old. He is in the autumn of his twenty-fourth year when he observes the first simple organisms. Before this he could see nothing but the dead ball of the earth, an earth sometimes veiled in clouds or shaken by raging storms. Over the years this spectacle has become wearisome. Not until the man is sixty does he observe something new happening to the earth. The earth's surface changes shape, folding itself to form mountains, and the shapes of the oceans change. The man sees the onset of what geologists call "algomic mountain formation."

When the man celebrates his seventy-first birthday (around 600,000,000 years ago), he can see a wealth of plants and animals, although none of the animals is a vertebrate. Then 300,000,000 years later he sees vast quantities of large green ferns and shave grass growing up before his eyes. Insects are flying around, and reptiles are walking on the land and creeping through the giant forests. But our observer, who is now in his seventy-fifth year, will witness events that are even more spectacular. Flying dinosaurs rise into the air.

When the man becomes seventy-eight, these animals die out as suddenly as they appeared. But something splendid happens to compensate the old man for this loss: colorful blossoms begin to bloom in the broken land!

One year later the whole earth is blooming. Palms, oaks, and giant redwoods rise from the ground. There are many mammals, and the man can even discern some ape-like creatures. Unfortunately, there are fewer birds.

The months pass, and now another exciting event occurs. By now the man is well over seventy-nine years old, and in another four months he will celebrate his eightieth birthday. Ape-like creatures appear which walk on their hind legs. The appearance of these animals continues to change and they become more and more like human beings. Now the old man sees other human beings like himself.

These new creatures do remarkable things. Just an hour ago they began to pile up stones to form tall pyramids. A half an hour ago they were melting iron in furnaces. Now they create flashes of atomic lightning which dazzle the old man's eyes. He has grown weary of watching. In the future someone else will see what happens on the earth.

Chapter Twelve

THE GROWTH OF KNOWLEDGE

Peaceful research

THERE IS nothing man fears as much as his fellowman. The blazing light of exploding atomic bombs is the product of modern weapons technology, and it bears witness to man's striving to protect himself from "others," either by attacking them or by defending himself against them. When "the other" comes to pay a visit, even if he is represented only by a single individual, he is greeted by an immediate demonstration of power. The honor guard marches before him, he is introduced to powerful members of the government, cannons are fired, he is served quantities of the most delectable food in magnificent buildings, and finally he is shown factories and research institutes which are intended to demonstrate the material and intellectual power which can be summoned to work for or against him. For thousands of years, in both their public and their private lives, human beings have strived to impress each other with their power. This behavior derives from the animal kingdom.

Heads of government are particularly proud of showing off their physicists, chemists, and engineers, for these are the people who produce the newest weapons. Weapons technology often demonstrates the maximum potential of science and technology. Governments readily supply funds and labor for projects involving "defense," and scientists and industrialists have frequently taken advantage of this fact to pursue peaceful research under the guise of developing armaments.

The kinds of research which please generals and heads of government generally involve nothing more than old knowledge in a new form. The fact that an arrow, a stone, a bullet, a bomb, or a grenade can be hurled at a target is old hat to a scientist, for he recognizes all these tricks as applications of the law of gravity, which man has known about for centuries. Devising new "experiments" in physics in order to create new armaments does not increase the sum of knowledge. To be sure, for the scientist, war can be the father of many things, for it brings him money and recognition. However, knowledge does not grow during wartime. It grows only in peaceful studies and laboratories. The wars of scientists take place in an atmosphere of peace.

Habitual thought patterns hinder progress

Let us choose a simple example, such as the dispute about water. Every schoolbook states that water is a simple compound represented by the formula H_2O. But do we really know what water is? Is the formula correct? It is a simplification, and strictly speaking it is even false! We still do not know enough about this substance, which is basic to all life. We are surrounded by oceans of water, yet we know neither where the oceans come from nor what the water in them is.

The ancient Greek philosophers saw the awesome waters of the sea and decided that water was an element like earth, air, and fire. Everything in the world was composed of these four elements. This was an impressive theory, and people continued to believe in the existence of four elements until the seventeenth century.

As late as the year 1770 scientists enjoyed creating oxyhydrogen gas explosions—that is, they enjoyed burning oxygen and hydrogen to form water by a kind of synthesis. However, little attention was paid to the small amounts of moisture created by this process. Instead, scientists debated the question of whether water could be transformed into "earth." They were so serious about this attempt that a chemist as brilliant as the French tax collector Antoine Laurent Lavoisier (1743–1794) spent three months distilling water to see whether it would turn into earth.

The so-called phlogiston theory, an appealing and venerable mass of inherited beliefs and conjectures, prevented scientists from thinking in more progressive terms. This theory stated that a substance called phlogiston is given off by matter when it burns. Lavoisier discovered many new facts. He found out that diamonds are made of carbon, he investigated mineral waters, and he was among those scientists who disproved the phlogiston theory. But he did not find out what water is, despite the fact that this information should have lain within his area of expertise.

The first person to understand what water is was a man who was not a chemist, who was not conducting experiments in this area, and who succeeded because he attacked the problem with an open mind. He was the engineer and builder of steam engines, James Watt. Watt, who was born January 19, 1736, in Cartsdyke, Scotland, experimented successfully in several areas. He built mathematical apparatus, astronomical equipment, and models of steam engines. His building experience eventually led him to construct an improved steam engine. This was unquestionably a useful invention. However, Watt knew little more about water than the fact that it could be made into steam. Thus, when he heard about the experiments of contemporary chemists, he had no preconceptions about the subject. He was the first to understand the nature of water. On April 26, 1783, he wrote a letter to J. Priestley (1733–1804) on the subject of Priestley's experiments. In the letter he asked whether it could not be assumed that water is composed of phlogiston (today we would say hydrogen) and dephlogistonized air (today we would say oxygen).

Watt's idea was well received, and in July of the same year English scientists were so convinced of the truth of Watt's theory that when a young assistant working with an English research group made a trip to France, he told French scientists about the theory, too. Among others, he told Lavoisier. Lavoisier repeated the relevant experiments, understood the significance of the new theory, and reported his findings to the French Academy of Sciences. He did not bother to mention that his findings had first been discovered by British scientists. After this coup, Lavoisier was considered *the* great researcher on the continent. Soon a battle began to rage over who had made the discovery first, a battle known as the "water controversy." The debate lasted for decades. Watt died on August 5, 1819, but it was not until sometime after his death, in 1835, that scientists everywhere acknowledged who really deserved the credit for discovering the composition of water: the engineer James Watt.

During the water controversy, revolutions raged all over Europe. On May 8, 1794, Lavoisier was guillotined, or had to "sneeze into the sack," as people used to say then. Wars came and went, empires crumbled, yet today we still know very little more about water than what Watt knew in 1783.

We *do* know that the composition of water is not as simple as Watt thought it was. About two hundred fifty years after his discovery, scientists recognized that individual molecules of water do not exist at normal temperatures. Water is unquestionably a liquid, but it possesses a definite structure. Clearly, great numbers of H_2O molecules cling together in organized "clumps." Water is a liquid composed of crystal-like groups of H_2O.

It would be nice if a liquid existed in which these "water crystals" could be dissolved the way we dissolve salt or sugar. In this case we could study water more closely. However, no one knows of a solution in which water will dissolve. Thus, scholars are still debating whether a "water crystal" contains eight, twelve, or three hundred molecules of H_2O. Or is water composed of large and small groups of H_2O? And how is its composition related to the temperature of water? What methods of measurement can safely be used to study water, and which methods are unreliable? Questions and more questions! However, scientists still hope that with time and patience they will find some answers.

Productive errors

In 1970 a Russian joined in the battle over the nature of water. He was Boris V. Deryagin, a Moscow physicist and chemist, and he suggested a new theory involving a new type of water, "polywater."

Deryagin did not do anything very remarkable. He condensed water vapor into water in a small quartz tube, a capillary tube. Through this experiment he believed that he had found traces of a hitherto unknown kind of water which is up to forty percent heavier than normal water, which remains unchanged at a temperature of $+500°$ C, but which "melts" to form "normal" water at a temperature of $+700°$ C, and which hardens to form a vitreous ice at $-40°$ C. Other scientists believed that Deryagin had made a mistake and that his results derived from careless experimentation. Not until the newspapers enthusiastically hailed the discovery of "polywater" did other scientists begin to take the Russian seriously. Had he really discovered something new?

Several theoreticians began to wonder whether some of their ideas and computer calculations did not suggest that polywater might really exist. Then other scientists began to experiment, and some of them decided that Deryagin was right, that he had really discovered a new kind of water! Soon scientific periodicals in Western Europe were filled with accounts of the new polywater. Some scientists supported and some refuted the existence of the new water.

Polywater seemed to be a simple phenomenon. A synthetic product contains countless building blocks which form a "polymer." For example, many ethylene molecules unite to form polyethylene. Thus, in the same way, scientists reasoned, water could unite to form polywater—or could it?

One might imagine that scientists would find it easy to settle this kind of debate by means of an experiment, but this was not the case. If one proceeds exactly as Deryagin did, one finds the same results; but if one tries to expand on the experiment, the results are different, if not quite contradictory. If we knew more about water and its structure, we would not need to experiment further, but as of 1973 scientists still did not know exactly what water was. Desperate researchers sought to arrive at a compromise. They said that if water is placed in a capillary tube, it forms a layer several thousandths of an inch thick, which causes the water to behave in the strange fashion described by Deryagin. Naturally, this theory is nonsense as long as scientists have not seriously studied the legendary layer of water.

In the summer of 1973, an international group of water researchers met in the little university town of Marburg, West Germany, to discuss water. Major scientific articles were planned, and other articles were just appearing in print. Then Deryagin, the discoverer of polywater, announced that the whole question was not really very important to him. "Perhaps," he said, "the phenomenon I observed has nothing to do with the structure of water!" How true.

The debate about polywater is not over, although the lively discussion has stopped for the moment. Some unexplained measurements have been discovered, and someday someone must and will explain them.

Just three months after the polywater affair, a Chinese-American scientist in Philadelphia conducted experiments which led to a new discussion. Deryagin believed that he had discovered peculiarities in the behavior of water inside capillary tubes. His American colleague studied works written in 1895 and decided that the water in the membranes of a living organism possesses an unusual structure. Instead of "polywater," scientists have begun to discuss concepts like "structured water" and "polarized multiple layers." This time it will be even more difficult to prove anything by experimentation, for when we experiment in a living organism, the results are even more uncertain than when we experiment in a glass capillary tube.

Seventy-five to ninety-five percent of human, animal, and plant organisms consists of water. This fact makes it clear why it is so important that we learn more about water.

We know a great deal about our body metabolism, about foods, drugs, vitamins, and hormones, and we can keep astronauts alive for weeks by feeding them artificial food. However, we know relatively little about the water which makes up most of our bodies. Often it is breakdowns in the metabolism of salts in the bodily water which lead to illness. If we knew more about water, perhaps we could devise means of alleviating or curing many diseases.

Other unknowns

Let us consider a second example, the bones in our bodies. Eighty-five percent of our bones consists of an inorganic compound, calcium phosphate. Chemists know comparatively little about how calcium phosphate is stored in bone, how it is formed, and how it composes a solid structure. Doctors cannot tell why some patients suffer from osteoporosis, a "softening of the bone," or how to cure them. More research is needed in this area, too.

The bones supply the framework of human and animal bodies, and lignin does the same thing in plants. Modern books state that lignin, a yellowish powder, can be extracted from plants and that it comprises up to thirty-three percent of the material composing them. But is this true? We can fill whole libraries with learned treatises on lignin. We can describe what appears to be the chemical composition of lignin and we have many clever theories about how it develops in the plant. However, we cannot describe in detail what lignin actually *is*. The forests are full of trees, and every day thousands of tons of lignin grow inside them, and every year some 40,000,000 to 50,000,-000 tons of lignin are obtained from wood that undergoes processing—for example, wood that is made into wood pulp. Yet we cannot totally explain the structure of this important substance. Some people question whether lignin actually exists. They suggest that the substance we chemically extract from wood may derive its chemical form from the process of extraction itself. What is even worse, we do not know what to do with these vast quantities of lignin! The best thing we can hope for is that workers can get rid of the "waste material" without damaging the environment.

Another example of everyday substances we know little about is cellulose, which is even more important to plants than lignin. It plays an important role in the structure of plants and is the organic compound we encounter most frequently in nature. Yet we still do not know how cellulose forms in plants.

However, our ignorance of phenomena such as water, bones, lignin, and cellulose should not lead us to conclude that fields like medicine or chemistry are backward in comparison with other sciences. In fact, just as many unanswered questions exist in other branches of science. Scientists gladly forget about them and, intentionally or not, concentrate on solving smaller problems to which they can find answers.

Medicine and chemistry have made great strides in the past few decades. Natural substances from the plant and animal kingdoms have been isolated and serve as medication. They have been studied, created synthetically, varied, and often improved on, and now they belong to our standard storehouse of drugs. If colds, pneumonia, venereal disease, diabetes, and tuberculosis have lost much of their terror, it is due to the successful research of physicians and chemists. Man can surpass nature in the creation of medicines!

We have had the same success in improving natural foods. We now artificially breed and grow superior plants which produce larger harvests and healthier food than ever before. We have learned to breed plants and animals in such a manner and in such numbers that we can now feed more people than it seemed possible for us to do just a few decades ago. Because of advances in chemistry, biology, and medicine, epidemics and famines no longer occur in most places during peacetime, and we no longer encounter deserted towns whose inhabitants have all perished.

The myth of the good old days

Apparently people cannot escape the superstition that earlier generations lived a healthier existence than they do. However, all the evidence indicates that the past was marked by poverty, disease, hunger, wretchedness, and filth.

The "high culture" of the ancient Egyptians was an age of unspeakable filth. Large families lived with their servants and every type of "Egyptian plague"—bugs, mice, fleas, flies, midges, and snakes—in primitive buildings along unpaved, crowded streets. Lice must have been widespread, for lice eggs have been found in the hair of the mummies of high-born persons. Priests used to shave their entire bodies every other day in order to get rid of the lice. Waterways and all other suitable places were used as toilets. What was not carried away by streams, rivers, and irrigation systems evaporated in the sun. Infectious diseases of all kinds were rampant, including worm infections and metabolic diseases. Often people were starving. Craftsmen did not have any idea of how to protect themselves against the smoke and poisonous gases to which they were exposed when they smelted ore.

Things were not much better on the American continent when Mexican culture was at its height. The account of an explorer in 1542 may describe typical conditions in Cenral and South America. When he landed in San Pedro

Bay, he could see the tops of mountains but not the valley that lay before them, for atmospheric conditions prevented the smoke of the natives' campfires from rising into the air. Thick deposits of charcoal or soot were found in the lung of a mummy from the Canary Islands. In the past the environmental pollution which we consider so distressing today was so extensive that we cannot even begin to imagine it.

In Roman times, even elite troops of soldiers could not stay longer than five days in one place, for if they stayed longer, the incredible filth caused diseases, probably typhus and dysentery, to break out. It is reported that Tamerlane, the great leader of the Kirghiz, forbade his soldiers to drink water that had not been boiled. Alexander the Great drank water from silver goblets, and silver does to some extent destroy bacteria. Army camps were breeding grounds for pestilence, and often the conditions which reigned in any army were so dreadful that inhabitants of a besieged city could simply stay behind their walls until the besieging army was forced to leave.

The condition of medieval European cities was little better. Different cultures built their cities on the same foundations, and from the medical point of view, a great conflagration was often the salvation of a city. Cities could be smelled from miles away. Workshops, households, and farmyards bred filth and stench.

They lived in their own filth

A description of a siege has come down to us from the time of the wars against the Turks. After several unsuccessful attacks, the Turks began to build large siege towers which they hoped would help them to cross over the walls, fortifications, and ramparts. As soon as the people in the besieged town saw the towers were about to roll toward them, they gathered all the filth they could find. When the attack began, they opened the sewers, and the heavy siege towers stuck fast in the sticky brown flood that poured out.

When Henry V crossed the English Channel to conquer France in 1415, he had 15,000 soldiers under his command. On the evening before the decisive battle of Agincourt, only 9,000 of these soldiers were capable of fighting. The others were stricken with dysentery.

Things have not changed so much in our day. Of the 100,000 Allied forces who served in Italian East Africa between June 1, 1940, and June 1, 1941, 74,250 fell ill. On the other hand, only eight hundred twenty-four men were wounded.

Today we still have a good chance of dying in our own filth. For example, consider all the dirty trains, buses, and streetcars which are traveling carriers of infection. We still live in towns and cities built on the ruins of past cities, and we still transport garbage, sewage, feces, and rubbish somewhere out of sight, counting ourselves lucky if we no longer have to look at it all.

To be sure, things smell less than they used to, but "good," unused air no longer exists on earth, full as it is of heavily populated areas that resemble army camps. In the end, air may prove the most crucial commodity in our struggle to survive. Water can be purified and extracted from the oceans, but our air supply is limited. All students should carry out the computation which shows them how small a molecule is, for this computation reveals the limits of our air supply. Sir Robert Robinson, who won the Nobel Prize for chemistry in 1947, used to say that when Shakespeare wrote the first line of the second act of Hamlet, he breathed once in and out. Since that time, wind and storms have mingled Shakespeare's breath with the rest of the air. Thus, when someone breathes in today, the air he breathes contains two molecules of the air which Shakespeare breathed out long ago.

This computation appears to be correct. We breathe air which has been breathed in and out countless times, just as we drink water that others have drunk before us and eat food which grew from soil whose humus grew from the remains of earlier generations. The earth has truly been lived in, and we ourselves are only recapitulations of organisms which lived in the past.

The richest scholar—an eccentric?

Let us spend a little more time examining the air which surrounds us, the atmosphere we breathe. We owe much of our knowledge about what air is to one of the strangest scholars the world has ever seen, Henry Cavendish. We know little more about his youth than the fact that he was born October 10, 1731, a member of English nobility. His father was Lord Charles Cavendish, and his sickly mother was the daughter of the Duke of Kent. After attending school, Cavendish entered Cambridge University without taking any preliminary examinations. He became a member of the Royal Society, and, after that, all we know about him is that he worked both weekdays and Sundays.

Today we would consider Cavendish eccentric. He inherited vast wealth, but he lived on a modest scale. He was unassuming in his dress, ate simple fare, and when he invited friends over, he fed them simple fare, too. His large scientific library was open to everyone. When he wanted to read a book, he signed out for it like everyone else. When he died February 24, 1810, a contemporary wrote an obituary notice saying that Cavendish was the richest scholar and probably the most scholarly of rich men. This tribute still appears to be true. Perhaps Cavendish simply had no sense of the value of money. When he heard that one of his former librarians was having a hard time, he stuttered in embarrassment, "What can I do? Will a check for £10,000 be enough?"

If Cavendish had published his results more frequently and faster, he would have gone down in scientific history as a much more important researcher. His most important work is probably *Experiments on Air,* published in 1784. The year before this he had described a eudiometer, an instrument for measuring the purity of the air. In four hundred experiments he determined that pure air contains 20.84% oxygen. Today, around two hundred years later, we consider air pure when it contains 20.94% oxygen. Cavendish's results have been improved by only one-tenth of one percent.

Cavendish also made another epochal discovery. He was the man who *proved* that James Watt was correct in thinking that water is composed of hydrogen and oxygen. It was Cavendish's assistant Blagden who told Lavoisier this fundamental fact in 1783, the fact for whose discovery Lavoisier took credit himself.

Fatal zeros

We know a great deal about our earth's atmosphere. We have divided it into layers, measured the chemical composition of these layers, recorded their temperatures, studied the influence of sunlight on chemical reactions which take place among the various components of the air, studied tidal effects, flown through the atmosphere in planes, and traveled through it in rockets to reach outer space. Thus, we ought to know enough to answer all possible questions about the atmosphere—but we do not.

For example, we desperately need to find out more about air pollution. Some of the numbers involved in the problem of air pollution contain a frightening number of zeros. These numbers are not frightening because of their size. We could choose larger units of measurement, such as the weight of a corresponding number of Eiffel towers instead of tons, and the numbers would have fewer zeros. No, the zeros are frightening because they make it clear that our knowledge is very uncertain, that we do not know the exact figures involved, and that we have to round numbers off to zero. We believe that each year all of nature, including man, emits 1,000,000,000,000 tons of material into the air. Some 500,000,000 tons of this material represent industrial waste products. This is not an especially large quantity, for it constitutes only .05% of the quantity of waste gas which nature introduces into the atmosphere.

We do not know exactly what substances in what quantities make up this .05%. It is impossible for us to compute the figures exactly. We know the air in large cities is very impure, full of noxious exhalations, but we cannot do anything about it. As long as we continue to live and work in cities, we continue to use and reuse the air, and this use does not improve it. An automobile emits exhaust fumes in the city just as it does in the country. Automobile emissions cause discomfort in the city because there is not enough fresh air available, and this in turn results from the fact that our cities are built like medieval cities and are not planned with the automobile in mind. As long as people believe that they must live and work in close proximity to their neighbors, they must be prepared to endure the dirt, garbage, and noise their neighbors create. There is enough room on earth so that we could be free of this discomfort, for the surface of the earth comprises 57,469,000 square miles.

Assuming that we wanted to inhabit only fifty percent of the most pleasant regions on earth, only three or four families would need to live on every square mile. If we made all the deserts and mountains habitable, human beings would be so thinly settled that they would have difficulty in finding each other. It will be some time before the earth becomes overpopulated. *We do not suffer from lack of space so much as from laziness.* Everyone wants to have a quantity of services performed for him, and this means that he wants to have his neighbors, who can perform these services, nearby!

A soft bed of mercury

On the other hand, of course, we should not fail to take environmental pollution seriously. Our organisms are complex and therefore very sensitive. Even minimal concentrations of certain substances can harm our metabolic and other bodily processes and result in illness and premature death. We react adversely to metals like lead, cadmium, and mercury, all three of which are present in sea water. The oceans, which contain enough gold to attract miners, contain more mercury than gold. However, the quantities of mercury present in sea water are still minute, and they pose no danger to humans.

Pure mercury, which is a liquid metal, has almost no poisonous effect. One can even play with it without ill effect. When a nurse attempted to commit suicide by injecting herself with ten cc of mercury, it did her no harm, and the liquid metal could be retrieved from her bloodstream. But air infected with mercury vapor in a closed room is poisonous, and many chemical compounds containing mercury are very dangerous. Yet human beings have shown little concern about the possible dangerous effects of mercury. The first chemist to be concerned about the harmful effects of mercury fumes was the German Alfred Stock, who contracted mercury poisoning in his laboratory. He established what kinds of chemical reactions occurred when mercury fumes mingled with the air. However, around the year 1000 it was considered particularly "chic" for Arab caliphs to fill ponds in their gardens with mercury. They spread pillows on the silver surface of the pond and peacefully rested on them. In their day no one worried about polluting the environment.

As long as it does not affect our comfort, we do not worry much about environmental pollution, either. For decades we have been heating buildings with coal and converting coal into electrical current, and no one seems concerned that this process creates and releases poisonous mercury fumes into the atmosphere. On an average, one ton of bituminous coal contains only three hundreds of an ounce of mercury, but it can contain over an ounce. This means that in the United States alone, 1,000 tons of mercury fumes are released into the air every year. A total of 3,000 tons of fumes enters the air every year from the world as a whole. Fortunately, the mercury does not remain in the air but finally disappears into the soil and bodies of water.

When the filth becomes visible

We usually do not mention or do anything about air pollution until the pollution reaches a high local concentration and causes some distress. And yet sometimes our reactions to pollution are irrational. For example, a battle has been raging over the presence of sulfur dioxide (SO_2) in the air. Sulfur dioxide is a colorless, pungent gas which develops in a variety of ways. It can be created by the burning of coal and oil, or by the chemical conversion of sulfur or sulfur compounds combined with oxygen. We can read in any chemistry book that this gas is poisonous. However, sulfur dioxide is by no means the only poisonous sulfur compound in our atmosphere! Nature itself releases into the air hydrogen sulfide, a colorless, poisonous, stinking gas, along with a vast number of other sulfur compounds. If we add up all the sulfur which nature releases into the atmosphere, it comes to around 220,000,000 tons of sulfur per year, or seven times as much as the 30,000,000 tons produced by world industry. In fact, half of the air pollution caused by sulfuric gases can be attributed to the hydrogen sulfide created by nature, and only one-third of it, at the most, is sulfur dioxide.

Another erroneous conclusion which people frequently draw about air pollution is that poisonous gases remain in the air and thus continue to increase in concentration. Actually, within a few days after they are created, all these gases have changed into sulfates, which are salts that are difficult to dissolve. Rain or snow washes them into the ground, they are incorporated by plants, which need sulfur, and they enter into the cycles of nature again.

We do not know exactly how many sulfur compounds exist in the upper levels of the earth's atmosphere. But we believe that the quantity of sulfur is small. If this is true, we can diagram the sulfur cycle of nature. (See diagram.)

Naturally, we can only estimate the various quantities shown in the diagram. Amazingly, the diagram shows that the natural production of sulfur is insufficient for our purposes and that we need additional sulfur compounds

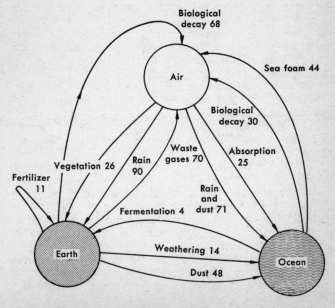

The sulfur cycle in nature. The numbers represent the annual turnover in millions of metric tons.

to serve as fertilizer. In particular, we need fertilizer to use in growing grasses, a group which includes all our grains. Nitrogen, phosphorus, and potassium alone cannot produce a good crop. If one day we succeed in eliminating the pollution of the air by sulfur dioxide, what will we use as a substitute for sulfur fertilizer, and how much money will the substitute cost us?

Wishes alone accomplish nothing

It is easy to wish for things, but we rarely think about the consequences of our wishes. We know very little about the true significance of air pollution, and it is all too easy to understand why. First, the concentrations of pollutants are usually minimal, and second, the earth's atmosphere is not like a laboratory, where it is easy for us to conduct experiments. Nevertheless, we must experiment, for computations and mental models can tell us only so much. Also, we cannot learn anything without taking the influence of the earth and the oceans into account. It seems impossible to design a realistic reconstruction of the manifold reciprocal influences of atmospheric pressure, moisture, movement, temperature, etc. in a laboratory.

We can easily draw up long lists of questions about air pollution which we would like to have answered. I will mention only a few.

1). Which air pollutants are absorbed by the oceans, and how and in what quantities does the absorption occur?

2). The atmospheric content of nitric oxides seems to derive from the oxidation of ammonia. How does this oxidation occur, and what quantities does it involve?

3). We know the source of methane (marsh gas) in the atmosphere, but what is the source of the other hydrocarbons? What percentage of the hydrocarbons emanates from forests?

We do not know the source of the astounding quantities of natural hydrocarbons, nor do we know where they are stored. They may serve a useful function in the cycles of nature, like ethylene, which is created by plants and which even in minimal concentrations helps fruit to ripen. Because we know so little about hydrocarbons, it is senseless to blame automobiles and filling stations for the hydrocarbon content of the air.

Once again, it seems amazing that we have hitherto devoted so little time to studying basic problems. *Have we neglected true research, the investigation of the world we live in, in favor of applied research,* the results of which are supposed to make our lives more pleasant and which we perhaps ought rather to call "comfort research"?

The great cycle

And what about other substances with which nature supplies us and which we consume? The narrow habitable layer around the earth is continually used as raw material. It undergoes a cycle that leads from the earth to plants to animals and men, and then it decays and returns to the earth, becoming raw material again. The topsoil, the place where life blooms, long ago turned into humus, the rotting remains of once-living organisms. We do not so much live "on the earth" as we do on a giant cemetery. The living organisms we see around us once formed a part of other organisms, formed part of their bodies, embodied beautiful or ugly, useful or useless creatures, were incorporated into their various organs, were eliminated during their lifetimes or decayed after their death.

We can be happy that organic matter is so quickly converted into a new form. Because it does so, it is ever new and for billions of years has served as the inexhaustible raw material of new life.

The inorganic matter produced by the earth is not so inexhaustible. We are mistaken if we believe that infinite quantities of this matter exist. We often imagine gigantic mountains of minerals to be embedded in the depths of the earth. But what is the source of the inorganic matter which we use? Unlike organic matter, which is swiftly replenished by the cycles of nature, mineral beds develop very slowly. Within a few decades organic matter once again stands ready for our use, but the natural cycle of rocks takes *millions* of years to complete.

Man has not for very long been concerned about mineral supplies, for his need for minerals used to be minimal. A man who makes a flint tool sees fields of flint before him and does not reflect that although he can break stones apart, he does not know any way to join them together again. During the approximately 2,000,000 years that primitive men made tools, they did not, in fact, use sizable quantities of minerals.

However, the situation changed with the advent of farming. This new technology, which marked the end of the age of hunters and gatherers, enabled people to live who did not procure their own food. Instead, these people could live in groups and practice a trade. They could form communities which later would grow into cities. The first cities grew where farming was easy and highly productive, in the climatically favorable zones along the banks of the Euphrates, the Nile, the Indus, and the Huang Ho.

With the advent of farming, men began to use comparatively large quantities of stone, clay, and various kinds of ore to build houses and monuments. The Tower of Babel may serve as a symbol of this period. Modern archaeologists have uncovered layer upon layer of structures built by different cultures. Thus, it is only too easy to understand why cities sometimes suffocated in their own filth. Mountains of debris, clay, dressed stone, baked ceramics, and glass testify to man's use of inorganic material that can never be replaced.

The exploitation of minerals

Strangely enough, copper was the first metal which man began to strip from the earth. Copper is relatively rare. Probably what made it seem so desirable was its splendid, glowing red color, the ease with which it could be processed, and its low smelting temperature. The demand for copper rapidly increased. It was not long before supplies of copper close to the large cities were exhausted. The Egyptians were soon compelled to travel long distances to search for the precious metal.

But then new, improved blast furnaces made it possible for men to smelt iron ore and obtain the hitherto unknown metal iron. In the past, iron had been known only in the form of iron meteorites (a nickel-iron alloy), a sort of divine gift from heaven. Iron was a fascinating metal. It shone with a silver glow, it was much harder and denser than copper, it was inexpensive, and inexhaustible quantities appeared to exist. Soon the new metal proved to be such a good value that even farmers could afford it. Its use became increasingly widespread.

The consumption of inorganic materials was still relatively small, but this was destined to change. What brought about the change was the disappearance of the large forests. For centuries wood had served as a source of energy, but then it began to be used in smelting and became rare and expensive. Could something be found to replace it? The English had burned their forests to smelt iron. Now what were they to do? They began to use coal and learned how coal could be used to produce iron. But in reality it was not the increasing production of iron which brought about "progress," but the possibility of using coal to create higher temperatures and greater quantities of energy than had been possible with wood.

The sun's energy, which was used to obtain salt from sea water, windmills, waterwheels, and firewood all produced small quantities of energy per unit of time. However, coal could accomplish much more. It could supply the energy needed to run steam engines! Coal, iron, and steam formed the basis of a new age. Once again man's spirit of invention, fired by necessity and by the desire for a more comfortable life, overcame limitations which no one had known even existed. To clarify this development, I will describe a prediction which someone once made about future economic conditions. This tale shows what happens when we make predictions without taking into account what human skills, reason, and research can accomplish.

Predictions which do not take research into account

In 1870, U.S. farmers had to rely almost exclusively on horses and mules to do their farmwork. For decades one horse or mule had served as the basis of energy needed to produce food for four people. In 1870 an economic expert would have predicted that by 1975 there would be 50,000,000 to 55,000,000 horses and mules in the United States. However, an engineer in 1870 would have realized that soon steam engines would influence the economy and that it was only a matter of time before they began to create energy for farm labor. Instead of predicting that the number of horses and mules would increase, he would have predicted their disappearance. On the other hand, neither an economist nor an engineer could have known that in a few years the internal combustion engine would render both horses and steam engines superfluous.

Technological and economic forecasts made for a period of more than five years are unqualified guesswork. The "oil crisis" of 1973 showed our generation how unrealistic economic forecasts can be.

The new energy sources—coal, oil, and natural gas— simplified the task of mining for minerals to a degree that a medieval miner could never have imagined. Now it was not only possible to realize men's dreams, but it became necessary to create new dreams so that people would use all that was produced. The artificial acceleration of consumption created a real danger, for the minerals we remove from the biosphere will disappear for a longer time than men will exist on earth!

The question of how men will manage the earth's supply of raw materials is a fundamental one, and scientists have attempted in various ways to find an answer. Perhaps the most pessimistic answer was that of an English minister. His theory is old and traditional; thus, people continue to be frightened by it and to discuss it. The English minister did not invent the theory. Other people arrived at the same conclusions before he did; in fact, he was accused of stealing the idea from them.

People often ignore the fact that this English minister, Thomas Robert Malthus (born February 17, 1766), was actually more concerned with problems like vice and misery, proverty and hunger than he was with the scientific and technological aspects of the future. He published his ideas in 1798, and his work reflects the impression which he as an Englishman had gained of the horrors of the French Revolution. His theory was this: the optimistic belief that humanity can become better and free itself of vice and misery is doomed to disappointment, for human beings multiply faster than their sources of sustenance.

Today some people still believe in this theory and foresee horrible periods of famine. But are they and Malthus really correct? Malthus's theory was based on statistics describing the increase in the population and the stasis in food production. He did not suspect that the prairies of North America would be turned into fruitful fields of wheat or that new species of plants and animals would be developed which would produce high yields. In his time artificial fertilizer and new farming techniques were unknown. If he had had more imagination, he would surely have been less pessimistic. Or would he have feared the future even more?

In Malthus's day many people—especially young mothers, infants, and small children—died young, and medical skills were less highly developed than they are today. Now medicine helps to preserve human life to a degree which Malthus never imagined possible. Malthus also failed in another respect to foresee what science would accomplish. He did not believe in "'moral restraint," in the possibility of keeping people from having too many children. We who are alive today, on the other hand, know that the pill and other forms of birth control can help to prevent overpopulation.

Malthus impresses us as a shrewd thinker, a philospher who thought about the future but who did not know what man's intellect and inventiveness could accomplish.

Thus far Malthus's predictions have not come true, and it remains to be seen whether they will come true in the future. The fact that we cannot answer this question right now shows how little we know about the world. Every time we hear of a famine, we remember his words. Nevertheless, over a period of thousands of years, whenever it was necessary, man has always devised means of preserving his species and even of improving his existence. Even the catastrophic famines of history,

    1770: 10,000,000 dead in India,
    1877: 10,000,000 dead in China,
    1918: 5,000,000 dead in Russia,

have not proved Malthus correct.

Nevertheless, all of us sense that someday the life of man on earth will come to an end and that his end may be long and bitter.

Chapter Thirteen

FACT AND FANCY

The cosmic accident

ONE DAY human beings will become extinct just as other species have become extinct before them. Anyone who denies this is either ignorant of the facts or afraid to confront them. The question is: What will bring about the end of mankind? A disease, a cosmic force . . . or the nature of man himself, his indomitable drive for power and prosperity, the struggle of men against men, their innate envy of each other?

We do not know when, how, or why the human race will perish. However, probably it will not die from the effects of atomic explosions, for these explosions will not appreciably change the earth. Radioactivity may sometimes be increased by the use of nuclear weapons or the breakdown of nuclear reactors, but there is no real threat of wide-scale disasters. As terrible as the consequences were when atomic bombs were dropped on Hiroshima and Nagasaki, these consequences were limited in scope, and the truly remarkable thing about the bomb dropped on Hiroshima was the fact that human beings permitted a second bomb to be dropped after they saw the results of the first.

Human beings have not changed since Hiroshima; thus, we must expect similar disasters to occur in the future. For example, we should remember what happened to the *Happy Dragon,* a Japanese fishing boat, in 1954. The boat was surprised by radioactive fallout from an atomic-bomb test in the Pacific. Most of the crew died after a long illness. We should also recall the U.S. bomber which "lost" a hydrogen bomb in 1966 off the coast of southern Spain, and the bomber which crashed in Thule, Greenland with four hydrogen bombs on board. However, even if such accidents exploded the weapons on board the planes, the results would be comparatively insignificant.

It is the forces of nature which could present us with unexpected danger. The American Nobel Prize winner Harold C. Urey has theorized that a cosmic collision such as the collision of a comet with the earth has always brought an end to geological eras on this planet. Moreover, Urey has attempted to compute the probable consequences of such a collision. For example, he has taken into account the fact that the severity of a collision depends on the speed at which the colliding objects are traveling. (Everyone who drives a car knows that this is so.) The earth travels at exactly 18.5 miles per second. The speed of a comet can be as much as 26.1 miles per second. Thus, a direct frontal collision between the two would involve a speed of 44.6 miles per second.

If the comet grazes the earth, the speed involved may be only 7.6 miles per second. If the comet sideswipes the earth, the speed at the moment of collision must be estimated as lying somewhere between 44.6 and 7.6 miles per second. Urey believes that on an average this speed would be around 28 miles per second. The next question is: How heavy is the comet which strikes the earth? We do not know the answer to this question, and thus we must estimate it as well as we can.

Halley's comet appears regularly in the sky. Men have known about this comet since 466 B.C., and we will see it again in 1985–86. Urey has been guided by Halley's comet in his estimate of the weight of comets. In his computation he accords the comet a weight (mass) of 1,000,-000,000,000 tons. This sounds like a great weight, but if we convert it into cubic miles of water, it comprises "only" 300 cubic miles. However, a comet might easily possess a mass 1,000 times greater than this.

Urey estimates the energy which will be created by the collision between the earth and a comet at 10^{31} ergs. An erg is a minute quantity of energy whose meaning it is difficult for non-physicists to grasp. The thirty-one zeros involved in this estimate need not be written out, for they

Nobel Prize winner Harold C. Urey at a scientific conference.

would not help to make the number comprehensible. However, we can understand this number better if we think of how hot the sun is in the summer. The quantity of energy which the sun radiates to the earth in one year, thereby giving life to animals and plants, is about three and a half times the quantity of energy which would be created by a collision betweeen a comet and the earth!

The number 10^{31} ergs is still not very graphic, but if we examine what this quantity of energy can accomplish, its meaning becomes clearer. This amount of energy could raise the temperature of the earth's atmosphere by 190° C and raise the temperature of a five-meter-thick layer of ocean by 5° C. It could cause a cube of water forty-six miles on a side to evaporate. It could cause 500,000 earthquakes with a strength of nine on the seismic scale to shake the earth. Moreover, this quantity of energy is two times strong enough to tear away the earth's atmosphere.

The different effects I have mentioned would occur to different degrees depending on whether the comet struck the ocean or the land. No matter what the combination of effects, the results would be apocalyptic in scope. Let us examine the possible consequences of a collision between a comet and the earth.

The end of the world?

The first effect would be earthquakes, which would be felt all over the earth no matter what the circumstances of the collision. Earthquake waves would roll over the earth's crust and in some places would meet and intensify each other's power. Smaller quakes would occur for a long time to come. All tall buildings would collapse. Avalanches and landslides would choke vast regions with rubble. Cracks would open in the earth and fill up with water, creating lakes and rivers and changing the courses of rivers which already exist. Urey believes that the collision would activate volcanic forces and cause giant rivers of lava to pour out of the depths of the earth.

The higher temperatures would make it impossible for men and animals to breathe. Plants with leaves would wither, although the seeds of certain plant species might survive. Reptiles, snakes, crocodiles, and lizards which live in the water may also have a chance to survive. Beetles and ants and other creatures which live beneath the earth's surface would not necessarily be doomed. If they survived the shock of the earthquakes, were not buried under mud and volcanic ash, did not drown in the floods of water, and could continue to find food, they might preserve their species.

If the comet crashed into an ocean, the continents would be flooded, and few living creatures would survive the catastrophe, except animals and plants that could live in salt water.

All myths about the end of the world and the twilight of the gods pale in comparison with the reality of a genuine cosmic catastrophe. Not only would human beings vanish from the earth, but there would be only just enough living things left to keep the earth from becoming a dead planet. These creatures might be the start of a new evolutionary chain.

Is this description sheer fantasy, a fantasy designed to terrify us, or will the events it evokes come to pass? Have similar events taken place in the past?

Urey considers it possible that such cosmic catastrophes have taken place not once, but several times. He even has some evidence which may suggest that this is true! The evidence involves the so-called tektites, droplets of dark, gray-green glass the length of a finger, shaped like teardrops or dumbbells. They are only found in large fields containing masses of them. For example, in Brünn, in western Slovakia, there are such quantities of tektites that they are made into glass jewelry. What created these masses of glass ("tektite" comes from the Greek *tektos,* meaning molten), and why are they found only in certain clearly defined areas of the earth?

Scientists spent decades trying to unravel the mystery of these strange droplets of glass. Today most agree that when large meteorites struck the earth, they melted the stone at the point of impact, and drops of this molten stone spurted long distances away. The tektites which are found near Brünn must have come from the region where the town of Nördlingen is situated today—that is, they must have traveled through the air for a distance of around four hundred kilometers!

How could the drops of glass have flown such distances through the air without cooling off? Their form shows that when they landed on the earth they were still in a semi-liquid state. Urey has supplied an answer to this riddle. When meteorites strike the earth, the air becomes so hot that the tektites do not cool as quickly as it had originally been assumed they would. Moreover, Urey's computations suggest that the energy created by the impact is sufficient to compress the air and to send the glowing tektites flying through a vacuum.

Periods of the earth's history

However, Urey wanted to establish more than this. His comet theory is designed to explain something which has always been a source of embarrassment to geologists: the reason why certain geological epochs come to an end and other epochs begin. Urey considers it possible that the collision between a comet and the earth instituted each new epoch. He links the age of tektite fields, which can be dated fairly exactly, with the various geological epochs. (See diagram.)

Age in millions of years	Tektite fields	Geological epoch
		Pleistocene
.7 to 1.2	Australia Ivory Coast	
		Pliocene
14.7	Brünn	
		Miocene
25	Libyan glass	
		Oligocene
36	U.S.A. (south)	
		Eocene

Reading from the bottom up, the timetable states that around 36,000,000 years ago, during the Eocene epoch (the time when the older type of lignite was formed), a large cosmic object, possibly a comet, fell to earth. The collision concluded this geological epoch. Now the Oligocene epoch began, when the younger type of lignite was formed. The earth today would still be much as it was then, covered with the forests of the lignite epoch, if another collision had not occurred 11,000,000 years later and shaken the earth to its foundations. As proof that this event occurred, Urey cites the pieces of yellowish glass (they are not considered genuine tektites) found in the Libyan Desert.

Once again disaster struck the earth. New geological conditions developed, the conditions which geologists consider typical of the Miocene epoch. The subtropical temperatures which had caused the forests of the Oligocene to flourish disappeared and other plants replaced these forests. Then another heavenly body—perhaps the one which struck Nördlingen, for they are about the same age—ended the Miocene epoch, and the Pliocene began. Finally, another collision ended this epoch, and the various ice ages began to come and go.

What Urey suggests is less a theory than a hypothesis. It challenges us to think about a certain possibility. Is it true that a comet periodically collides with the earth? No one knows exactly what cosmic phenomena are involved, how they arise, where they come from, and when new comets, if comets they are, may appear. These bodies must somehow be related to meteorites or asteroids. Our planet whirls in space, apparently unchanging. We tend to imagine that for at least several hundred million years its climate and surface have remained the same. But this is not the case, for the geology of the earth changes again and again.

Why does this happen? We do not know why particular geological conditions have succeeded each other on the earth, and no one can predict what the next geological period will be like. Scientists are still debating the question of whether we are facing another period of cold. Until we learn more about the periodic geological transformations of the earth, we will continue to suspect that they may be caused by cosmic forces; and until we know that they are incorrect, Urey's theories will continue to stimulate discussion.

The cosmic ice theory

Naturally, scientific debates sometimes stimulate eccentrics like the devotees of the cosmic ice theory. When they heard that comets were probably composed of "dirty snow"—in other words, that they were made of ice, cosmic dust (micrometeoric material), and frozen gas—certain people devised bold theories of their own.

On November 20, 1860, Hanns Hörbiger was born in Atzendorf, in southern Austria. When he died on October 11, 1931, in Mauer, near Vienna, just a few weeks before his seventieth birthday, he could look back on a successful life. He had two sons who were on their way to becoming famous actors, his work as a mechanical engineer had prospered, and he had invented a new type of ventilator.

However, Hörbiger did not confine his inventive spirit to ventilators. Around 1910, scientists were discussing something that they still do not know enough about, the rings around the planet Saturn. The first man to see them was probably Galileo, who glimpsed two "handles" at the edge of the planet. The engineer Hörbiger thought a lot about the rings around Saturn, and he began to wonder whether they might not be made of ice. Believing that he had discovered the key to unlock countless mysteries, he concocted a bold theory. He said that the inner planets of our solar system—Mercury, Venus, the earth, and Mars—are made of heavy stone, but the outer planets are principally composed of ice. He also believed that there was ice on the moon's surface. Comets, he thought, were likewise composed of ice, and were, in fact, "ice planetoids."

Scientists were annoyed by Hörbiger's cosmic ice theory and showed how the theory conflicted with scientific observations of heavenly bodies. For example, they said, how could comets shine as brightly as they did if they were made of ice? As far as we can tell, Hörbiger was correct in his theory about comets, but unless the furrows in the moon's surface were caused by ice meteorites, he was completely wrong about the ice on the moon. However, if a non-scientist constructs a theory that is comprehensive enough, some of it is bound to turn out to be correct: thus, the theory appears to be prophetic.

The cosmic ice theory shows how tenacious scientific speculations can be. Devised in 1912, it survived the first and second World Wars. In May, 1971, devotees of the theory began to publish the *Reports of the Hörbiger Institute* again. They had ceased to publish this periodical when the Allies invaded France in the summer of 1944, when no more paper was available for scientific periodicals.

The hollow-earth theory

The hollow-earth theory, a comical notion which may still have its secret adherents, persisted even longer than the cosmic ice theory. We know exactly when the theory was devised. On April 10, 1818, a letter was sent to the members of the U.S. Congress and several scholars. It stated that it was addressed to the entire world, and the author declared that the earth was hollow and that its interior was habitable.

The presumptuous author of this letter was an off-duty infantry captain, J. C. Symnes. He believed that we would find an entrance into the earth at the poles. If he has been correctly understood, he believed that the ten lost tribes of Israel were living inside the earth. Apparently we must imagine his hollow earth as being like a pasteboard globe. One can live on the outside, but there is a hole at the poles, and if one walks through one finds another earth "surface" inside.

Thus far no one has found the holes leading into the interior of the earth. Nevertheless, the hollow-earth theory has been expanded upon. A man named Bender, who apparently seized on this insane notion while he was a prisoner of war in France during World War I. With German thoroughness he incorporated recent scientific discoveries into the hollow-earth theory. He concluded that we live in a bubble inside the stone composing the earth. In the middle of the bubble float the moon and the sun and something which gives us the illusion of living in a universe filled with stars. When this thing moves between us and the sun, we experience night. Not long ago there were people who did not consider the hollow-earth theory completely incredible. This fact confirms the statement of the Count of Schlabrendorff that "Humanity should be named Stupidity."

Tall tales?

The legend of the Trojan War, recorded in the form of a poem, seems spurious, indeed. After all, the poem describes how the gods themselves intervened in the struggle. However, in essence this 3,000-year-old account of war, victory, misery, and death proved accurate.

No one dares to exclude the possibility that one day Siegfried's Nibelung treasure may be found.

The gold country of "Ophir," where Solomon sent his servants and from which they supposedly brought back around 4,400 pounds of gold, has been found. It lies in Africa, opposite the southern tip of Madagascar. Anyone who wants to can see the old mines there.

The Babylonian tower, which is not only mentioned in the Bible but also described by Herodotus, did not reach to heaven, but it was so large that archaeologists have been able to excavate its remains.

Marco Polo's account of the Far East and particularly of the life, manners, and customs of China (Polo lived from 1254 to 1324 in Venice) was for a long time considered sheer fabrication, but every line of it has been proved true.

For a long time it was believed that the tale that the Vikings had discovered America around 1000 A.D. was false. However, it has now been proved true.

No geologist doubts that there may be a core of truth to the biblical tale of Sodom and Gomorrah. The Dead Sea is a branch of the Red Sea, the trench which is opening up and separating Africa from Asia. Forces inside the earth are active in this region. Glowing volcanic ash which stank of sulfur may easily have covered the area. Earthquakes, gas eruptions, cloud-forming fumaroles, and splitting rocks and mountains may have produced the effects described in the Bible. Probably what we read in the nineteenth chapter of Genesis is, in fact, a description of volcanic forces at work:

Then the Lord rained upon Sodom and upon
Gomorrah
brimstone and fire from the Lord out of heaven . . .
and, lo, the smoke of the country went up as the
smoke of a furnace.

—Genesis 19:24–28

Atlantis

Plato, the great Greek philosopher who lived in Athens from 427 to 347 B.C., left us an account of Atlantis, but experts disagree as to its accuracy. The real name of the Athenian noble we know as "Plato" ("the wide") was Aristocles. He could hardly have been the friend of contemporary democracy, for the people of Athens had voted by democratic process that his friend and teacher Socrates be forced to drink a cup of hemlock. (The vote was two hundred eighty to two hundred twenty.) Plato is known as a moral philosopher and mathematician. After the legal murder of his teacher, he traveled widely. In the *Critias* dialogue (Critias was Plato's uncle) he writes about a strange legend, apparently ancient, which supposedly derives from Egypt.

The legend of Atlantis suggests that a wealthy island once lay beyond the "pillars of Hercules" (the Straits of Gibraltar). At one time the people of the island attempted to conquer the lands of the Mediterranean. Their island was only about twenty kilometers in diameter, but it was rich in temples, golden statues, etc. Later it is supposed to have sunk beneath the sea in a single day.

Ever since Plato wrote about Atlantis, it has stirred men's imaginations. What was its location? Treasure-hunters, historians, geographers, and visionaries have repeatedly gone in search of this legendary land. They were convinced that it lay in Africa, in North or South America, along the coasts of Greenland, in Korea, or even deep in the heart of Asia. Around 1950 a German minister believed that he had discovered Atlantis east of Helgoland on the floor of the North Sea. We do not know when and where the next "discovery" will take place or when another adventurer will come along who completely misunderstands Plato. The fact is that Plato was a political theorist; thus, his edifying dialogue may have been nothing but a political and moral fiction which might benefit our age if we would take the trouble to understand it.

Everyone knows that wealthy trading centers often develop on islands, and that islands are sometimes flooded and even sink beneath the sea. Legends about such islands are widespread. For example, there is the legend of Vineta. In the case of Atlantis, a philosopher simply made one of these legends into an edifying story.

What has driven men to search for Atlantis is the same unbridled flight of imagination which led to the creation of the hollow-earth theory. When scientists do not know enough about a subject, imaginative and credulous men concoct pseudoscientific mobiles which sparkle and turn and catch the eye until they are covered by dust and end up in the rubbish heap of time.

The philosophers' stone

Naturally, there is nothing new about theories like those involving the hollow earth and Atlantis. False prophets, charlatans, and lovable cranks have always existed in abundance. This is especially true in the field of science, for in science great labor often produces few results, and frequently the true value of these results is not immediately recognized. A case in point is that of the alchemists.

Originally the alchemists were not deceitful makers of gold who were interested in obtaining riches. In fact, there is some doubt as to whether medieval men who claimed to be able to make gold should be considered alchemists at all. The origin of alchemy was the struggle *to understand* the world. The inhabitants of the Mediterranean region were not satisfied with their traditional religions, and so some of them fell prey to specious thinking. They reasoned as follows: we do not know enough, but in the past, gods, prophets, and "the ancients" possessed extensive knowledge, and we must rediscover it. Thus they searched for old writings, sometimes forged them, invented imaginary people, twisted historical data, misunderstood commonplace facts, founded secret societies, and ended up far from their original goals. One alchemical formula reads as follows:

> Take quicksilver, as much as is necessary,
> put it in the vessel you know about,
> cook it in the way you know how,
> add the substance of which you have heard
> in the quantity mentioned
> this is the secret of the fixation of quicksilver.

The alchemists' search was philosophical and mystical in nature. They believed in the existence of a "tincture" which conferred health, youth, and strength on men. Some of them searched for the famous "philosophers' stone." There was no end to the things they believed the stone could accomplish. Above all, they believed that it could confer power and knowledge on its possessor. It linked everything in the world and related all things to each other. When modern chemists speak of certain elements and substances as "related," they are unconsciously perpetuating alchemical conceptions.

The prototype of the alchemist is Arnaldus of Villanova (c. 1240–1319). Famous and infamous, adventurer and physician, denounced as a heretic and a revolutionary, he served as instructor of medicine and alchemy in Barcelona, was the court physician of the King of Aragon, traveled in France and Italy, and turned against the Roman Catholic Church. Despite his attitude toward the Church, he was consulted by Pope Clement V. He died on a sea voyage. Besides knowing a great deal about chemistry and alchemy, he appears to have been the man who taught people to cure goiter with iodine.

His pupil was Raymond Lully (1235–1315), whose grave may be visited by travelers to Palma, Mallorca. (Another monument to Lully stands in the harbor.) Lully loved traveling as much as his teacher. He even traveled as far as Palestine and Armenia and was always concerned with converting heathens. He promised the King of Scotland and England the philosophers' stone and was housed in the Tower, where he worked at making gold. He was finally slain by pagans in Tunis.

The alchemists were extraordinary men. With boundless passion they devoted their strength, their wealth, and their lives to bringing all known substances, thoughts, ideas, and moral concepts into touch with each other. Amazingly, alchemy continued to flourish for centuries, winning new devotees from all levels of society.

Our modern belief in scientific "progress" may be no more than a pale imitation of the adventurous attitude of our alchemist forebears. Considering the stormy, "revolutionary" role which science played in the past, we live in an age of peaceful development. Modern science changes material circumstances more than it does intellectual attitudes.

What did this mystical and religious and yet so earthly "science" of alchemy really accomplish?

The alchemists assembled an astounding number of facts about chemistry, including an exact description of the element antimony and less exact information about acids, the effects of heat, and other matters. The trades profited from alchemy, too, when alchemists developed the art of manufacturing porcelain and ruby glass. However, more important from the scientific point of view was the fact that the alchemists learned to experiment. Before their fireplaces they worked with crucibles and tongs and instruments of glass and clay. They understood the arts of distillation and sublimation, they understood the importance of mixing the correct amounts of various substances together, and they knew not only that it was necessary to maintain certain temperatures while performing certain processes, but also how to create and maintain such temperatures. They developed the retort, an instrument used in distillation, to such a degree that today it is the symbol of chemistry.

That there were charlatans and gold-makers among the alchemists means little, for even today dishonest people sometimes pass themselves off as scientists. And in the end, there is not much difference between trying to make gold for some potentate and accepting money to carry out a less than honorable scientific project for some government.

Stone Age computer

Some historians of primitive cultures believe that we do not know a great deal more about science than our ancestors did. For example, Alexander Thom, professor emeritus of Oxford University, spent years investigating how much Stone Age farmers knew about astronomy. Among other things he studied and surveyed the great stone monuments in the area of Carnac, Brittany. He

One of the most massive of stone monuments is the menhir of Dol, in Brittany. It is 9.3 meters high, and we do not know how deeply it is sunk into the ground. Reportedly, the rock sinks the width of one finger every one hundred years, and when it has disappeared, the Last Judgment will begin. (Photograph by F. Boschke)

believes that the large granite blocks serve as a sort of gigantic astronomical computer 3.5 miles wide. If he is right, this would mean among other things that Stone Age lunar astronomers possessed knowledge of astronomy and geometry which they could not actually have possessed until 3,000 years later.

Moreover, those Stone Age men dressed in furs would have had to been able to make more exact measurements than we can make with a measuring tape. They must have made their measurements with an oaken surveyor's rod or a whale bone. Certainly at that time bodies of scientific experts must have existed that tended to the business of establishing a unified system of measurement; for apparently a Stone Age linear measure of 32.7 inches was used for all the stone monuments all the way between France and the Orkney Islands. This kind of international cooperation must have enabled the Stone Age scientists to set up the great menhir east of Carnac which has now been split open, but which was originally more than sixty-five feet tall and weighed around three hundred fifty tons.

The upright stones of Stone Age monuments are sometimes arranged in circles. The stones themselves are massive and somewhat rounded. Sometimes a circle consists of just half a dozen giant stones. Occasionally double or even triple circles rise from the landscape. At Stonehenge there are several circles, the outer circle consisting of smaller rocks, the next of larger, and the inner circle of giant stones. There is also a ring of holes where poles may or may not once have stood. When so many rings are present, one can connect the different stones and holes by 1,000 or 10,000 imaginary lines. To our generation is left the task of computing along which of these lines the sun rose or the moon set in 1,500 B.C. Many people have interpreted Stonehenge as a Stone Age astronomical observatory. In recent decades, when men succeeded in building computers, someone soon claimed that the stone circles at Stonehenge represent a "neolithic computer." Surely the next time we make an important discovery, we will decide that Stonehenge really served some other purpose.

At a certain point the erecting of stone monuments seems to have become fashionable. It appears that the custom may have begun in Iran around the middle of the

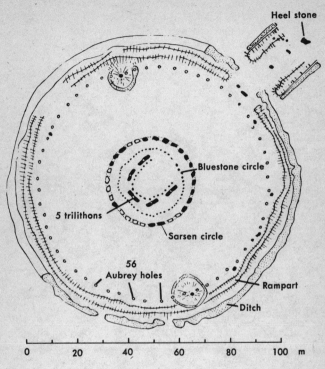

Ground plan of Stonehenge. Is it a Stone Age computer? An astronomical observatory? A fortification? A place of sacrifice?

Ship-shaped arrangements of stone in northern Denmark.
(Photograph by F. Boschke)

third millennium before Christ. From there it spread across Europe and the rest of Asia so that stone monuments, menhirs, and stone circles are known from the Hebrides to Sicily and from Spain to Japan and Korea. A fanatical, obsessive desire to build must have driven men to erect these landmarks. The giant squared stones at the center of Stonehenge are estimated to weigh around 2,500 tons. About fifteen miles north of Stonehenge lies a similar stone circle which travel guides rarely show to tourists, the monument of Avebury. Is it a second Stone Age computer?

Pretty pictures

Among the most intriguing creations of primitive societies are the pictures scratched in the ground in southern Peru. Scientists freely admit that they do not understand the purpose of these pictures.

As geometrical constructions, the pictures scratched in the plain of Rio Grande de Nazca y Palpa are related to the stone circles and other stone monuments of Europe. But what we find in Peru far surpasses simple geometrical forms. We see the outline of a bird four hundred twenty feet long. We also see other strange animals which may be dogs or apes. These creatures are equipped with large hands or paws, with four or five extended fingers. As a rule, the lines of the drawings are straight and overly long, as if the painters of the pictures had never seen them from above and did not know what they were producing. Only the picture of a spider with a thick, rounded rear is drawn in something approaching normal proportions.

These pictures recall the earth pictures in England, the "white horse of Uffington," three hundred ninety feet long, the "long man of Wilmington," in Sussex, two hundred feet tall, and the "giant of Cerne Abbas" in Dorset, one hundred eighty feet tall. In England the green grass was removed to reveal the white, chalky ground underneath, but the people of the Peruvian Nazca culture (c. 300–900 A.D.) removed dark stones from the ground creating light-colored lines which have been preserved by the desert-like climate.

What moved large communities in England and Peru

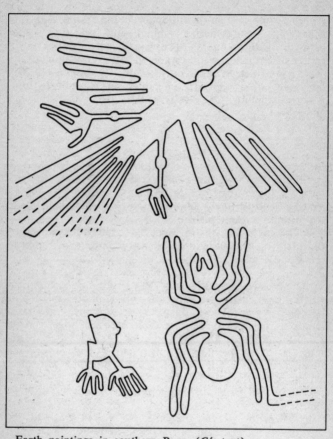

Earth paintings in southern Peru. (*Cf.* text)

to create these extraordinary figures? Did they want to decorate the ground? Were their pictures, like cave and rock paintings, designed to confer success in hunting? Or was it simply pleasure in discovering a large, empty space which impelled them to fill it with pictures? And why are the pictures so large? They are so big that they are visible in totality only from the air. (Incidentally, during World War II the English had to camouflage their primitive rock paintings so that they would not be used to orient enemy planes.)

Baroque gardeners were also driven by the urge to create pictures in the landscape. This urge seems innate to man. The first inhabitants of North America created bas-relief figures out of earth. Before grave robbers, farmers, and amateur archaeologists destroyed them, there must have been thousands of effigy mounds in the Mississippi and Ohio valleys. Just as straight lines are characteristic of the pictures in Peru, curving lines characterize the close to 5,000 effigy mounds in the state of Wisconsin. Spirals, serpents, round bears, and numerous other animals can be found on these mounds. In Colorado we find ground drawings of human beings up to ninety feet in length. They are badly proportioned figures, with long, thin legs, thick, swollen knee joints, short bodies, long necks, and tiny heads. The arms are stretched wide. The images look like the pictures children paint in the first grade.

Silbury Hill, near Marlborough, a round hill of earth one hundred thirty feet high, may be related to these pictures. It was constructed around 1,000 B.C., and the Roman occupation army in Britain had to build their road around it. It resembles the other phenomena I have mentioned in that no one knows why it was built.

We should avoid trying to read meanings into earth mounds, prehistoric graves, menhirs, dolmens, pyramids, or circles of stone. Any interpretation of ours would be sheer nonsense, for we live in another time and hold a different view of the world. Instead of trying to interpret these phenomena, let us look at the image of an early Aztec astronomer. The picture is not really old (1550 to 1553), but it constitutes an early example of the scientific investigation of nature. A peaceful and serene observer is seen gazing at the night sky without the aid of a telescope, quadrants, or a stone monument. He is a reflective, wise man observing the stars. (See illustration.)

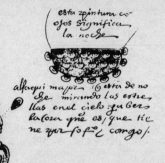

Aztec astronomer observing the night sky (from the Codex Mendoza). (From G. Lanczkowski, *Aztekische Sprache und Überlieferung*, Springer Verlag, 1970)

The belief in UFO's

As long as science has nothing definite to tell us about the origin of "landscape art," we may assume that the creators of these "art works" were moved by a childlike joy in creation. Those who desire more complex interpretations may concoct as many theories as they choose, but it is absurd to link landscape art with the visits of extra-terrestrial beings and cosmic space travelers.

It would be more profitable to listen to people who believe in the existence of UFO's or flying saucers. (UFO stands for "unidentified flying object.") These people collect and seek to interpret reported sightings. For the most part, the sightings are of meteorological or astronomical phenomena. However, some strange things have been observed for which we have not yet found a scientific explanation. The subject of UFO's deserves some attention, for there is a chance, albeit a minimal one, that they may involve a new phenomenon. How else could scientists learn about the world than by observing new phenomena and asking what caused them? And naturally non-scientists, as well as scientists, can observe new phenomena.

It is absurd to believe that flying saucers or UFO's could visit earth with a crew similar to humans in their shape, their knowledge of technology, and their moral concepts. Quite apart from the technical difficulties involved in such a flight, the time factor would prevent beings resembling us from coming to earth. We would be happy to talk with aliens who have reached our level of development, beings with whom we could exchange knowledge. However, we have little interest in the sort of creatures which lived on earth 1,000,000 years ago. Moreover, humanoid beings whose evolution was 1,000,000 years more advanced than our own would be even less interested in us than we would be in the creatures of our remote past. To them we would be little more than primitive, "early" life forms. Aliens and earth people could devote themselves to studying each other only if their levels of development were no more than around 1,000 years apart. Only then could they understand each other, engage in a fruitful exchange of ideas, and examine problems common to them both.

The next point in the universe where beings similar to humans might exist may lie thousands of light-years away! The hope that the beings who live there have the same interests as ourselves, that we could understand each other, and that it would be worthwhile to visit each other is nonsense from the point of view of both parties. Extraterrestrial UFO's do not visit the earth. Even if we and an alien civilization wanted to "talk" by radio on the famous twenty-one-centimeter band which extends through the universe, it would be a strange accident indeed if the radio signals we sent and received arrived when the alien culture was at approximately the same level of development as our own!

Are we living in a zoo?

In 1959 and 1973 scientists searched for signals from space on the twenty-one-centimeter band, but they searched in vain. No matter which stars were tested, we found no signal which might have been sent by alien "men." If we assume that intelligent life exists near one of these stars, the results of the experiment are even more depressing, for this would mean that the aliens have advanced so far technologically that they consider us primitive and have no interest in communicating with us. On the other hand, the aliens may be unable to communicate on this wave length because they are less advanced technologically than we are. One way or the other, these aliens would not be our partners in the universe. Or is there some reason why they are deliberately refusing to speak with us?

A Harvard student who had apparently read a great deal of science fiction suggested that we might be living in some sort of galactic zoo. Have members of a highly advanced civilization been living in our galaxy for some time, and have they assigned our solar system the role of a national park? Are the scientists who run this zoo conducting an experiment in "the Behavior of Life Forms in the Galaxy," and do they refuse to let themselves be seen because they do not want to disrupt the normal course of the experiment? Are we a species of wild animal which the aliens do not speak to, but only observe?

All this sounds slightly insane, but scientific periodicals contain many references to the idea. And isn't what the Bible tells us a variation on this idea? So, now everything is created, get out of the breeding place (Paradise), and let us see what you make of yourselves! The notion that we are living in a cage in a zoo or a natural preserve, or vegetating like an experimental animal, is so depressing that it challenges us to do something to counteract the experiment. We must somehow sow the seeds of life outside this zoo and inject the "dead" universe around us with living creatures.

We almost have the opportunity to do that now! Around the year 2000 a small spaceship powered by nuclear energy and carrying various sorts of microorganisms may be sent to a distant planet in our galaxy to sow the seeds of new life. This sounds like science fiction, but scientists have actually talked about doing it!

Many things about this plan seem logical. Microorganisms are not only small and light, but they need little nourishment. For example, all that blue-green algae need is carbon dioxide, water, and sunlight. Or perhaps we could freeze the microorganisms for their cosmic journey. At a temperature of 0°C, algae might possibly be protected and conserved for 1,000,000 years.

Even if the spaceship traveled at a moderate speed, in 1,000,000 years the living cargo could travel quite a distance. But where would they go? Scientists have an idea about this, too. They would have to send the microorganisms to a planet similar to the earth, or the organisms could not begin to evolve into human beings. The astronomers who are discussing the project have suggested that the microorganisms be sent to one of the planets of the Barnard star. This star appears to fulfill all the necessary conditions and possesses two planets similar to the earth.

The Barnard star is 30,000,000,000,000 miles away; thus, in astronomical terms it is very close, but it is still far enough away so that we could sow life there. If the plan is carried out, the man who discovered the Barnard star, astronomer Edward Emerson Barnard, will have another claim to fame. The Barnard star, a star of the tenth magnitude, is famous only because it "rocks" in the sky. The planets which orbit the star cause it to describe small ellipses along the path of its flight.

Proof awakens doubts

But let us return to those UFO sightings which contemporary scientists cannot explain. We should keep one thing in mind: the fact that we cannot explain these sightings *today* does not mean that we will not be able to do so in another five or fifty years. Moreover, our theories may not involve extraterrestrial visitations or other fantastic explanations. We should think back to all the things which seemed inexplicable fifty years ago, things which we now understand in detail. Perhaps we do not know enough about physics to understand UFO's. How much will we know in the year 2000 or in 2100? However, we should realize that if it is possible for us to send spaceships bearing microorganisms deep into space, it may be possible for alien cultures to do the same thing. Thus, the number of people who believe that UFO's may exist continues to multiply.

Some UFO sightings have actually been photographed. These photographs are of doubtful value, because it is easy to tamper with photographs. An unclear photograph can easily be "improved on." When someone tampers with a photograph, his eyewitness account is valueless, too.

Radar has also recorded UFO's. Most of these radar sightings occurred in the Fifties. Anyone who knows anything about the development of radar instrumentation during that period will realize that such sightings do not really prove anything.

The most convincing evidence of the existence of UFO's lies in the statements of eyewitnesses. On the other hand, every lawyer knows that witnesses are capable of making mistakes.

In a few cases sightings of UFO's have also been confirmed by radar. For example, a UFO was sighted in England in 1956. A radar station recorded the object for almost an hour, and it was also observed by the pilot of a fighter plane. Military personnel on the ground also claimed to have seen the UFO. In September, 1957, U.S. Air Force radar technicians observed a UFO while engaged in a military exercise. One pilot saw a "giant, glowing white ball." This and similar accounts may offer a key to the superstitious belief in UFO's. Perhaps many sightings were made by military personnel because the objects they saw were, in fact, military in nature.

Whether they are military vehicles or new experimental machines, there is nothing miraculous about UFO's. They are not spaceships from distant stars, but terrestrial objects. In fact, they are exactly what their name says they are—unidentified flying objects. Many people will remember having heard about "flying disks" between 1939 and 1945. As early as 1937, young builders of model airplanes not only built arrow-shaped and triangular models which were capable of flight, but also disk-shaped airplanes with rings of propellers which were the next best thing to flying saucers. Who is building UFO's today?

"Bergships"

Science and imagination go hand in hand, but unless we are to waste our time in idle dreaming, both must be controlled by reason. However, sometimes a link develops between dreams and reality. An example of this is the secret project "Bergship." The military supplied the information and scientists struggled with the problem, but it was nature which finally solved it.

In 1940 German troops were planning an invasion of England, but they needed ships to do so. For a time they wondered whether they could not use barges made of concrete. This was an interesting experiment, but nothing more. Three years later the English needed ships for their outlying anti-aircraft guns. They used their imaginations, too, and made some progress when they decided to make ships from water. They wondered whether artificial icebergs could be used to carry anti-aircraft guns and even planes. Project "Bergship" was begun. The English developed a form of artificial ice strengthened by waste products from the paper industry. It was called "pykrete" after its inventor, G. Pyke. The pykrete was fitted with condensing coils and motors designed to move the "bergships." However, this project proved unsuccessful, like that of the concrete ships.

By 1962, nature had made "bergships" a familiar tool of research to all scientists, especially those of the Soviet Union. Soviet meteorologists had built a weather station on the ice, and then the ice on which it stood suddenly broke off and drifted away. From then on, weather stations were built on drifting icebergs, or bergships.

An antiquated novelty

Sometimes the same idea occurs to a number of people at different times before it finally proves useful. Moreover, sometimes a discovery is made *too soon*—that is, the discovery is made at a time when no one yet understands its significance. Some inventors and researchers are too far ahead of their times.

For example, Gregor Mendel, the Moravian monk who discovered the laws of heredity, presented his results to other scientists in 1865. In 1900, sixteen years after Mendel's death, the laws of heredity were discovered again, and fortunately people remembered that Mendel had been the first to discover them.

We owe our knowledge of how genetic material is fixed in the molecules, in the so-called DNA, to a Canadian physician whose importance is often ignored, O. Thomas

Avery (1877–1955). To be sure, other scientists knew that Avery had published his results, but for eight years no one understood what he was really talking about!

In other cases scientists have quickly understood what another scientist was talking about, but they have not realized that his ideas were correct. For example, in September, 1874, when the young Dutch chemist van't Hoff published his theories on the arrangement of atoms in space, other scientists not only failed to accept his theories, but they even made fun of him. Today van't Hoff's theories are basic reading in schools and universities.

Just make a plan

Clearly, imponderable factors determine scientific progress. We have to ask ourselves whether the planned scientific development which is so frequently discussed today can really take place. Can we control the progress of research and technology? Can we decide in advance: Now I am going to discover this or that? Should we, as many governments foolishly do, demand that our scientists do research in a certain *field?* Inevitably, we will neglect other fields, for every nation has a limited number of scientists and limited funds.

Moreover, when governments demand that scientists concentrate on solving certain problems, they are usually not demanding scientific analysis, but rather "socially relevant" technology. If we devote all our knowledge, technology, and money to getting to the moon, we will certainly get to the moon, but we will not arrive at any new knowledge. Scientific discoveries are completely different from technological developments.

Is it possible to discover something we know nothing about? Certainly we can finance thousands of well-educated people and so compel them to search for particular things. However, 1,000 Columbuses could not find America where no America exists. No well-informed body of experts can know where and when new terrain is ripe for discovery. Only one man can know, and he is the one who not only possesses intelligence, but *happens to hit on the right idea.* Knowledge and learning alone are not enough to ensure discoveries.

Money alone does not guarantee scientific progress. British biologist Professor K. Mellanby has stated that between 1942 and 1972, the money allocated to research increased two hundred times and in some cases four hundred times. If we subtract an inflation factor of ten, funds for science are still twenty times as great as they were previously. If we take into account the increase in the number of universities and similar factors, money for research is ten times what it used to be. And what is the result of this increased expenditure?

Research teams have grown larger, and 600,000 to 700,000 scientific works are published each year. But this is not ten times, but only twice as many new results as were published before the war. The so-called "information explosion" refers to the fact that scientific information is printed more extensively than it used to be. However, the increase in the amount of printed matter does not imply an equivalent growth of knwledge.

Beware of confusing quantity with quality

Increased numbers of assistants, more expensive laboratories, floods of students to be educated, and scientific committees and congresses cannot accelerate the growth of scientific knowledge. In fact, these things do nothing but take up the time of competent researchers. Mellanby believes that two things will help:

1). As regards research, we should take the same approach we took in the past.

2). We must understand that research can only be accomplished by researchers free to do research!

Perfect organization and management does not necessarily allow anyone to get any work done, and no committee, however eminent it may be, has ever given birth to an original idea. Unless one is seeking to confirm an opinion or simply gathering facts, to do research means to search for something one knows nothing about. And one cannot know beforehand whether the results will be "good" or "bad," pleasant, or even useful. Those who engage in the adventure of research must accept the response of nature as a law that their wishes and intentions cannot affect.

On the other hand, clearly no one does research in a vacuum. All research is based on a solid foundation of knowledge. But all research begins at the point where knowledge ends. When scientists begin to explore, they encounter questions.

Chapter Fourteen

"FOR WE KNOW IN PART . . ."

Faith is more certain than knowledge

SCIENTISTS TODAY can answer thousands of questions quickly and completely. However, we are still faced with many questions about basic matters which only *appear* to be simple. One day we will probably know the answers to these questions, too. To describe our situation in biblical terms, we can see the Tree of Knowledge and we hope one day to eat of its fruit. *Whether it will benefit us to do so is another question.* It is possible that the Bible may be right and that once we have seen the world for what it is, we will be sobered and terrified and will long to return to the paradise of ignorance.

In the past, hasn't progress brought us more fear than satisfaction? Our dissociation from nature has made us proud, but more than that, it has made us insecure. Weren't we happier with a secure faith than we are with the half-knowledge characteristic of the present age? Equating science with technology and both with "progress," we grow intoxicated with what we imagine to be the blessings of the present. Actually, we are seeing things backward. We claim that today's science is tomorrow's technology, whereas in reality today's technology is only yesterday's science, and every time we predict a better future we are really confessing the miseries of the present. The faith of the past not only brought us more peace, but was also more comfortable than the knowledge of today. It is not advantageous to exchange faith for knowledge.

But we are curious, and so we embark on the adventures of research. This journey into the unknown has an irresistible lure. The urge to gather knowledge is innate in man, and when we obey it, we play our ordained role in nature. This may sound as if man's investigative spirit were something exceptional and unique in the universe. We cannot be certain this is true. Probably it is our own arrogance and ignorance which lead us to assume that it is. After all, by the end of their lives haven't some animals learned a great deal about the world? A city dog which carefully observes the streetlight and does not cross the street until the light turns green has reached a level of knowledge which—comparatively speaking—many of our contemporaries never attain.

We know that we humans possess knowledge, whereas the knowledge of the dog seems to us insignificant. However, it is time that we realize how many gaps there are in our knowledge and how insignificant we ourselves are. Given the chemical makeup of the creation, it was natural and even inevitable that life should come to exist on earth. In fact, it was inevitable that the metabolic processes with which we are familiar should come to maintain the lives of all existing creatures. Some amazing correspondences exist between the quantity of chemical elements in the earth's crust and their quantity in blood. Like all life, our lives are part of the earth.

We know an incredible number of facts about ourselves. We know how we come to be, we know about our growth, our diseases, our metabolism, and the end of our existence. We know some things about our thoughts, our drives, and our behavior. However, we know little about what happens when we become old; the word "gerontology" is still new to us. And what do we know about learning, remembering, thinking, getting an idea—all the things we think of as so typical of a human being that he is not a human being without them?

We are inclined to regard people who differ mentally from the norm as being "mentally ill," but what does this phrase mean? Do seers, soothsayers, and parakinesis exist? What is mentally "normal" for a human being? We have a great deal to learn in this field, for we do not yet know all there is to know about ourselves.

There is no road back

Wherever we look, we see an interesting and exciting world. In fact, sometimes we are so carried away by enthusiasm that we forget how much we still have to learn. We have started to walk along the path of the investigation of nature, and now we have no choice but to continue on this path. Our knowledge has shaped our lives, and there is no road back unless we choose to, and are able to, forget everything we know.

We have the desire and perhaps the right as well to learn why our world exists and what it is like. We want to learn the answer to the question: Where am I? When we learn this answer, we can face the ancient philosophical question: What am I, what is man? Only unfeeling and unintelligent men can fail to ask themselves these questions.

Centuries may pass before we learn enough science to answer the first of these two questions. Then more centuries will pass before science can help us to answer the question about ourselves. It is the most human of our attributes, hope, which enables us to risk our faith and engage in the experiment of science.

It would be easy and comfortable for us simply to admire the world around us, for it is a wonder. However, we need a hope which will endure for generations if we are to undertake to understand, rather than simply to contemplate, this incomprehensible and miraculous world. Perhaps when the present geological epoch comes to an end, man will become extinct without ever having reached this goal, but what does that matter? We have received and accepted a challenge. Generation follows generation —schoolchildren, students, scholars, practical men, and thinkers—some of them providing us with the necessities of life and others fighting for the freedom to investigate and think. We have not come very far along our path. This book shows that our science is still rudimentary. However, all intelligent men understand that successes lie in store for us along our road and that along the way we will learn many things which will make our daily existence easier or more pleasant.

We have investigated, invented, and understood so much that we must now take the next step and decide the future course of scientific research. After we have taken stock of what we know, we should be able to found science on a new basis, the basis of what we have observed and recognized as true.

We began to do scientific research in the vain belief that life on earth was something extraordinary and that man was the final and the most highly evolved of terrestrial life forms. In fact, we believed that the earth, the best place in the universe, had been created expressly for man. We can now say with certainty that this belief is born of a deeply ingrained prejudice and immense vanity.

The earth is, in fact, a wretched and insecure place. Man's life on earth is nothing but one step in a natural process of evolution, and both as individuals and as a species, we have only a short time to live. *We must use this time to the best of our ability.* At the moment, man comes first in the pecking order of living creatures. It would be worth our while to make the effort to achieve all that we believe man is capable of.

INDEX